Jehovah's Witnesses –
The Good… The Bad…
The Deceptive…
And Worse!

An Exposé

Jim Staelens

Captain UAL Retired

Jehovah's Witnesses - The Good... The Bad... The Deceptive... And Worse! *An Exposé*
Copyright © 2013 Captain Jim Staelens, Sr. - LLC

ISBN: 148264780X
ISBN-13: 9781482647808

Library of Congress Control Number: 2013903943
CreateSpace Independent Publishing Platform
North Charleston, South Carolina

BIBLES USED:

Holy Bible, New International Version® - NIV ® Copyright © 2011; published by Biblica, Inc.™

New World Translation of the Holy Scriptures - NWT - © 1984; *THE BIBLE in Living English* - BLE © 1972; both carry Copyright © by Watchtower Bible and Tract Society, of PA - both are published by Watchtower Bible and Tract Society of NY; however, any Bible translation of your choice will be just fine for checking references.

DICTIONARIES USED: (on line and public domain):

Webster's Revised Unabridged Dictionary 1913 and 1828.
Wiktionary - (on line) date retrieved 4/2/2013

PICTURES: The front and back cover pictures belong to me.

COPYRIGHTED QUOTES: This book conforms to U.S. Copyright laws: There are not over 300 words quoted, from any © book, nor over 50 words from any © magazine, nor over 300 verses from any © Bible translation.

FAIR USE RULE: This work is protected under the auspices of Title 17 Sec. 107 of the U.S. Code - the *"Fair Use Rule"* for any "critical work," which does apply to this *Exposé*. All works published *before January 1, 1923* are in *"public domain."*

Website: www.jws-exposed.com
E-mail: info@jws-exposed.com

PROLOGUE

- What *lethal mentality* afflicted some airline crews during the 60's and 70's"?
- How did Crew Resource Management (CRM) concepts *overcome* this mentality?
- How could application of the *same concepts* correct a *faulty mentality* on the part of the Watchtower/Witness/Hierarchy (*W/W/H*) and prevent *similar abuses* by them?

DEDICATION

To all victims of the Watchtower/Witness/Hierarchy (W/W/H) and to those who may have been hurt due to such things as its failed prophecies, broken promises, deception, manipulation, tyranny of authority, and worse. This includes my six living children and their families, two of whom have been especially harmed by the W/W/H and its directives. It is my hope that they and many others likewise will be helped by this exposé—to enjoy true peace of mind and happiness based on truth!

SPECIAL THANKS FROM JIM STAELENS:

To my loyal wife, Dale, who for fifty-three years has loyally stood by me for the good, the bad, the happy, the scary, and sometimes even the tragic, times of life -

- Helping me to secure my job with United Airlines.

- Helping me transition from a private pilot to an airline pilot, with considerable help to me in my studying.

- Raising our seven children, many times alone, because I was at the other end of the world.

- Coping with me as we endured the tragic death of our twenty-two month old son, Ronald.

Special thanks are also due to the owners and providers of websites such as the following:

- www.airdisaster.com
- www.freeminds.org
- www.jwfacts.com
- www.silentlambs.org
- www.watchtowerdocuments.com
- www.wikipedia.org
- www.wiktionary.org

Many other websites have also been helpful in my research.

CONTENTS

PROLOGUE: . . . . **III**
Title, ©, Dedication, Thanks, Contents, The Author . . . . I–IX
Questions and Illustrations—Why? . . . . XI–XIII

INTRODUCTION **1–10**

CHAPTER TITLES
1. Recognize Accountability—Accept Responsibility! 11
2. Abuse of Authority: What Can Be Done About It? 21
3. Whistle-blowers Past and Present: The Threat of Exposure 41
4. Jehovah's Witnesses: "The Good…" 67
5. My Life: A Mixed Bag! 79
6. Over Thirty Failed Prophecies, During 131 Years:
   Grave Disappointments 109
7. Has the W/W/H Claimed to be God's Prophet? Yes, or No? 133
8. The Baptism Deception—for Youths: The Dark Side. 149
9. Double-talk, Deception, Hypocrisy, and Lying Have
   Been Rampant. 181
10. Disfellowshipping: The Dark Side Leading to the
    Destruction of Families 207
11. If Not Disfellowshipping: What Could Work, and
    Has Worked—and How?. 251
12. How and Why the W/W/H Hides Accountability and
    Evades Responsibility 273
13. If It Looks, Walks, Swims, and Quacks Like a Duck—It's a… 295
14. Escaping the Spiritual Abuse of Deception,
    Manipulation, and Tyranny of Authority. 303
15. The Conclusion of the Matter… 319

REFERENCES **335**

THE AUTHOR

I was born in Saginaw, Michigan, in 1941.

I started learning to fly airplanes in 1961, was hired by United Airlines in 1966 and retired as a captain in 1991. With nearly fifty years of flying experience, I have logged over ten thousand hours and five million miles, have handled several life-threatening emergencies and survived one plane crash.

During the past sixty years, I have read the entire Bible through numerous times, and I have studied many different translations with the assistance of *Strong's Exhaustive Concordance*, Greek-English as well as Hebrew-Chaldee lexicons, and Greek-English interlinear translations.

From 1957 until 2007, I served in every position of responsibility in congregations of Jehovah's Witnesses and also helped teach several schools for congregation elders and others. I served on judicial committees, was the assembly overseer for circuit assemblies, and was the program overseer for a district convention. I have lectured to tens of thousands of people at many large Witness district conventions; I am very well qualified for and feel *impelled* to write this exposé, especially for people such as the following:

- Persons curious about Jehovah's Witnesses
- Former Witnesses (for whatever reason)
- Active Witnesses (with serious reservations)
- Anyone thinking of studying with Jehovah's Witnesses
- ➢ Pointed questions for the next time a JW calls at your door

When I finally discerned the bad, deceptive, and worse, with respect to the W/W/H, how did I deal with it? How did I manage to get and keep those blinders off? The answers may help and surprise you!

Jim Staelens Sr.

Captain UAL Retired

QUESTIONS AND ILLUSTRATIONS—WHY?

- Questions and illustrations: powerful teaching tools.
- ❖ Flying: examples from nearly fifty years of flying experience, privately and with United Airlines.
- ➢ Pointed questions: for active Witnesses.

There are points throughout the text of this book that are accented with three types of bullets (shown above); they will serve as a prelude to and/or for emphasis of points being considered. Review Points numbered 1, 2, 3, etc., will be found at the end of this section and at the end of succeeding chapters.

If you, the reader, have children, you are already aware of the fact that shortly after they begin learning to talk, they learn the question, "Why?" From that time on, you will be bombarded with this question. "Why?" is so important because it leads to the reason, hopefully an accurate and satisfying reason, for what you say or believe.

If, for whatever reason, you do not or emphatically will not answer the question, "Why," you risk undermining your own credibility. If you cannot answer a question correctly, due to lack of knowledge about the matter, *say so;* do not try to wing it.

The need for illustrations is apparent when considering the need for understanding. If a matter is illustrated, the picture becomes much clearer, easier to remember, and less likely to be forgotten.

Consider an illustration involving the operation of an aircraft. Let's say that a person, *a new kid* who had just started learning to fly, told you, "I discovered what makes an airplane fly off the ground. It's like a giant surfboard, and as it starts moving down the runway, wind strikes the underside of the wings, and the plane becomes like a wheelbarrow being pushed up a hill, and the plane is *pushed up* to whatever altitude the pilot wants." Is that explanation feasible? Remember he's a new kid.

Can his statement be demonstrated? Is it true? The answer to all three of these questions is No.

But suppose, instead, that a flight instructor or an airline captain, for that matter, told you, "A plane is *lifted up* to cruise altitude because a giant vacuum is created over the top side of the wings as the plane accelerates down the runway, and the plane is literally *sucked up* into the air, as if by a giant vacuum cleaner." Would you believe that? Perhaps, and yet…

Maybe you are thinking, "You've got to be kidding! Do you really expect me to believe that a Boeing 747 airliner, weighing over eight hundred and fifty thousand pounds and carrying over five hundred passengers, is *sucked into the air* by a vacuum?" Could that be demonstrated? Could it possibly be true? The answer to these three questions is *Yes*. Really? Yes, really!

Let's try this experiment: Pick up the closest end of a sheet of paper with the forefinger and thumb of each hand. (Thumbnails should be facing up.) Holding those two corners, turn your hands toward you (ninety degrees) so that your thumbnails are toward your chest and the piece of paper looks like the leading edge of an aircraft wing, with the loose end draped over the top part of your hands.

Now, pull the piece of paper up to your mouth, even with your chin; take a deep breath and just blow over the top side of the paper. This creates a vacuum, and you will see that the sheet of paper begins to lift up off the back side of your hands. That is *exactly* what happens to an airplane; no matter what size the aircraft is, how much it weighs, or how many passengers it carries. When enough air is flowing over the top side of its wings, an airplane will climb.

When wing flaps are extended for takeoff or for landing and the plane is close to the ground (a situation called being in ground effect), lift will be assisted, to some degree, by wind under the wings.

But the point is that a plane is *lifted* into the air by a vacuum! That is the truth about what gets an airplane off the ground and up to cruise altitude.

So it is with illustrations. They have the effect of doing such things as 1) teaching us a fact we will likely never forget and 2) teaching us a point well enough for us to be able to demonstrate the truth of what we have learned to someone else. You will notice that questions and illustrations are used liberally throughout this book.

Many flying illustrations and examples will come from my nearly fifty years of flying experience, gained both privately and with United Airlines, making the points considered easy to remember and *difficult to forget.*

REVIEW POINTS:

1. If explanations about what one believes do not honestly and truthfully answer the question, "Why," what will likely happen to the credibility of the one(s) making the explanations?

2. If the reasons given as explanations by such one(s) turn out to be wrong, either by accident or by deliberate action, should one be inclined to believe such one(s) future explanations? Do you think that inclination would change if *false prophecies* were given instead?

INTRODUCTION

Can you think of things that started out *Good,* but ended up becoming *Bad, Deceptive,* or *Worse?* Consider the following:

THE SUBMARINE:
William Bourne published his submarine design in 1578. It was implemented in 1620 by Cornelius Jacobson Drebbel, a Dutchman who invented the first rudimentary submarine. That was followed by David Bushnell's *Turtle* submarine in 1775 and by Robert Fulton's *Nautilus,* 1793–1797. The *H. L. Hunley* submarine was used by the Confederates during the Civil War in 1864. The First and Second World Wars saw the use of many submarines for war purposes. The year 1955 saw the first nuclear-powered submarine, with most submarines now sporting intercontinental ballistic missiles with multiple independent nuclear warheads. *Good, Bad, and Worse!*

THE AIRPLANE:
December 17, 1903, found Orville and Wilbur Wright flying the first airplane at Kitty Hawk, North Carolina, U.S.A. Followed, in 1914, by pilots shooting at each other from airplanes during the First World War. The Second World War saw the dropping of two atomic bombs, the first on August 6, 1945, from a Boeing B-29, the *Enola Gay*, and the second on August 9, 1945. A total of 150,000 to 246,000 killed! Enter…the Nuclear Age! *Good, Bad,* and *Worse!*

OTHERS:
What about the computer? It's good, but has also become a tool for massive theft and spying. What about medicines? They're good too, when used to relieve pain, but when used for recreational purposes, the consequences can become devastating or even deadly. *Good, Bad* and *Worse,* yet again.

You get the idea, don't you? Along with the *Good* almost always have come the *Bad, the Deceptive, and Worse!* Is not the same true of us as individuals? Has every decision and action we have made been good?

Have some turned out to be bad, deceptive, or worse? We might wish that those decisions could be swept under the rug and forgotten. Do you think it would be any different if the decisions were made by a group rather than by an individual? Eventually the truth comes to light, resulting in the *exposure* of wrongs.

So, what about religion? Has it always been a force for good? Has it not also been a means to manipulate and control the lives and thinking of millions of unsuspecting and trusting people? The bad, deceptive, or worse! For example, the Crusades were responsible for some of the bloodiest pages of history. What about Jim Jones, who was called "the Mad Messiah"? His television ministries were propagated in 1980 from his organization, which was known as the People's Temple. For his followers, in Guyana, his sect brought deception, disaster, and death.

More recently, in 2011, we've heard about fifty-five-year-old Warren Jeffs, the head of a polygamist camp and a member of the Fundamentalist Church of Jesus Christ of Latter-Day Saints. He was exposed for his wrongs and was sent to prison. Would most rational people consider him to be a saint, even if he was the leader of a religious organization? Hardly!

Do you think one should consider deliberately joining an organization with such an infamous reputation? What if it looked or sounded good at first glance, but later, it was revealed that the organization had consistently lied, deceived, and been dishonest in other ways? Would it not be better to get all the facts first, if possible, before getting involved with such an organization? Research and thinking for oneself are a must, to avoid the disasters others have already experienced when victimized by such an organization.

A scripture very relevant to this exposé comes from King Solomon (c. 1,000 BCE). Ecclesiastes 1:9 says as follows:

> What has been *will be again,* what has been done *will be done again;* there is *nothing new* under the sun (NIV; italics added).

That which has come to be, that is what *will come to be;* and that which has been done, that is what *will be done;* and so there is *nothing new* under the sun (NWT; italics added).

In other words, history will continue to repeat itself. From its dawn, deception has been the card of choice used to enslave others by those with greater power or knowledge. Would the Watchtower/Witness/Hierarchy (hereinafter referred to as "W/W/H") be an exception? Its own history answers with an emphatic, "*No!*"

As is disclosed in *Jehovah's Witnesses Proclaimers of God's Kingdom* - (WTB&TS 1993), nearly 80% of present-day active JWs became such after 1970 (p. 717). The vast majority of these Witnesses are not aware of over thirty different prophecies, spanning the 131 years from 1844 to 1975; these prophecies were made and published by the W/W/H in its own literature, foretelling the end of the world and/or events related to it—all turned out to be failed prophecies! (See chapter six below.) Many honest-hearted, present-day active Witnesses are not even aware of what their hierarchy actually prophesied and published would happen in 1975, let alone the many others before and after that date. These facts will unfold as you read the above-noted chapter.

This book is an exposé, and it has been written to help readers choose to think for themselves. It provides facts, insight, and understanding into how and why the W/W/H has functioned as it has. The book includes honest details with clear and specific references to Watchtower/Witness publications, for easy checking. These will help any with the curiosity, concern, and courage to read them. You are reading a book that discusses the good—there has been some—but it is also an exposé of the bad, the deceptive, and worse, of the words and deeds of the W/W/H, of which I am ashamed to say, I was at one time an active part.

Chapter three, which discusses whistle-blowers, will provide considerable insight from the Bible into the problems that infected even those claiming to be God's people, the Israelites, from about 1313 BCE to the first century. Such facts make it clear that even they did not have the market cornered on honesty, truthfulness, and virtue. In reality, dishonesty, lying, and deception plagued them also. Eventually, they lost all; their beloved city and temple were destroyed again, and Jesus noted about them in Matt. 23:38, "your house is left to you desolate" (NIV) or is "abandoned to you" (NWT).

A noteworthy fact from the past regarding the foundation of the modern-day Watchtower/Witness organization is that C. T. Russell when 27 years old *founded* and became *editor* of *Zion's Watch Tower*, and continued as such for 37 years. He died at 64 years of age. He was the *president* of the Watchtower Bible and Tract Society for about *32 years (1884–1916)* (*Watchtower* December 15, 1977, p. 757). Clearly, C. T. Russell was the founder of the modern-day Watchtower/Witness organization presently known as Jehovah's Witnesses.

Upon Russell's death, he was succeeded by Joseph F. Rutherford as president on January 6, 1917. Then in 1931 at a convention in Columbus, Ohio, the Watchtower organization adopted the name: *Jehovah's Witnesses* by resolution (WTB&TS 1993, pp. 719, 720).

Throughout his life, "Russell had been the Society" (WTB&TS 1993, p. 63). So obviously he was viewed by those associated with that organization, from its very beginning, as its founder and leader.

However, notice the double-talk and deception from www.jw.org, the official website of the present-day W/W/H. The "FAQ section" presents the question, "Who was your founder?" The website's *deceptive* answer: "While Russell *took the lead* in the Bible education work at that time and *was the first editor* of the *Watchtower*, he was not the founder of a new religion" (italics added - retrieved from their website - www.jw.org 2/1/2013).

Did you notice how the website sidestepped the question? It asked, "Who was *your* [the Watchtower/Witness organization's] *founder?*" The question was not, "Who was the founder of Christianity?" The website's answer, which ignores and does not answer the question, is, "… since Jesus was the Founder of *Christianity*, we view him as the *founder of our organization*" (italics added). However, as the facts just presented clearly show, Russell was the founder of the Watchtower/Witness organization; the W/W/H's statement is deceptive double-talk, which has been the organization's usual practice and mode of operation throughout its modern history.

Clearly, the W/W/H denies facts that it has already published. You will see how the organization has done this over and over again, when you get to chapter six. Deception has often been the card of choice for many different religious hierarchies, especially when applying excessive control; the W/W/H has been in the forefront when it comes to such deception; they have become masters at it.

You no doubt have noticed that the modern-day W/W/H is trying to distance itself from Russell. Why do you think it vigorously tries to downplay Russell's influence as its founder? Notice this quote from a book penned by C. T. Russell in 1911. He called attention to the word "sect" in his book, *Studies in the Scriptures* (WTB&TS vol. 3, 1911, p. 185), and although he was defining the word "sect," he covered some of the earmarks of the word "cult." Mr. Russell noted as follows:

> When one joins a sect, *his mind* is supposed to be *given up* entirely to that sect, and henceforth not his own. The *sect undertakes to decide for him* what is truth and what is error; and he, to be a true staunch, faithful member, *must accept the decisions of his sect,* future as well as past, on all religious matters, *ignoring* his *own* individual *thought,* and *avoiding personal investigation,* lest he grow in knowledge, and be *lost as a member* of such sect. This *slavery* of *conscience to a sect* and creed is often stated in so many words, when such a one declares that he *"belongs"* to such a sect. (italics added, except for "belongs")

Note these six main points from Russell's definition, all of which involve both "exploitative" (Wiktionary) and excessive control, which are definitely sect-like and cult-like traits which identify the W/W/H:

- The mind must be given up entirely to the sect
- The sect decides what is truth or error, not you

- You must accept the decisions of the sect
- You must ignore individual thought
- You must avoid personal investigation
- Your conscience becomes enslaved to the sect

Did you notice that a sect as well as a cult steals the conscience as well as the quality of free will from its adherents? Both of these are God-given attributes that all humans have been endowed with. It is the height of presumptuousness for any religious hierarchy to snatch these God-given gifts away from its members.

Is it not clear that Russell's comments about a sect would be viewed as damaging to the W/W/H in the present climate? What is your conclusion? Did Russell indicate that sects exert excessive and exploitative control? Yes, or No?

These facts also negate any claims by individuals or by any organization, including the W/W/H that they are the only ones on earth who teach the truth and that therefore, they alone are entitled to absolute obedience and loyalty without question. These are ludicrous and dogmatic statements with no foundation whatsoever. This is made clear by the points Mr. Russell stated in 1911 regarding a sect as well as by the definitions listed below.

Notice these authoritative definitions:

> Sect: 1. A religious group or faction *regarded as* heretical or as deviating from orthodox tradition…a nonconformist Church. 2. A group with *extreme* or *dangerous* philosophical or political ideas. (italics added) *Webster's Revised Unabridged Dictionary* (1913, 1828).

> Cult: A group of people with a religious, philosophical or cultural identity sometimes viewed as a sect, often existing on the margins of society or *exploitative* towards its members. (italics added) *Wiktionary.org* - (retrieved: 4/02/2013)

INTRODUCTION

Did you notice that a cult is regarded as "exploitative towards its members?" Another way to say this would be: *it imposes excessive control.* But, do you think that sect or cult members regard themselves as being victims of such behavior? Likely they do not. Why not? Because those who have been victimized by them are usually too close to the problem to be able to see clearly or to discern that they are being manipulated and excessively controlled. You will see that such a mode of operation can have lethal consequences.

It is noteworthy that other current W/W/H publications present limited and incomplete definitions of both the words "sect" and "cult." See and compare *Reasoning From the Scriptures* (WTB&TS 1989, p. 202). Why do you think they omit giving complete and accurate data?

Russell's definition of a sect (which remember, unbeknown to him, included the earmarks of a cult) is remarkable, given information taken from *Wikipedia* (retrieved 4/02/2013 "Cult"), it notes that "the word cult…is first seen in the early 17th century…then during the 1930's cults were the object of sociological study." This was well after Russell's comments.

It is of special note that those who are exploited by others rarely recognize that they are being victimized. It is others who are likely to regard them as such; their own perception becomes clouded and obscured. Their own view and that of others come to be opposites.

Russell's definition is far more in line with the authoritative dictionary definitions for the words "sect" and "cult" than are the present-day definitions of the W/W/H.

It would certainly appear that Mr. Russell was trying to warn his readers of the very detrimental characteristics of a sect; these become even more extreme in a cult. These facts, along with the dictionary definitions (as well as common usage) for these words, should help one to be able to discern the dangers facing members of such groups.

Understanding these points will become very relevant and obvious in coming chapters; although applying to many similar groups, this exposé focuses particularly on the W/W/H. In the case of that organization, it is the group's own words, publications, and actions which identify it as having sect-like and cult-like traits. What can be done? The organization *could* learn from the many lessons contained in airline training and procedures. Clues will keep coming to identify such lessons.

Many fatal airline accidents of the 1960s and 1970s became a catalyst that, in 1980, precipitated the development of the concepts of crew resource management (CRM) (see chapter 2). Both NASA and the airlines felt compelled to adopt and implement such concepts with a view to saving lives. These same concepts *could* prove very beneficial; perhaps even lifesaving, if learned, applied, and practiced by the W/W/H.

My hope is that countless persons, will have an open mind to read this exposé for whatever, their, reasons may be. Hopefully, it will prove to be not just informative but also an eye-opener and helpful to any and all such readers; perhaps even some personally close to them, may be able to benefit greatly from the reading of this book also.

INTRODUCTION

REVIEW POINTS

1. Perhaps you are aware of the fact that the W/W/H has vigorously tried to prevent rank-and-file Witnesses from thinking for themselves and/or checking up on their record. Why? What is the W/W/H organization's agenda?

2. You may recall hearing one of these talks given at a Kingdom Hall or convention: "Avoid Independent Thinking," "Beware of Independent Thinking," "Don't Give in To Independent Thinking," or "Shun Independent Thinking." There have been these and various other titles used over many years. What do you think the purpose of these talks has been?

3. Although the titles have varied, has not the purpose really been the same—to stop rank-and-file Witnesses from thinking for themselves, let alone investigating the W/W/H's failures, deception, and wrongdoing?

4. Is that not exactly the kind of mentality and excessive control exercised by sects and cults, which Mr. Russell was warning his readers about in his book? Can you discern that his warning, penned in 1911, is very relevant to our day as well?

5. Have things really changed since that time? Is it not true that history shows Russell's warnings to be every bit as valid today as they were back then?

I am well aware that some of the information presented in this book could be difficult for anyone who is an active member of the W/W/H's organization to read in an unbiased way. Having been in that position myself I fully realize how one could feel it to be a personal affront to them; it is not.

Rather, this book is an exposé, not of rank-and-file JWs but rather, of the W/W/H (especially the upper echelon - their governing body). It is not the average JW who has been responsible for manifold false prophecies over a period of two life-times. Keeping these points in mind will make it more palatable for anyone reading this information, to do so without feeling major personal discomfort or guilt. *Understanding* is a help, not a hindrance, to learning, in all venues of life.

Haven't we constantly had to make changes in our lives as we have continued to learn more about ourselves and/or others? The venues and concerns may be different, but we must continue to learn from our experiences. You will see as you progress through this book that it has indeed been my experience too.

The first chapter will cover an actual in-flight emergency. It will provide some insight and actually set the tone for much of the information which will be considered throughout this book. It will also provide clues that could pave the way for much needed changes by the W/W/H, if only it would be willing to learn and apply them.

However, these same clues and changes can benefit any and all humble and honest hearted ones in all walks of life.

Stay with us as our flight through time continues:

Chapter 1

RECOGNIZE ACCOUNTABILITY— ACCEPT RESPONSIBILITY!

- How can accepting responsibility be disarming?
- Who benefits most from this trait?
- ❖ Flying: An in-flight emergency with a lesson!

I am going to draw on an actual account of an in-flight emergency that I faced as an airline captain in the late 1980s; you will find many such accounts in the course of this book. This account involves the issue of recognizing accountability and taking the responsibility for one's actions. Let me illustrate.

First, you will need some preliminary information about high-tech jets. Such planes are said to have glass cockpits because most of the flight and engine instrument readings are displayed on cathode ray tube computer-like screens. At the time, the only airplanes in United's fleet that had such technology were the Boeing 767 and the Boeing 737-300. I have had considerable flying time in both jets.

Both of these planes have what is called a flight management computer (FMC), which provides immediate flight and navigational data to the captain and copilot.

Additionally, if you have flown as an airline passenger within the past twenty-five years, you are aware of the safety announcement made by the first flight attendant (or a video presentation) as the plane begins its push-back from the gate. If you are on a domestic flight in the United States, it will also be a nonsmoking flight, and the announcement will include the fact that "there are smoke detectors in all of the lavatories. Smoking or tampering with a smoke detector in an aircraft lavatory is a federal offence."

One final noteworthy point involves the reason for this law. The airline industry worldwide has lost many airplanes because someone was smoking in the lavatory and put his or her still lit cigarette down the paper towel wastebasket rather than putting it out in the ashtray. Once the plastic in an aircraft lavatory catches fire, it quickly gets out of control unless the fire can be extinguished almost immediately. If it is not extinguished, the amount of time the captain has to get the plane on the ground is extremely limited—the average *maximum* time limit is only *sixteen minutes*. Hundreds of people have died because of such fires.

Some very graphic real aircraft crashes come to mind. We in the flight crews had all heard cockpit voice recordings and were shown pictures of cabin fires started by lighted cigarettes improperly disposed of in aircraft lavatories. These accounts were presented to us in Denver during our biannual flight crew proficiency checks. In one case where the plane had caught fire in the lavatory, the captain of a foreign carrier had opted to try to make it to an airport that was over *twenty-six minutes away*—well beyond any likely survivable time.

We all watched and listened in horror. The plane was about seven hundred feet in the air. The cockpit windows had been opened by the captain and copilot; they had their oxygen masks on. Dense black smoke was streaming from both windows and all of the passengers onboard had already died. The plane started a roll and then crashed upside down. I felt as though I had been there. At that time, I determined that I would never attempt a distance greater than twelve minutes away, if I were ever faced with that kind of situation.

That account became indelibly imprinted on my mind, much as the sinking of the *Titanic* on April 15, 1912, must have become etched for a lifetime on the minds of those who witnessed it from their lifeboats.

It has been said that "airline flying involves countless hours of sheer boredom interspersed with brief moments of stark terror." I have experienced the truth of that statement more than once. The above facts will help you to understand why the following events occurred as they did.

- It was about 2:30 a.m., and we were hurtling through space at nearly nine miles a minute and over six miles above the earth, on a flight from San Francisco to Chicago. Frank, my copilot, and I were settled back in our seats, nursing our cups of coffee and enjoying the truly first-class view of a moonless but star-studded sky. The flight attendants were doing a liquor service for any passengers still awake.

Then all hell broke loose! We heard the smoke alarm blaring from the aft lavatory. Two seconds later brought the flash of an amber call light on the throttle quadrant, and we simultaneously heard the chime of the flight attendants' intercom.

As I picked up the phone, I heard, "The aft smoke alarm is blaring! I'm on my way!"

I ordered Frank, "Grab the fire extinguisher and get back there!"

He bolted from his seat, extinguisher in hand, and dashed toward the back of the plane. The clock was ticking!

I instinctively punched the button labeled, "NEAREST," on the FMC. We were crossing the continental divide, at a place where the jagged Rocky Mountain tops reached to nearly sixteen thousand feet above mean sea level (MSL). The FMC confirmed what I suspected: the nearest airport that could accommodate us was *thirty-one minutes away;* even at nine miles per minute, there would be no way on earth to get to any airport in time if the cabin was on fire.

Can you imagine how I felt at that moment or what was going through my mind? As I prepared for a rapid descent, my right hand was resting on the throttles, and the thumb of my left hand was resting against the autopilot disconnect button on my yoke. I was ready!

There was no panic on my part as the seconds crept by, only a silent recognition of what would have to be done if the next call from the cabin was, "*The fire's in the ceiling, and we can't get to it!*"

I would have no choice. I would close the throttles and simultaneously disconnect the autopilot and extend the speed-brakes on the top sides of the wings. We would be in a rapid descent headed down at over four thousand feet per minute. There would be no airport, no runway, and no lights waiting for us—only jagged Rocky Mountain tops. There would be no time to prepare for an evacuation; we had nineteen thousand feet to drop in less than four minutes. I would slow the plane as much as possible to stay airborne and to prevent a stall, and then, as gently as possible, we would crash onto the mountaintops. If there were going to be any survivors at all, they would likely be few.

Three times previously, I had experienced this feeling, expecting that I would not likely be able to get out of the plane alive. I had survived those previous emergencies, but I didn't like the feeling; I was hoping that this would not be the time that I could not survive.

The amber call light on the throttle quadrant flashed, and I heard the chime and quickly answered. "It's OK!" the flight attendant affirmed. "Frank is double-checking the paper towel basket and all the panels; it looks like someone covered the smoke detector with a damp paper towel and smoked a cigarette. He should be back up there in a couple of minutes."

"Do you know which passenger it was that was smoking?" I asked.

"No," she replied. "We were doing our liquor service in First Class and didn't notice who it was."

I kept my right hand clear of the throttles and removed my left thumb from over the autopilot disconnect button, allowing the autopilot and computers to continue to do their jobs. I was thankful that it had been just cigarette smoke and not fire. I took a deep breath and began contemplating what kind of announcement I would make to my passengers. They had just heard a blaring smoke alarm, and many, no doubt, had been startled awake by it. They had witnessed a flight attendant and their first officer racing for the aft lavatory.

"What kind of a person," I wondered, "would have the stupidity to risk a felony charge, imprisonment, or worse yet, perhaps cause the loss of his own life and possibly the lives of all the rest of us, just for a cigarette?"

In a couple of minutes, Frank was back on the flight deck, and I had figured out what I was going to say. "You've got the plane," I told him. He slid his seat forward, preparing to take away control from the computers and autopilot, if necessary; I picked up the mike to make my announcement.

"This is Captain Staelens. I know you are all aware of the fact that we had a smoke alarm blaring from the aft lavatory. Everything is OK now. There is no fire, and we are out of danger. However, someone back there was willing to risk not only the possibility of a felony charge, with imprisonment, but he was willing to jeopardize his own life and the lives of all the rest of us by smoking a cigarette in the lavatory and temporarily disabling the smoke alarm.

"United has lost one airplane; the airline industry has lost several. Additionally, hundreds of lives have been lost due to fire caused by an individual who carelessly dared to smoke in an airplane lavatory and then improperly disposed of his cigarette. I want to know who it was that jeopardized the lives of all of us on this flight. I'll be standing at the door waiting to find out when we deplane at O'Hare."

I was more than just irritated; I was angered. My life, the lives of my crew, and the lives of over one hundred passengers for whom I, as their captain, was responsible had been put in jeopardy. My voice left no room for doubt as to how I felt.

I picked up the phone and called Joan, our first flight attendant, and advised her that if any passenger went into any lavatory for the remainder of the flight, I wanted one of the flight attendants to stand by the door and be alert for the smell of cigarette smoke.

"OK, Captain," she said, "we'll do that. But I'd be willing to bet that nobody is going to touch a cigarette for the remainder of this flight." And so it turned out to be.

We arrived at the gate after our landing at O'Hare, and I had briefed Frank to take care of the parking checklist after I shut down the engines. By the time the gate agent opened the forward cabin door, I was standing in the cockpit doorway, waiting. Few people on that flight made eye contact with me as they rapidly deplaned. A couple of passengers made the comment, "I am a smoker, but it wasn't me. I'll never smoke on any airplane again, especially after this flight!"

The plane was rapidly becoming empty, and it was becoming certain that whoever the guilty party was, I would never know.

Frank had finished securing everything in the cockpit and was prepared to leave. I stepped aside so he could deplane; then I reached for my own suitcase and flight-case. The flight attendants were in the back, getting their suitcases out of the hat racks.

As I prepared to leave, I noticed one more passenger coming toward me, approaching the First Class section. It was an older lady; she was small in stature and had her head down as she approached me.

I was holding a suitcase and flight-case in my hands, ready to deplane behind her. As she got closer to me, I could hear her sobbing. She stopped and looked up at me, and with tears in her eyes, she sobbed in a stammering voice, "I'm the one you're looking for."

I set down my baggage and gave her a hug. The top of her head barely reached to the middle of my chest. I was a giant, compared to her. "You're OK, you're OK," I assured her. "I am not going to report you or have you arrested. You're OK!" I reassured her. She was still sobbing, and my heart ached for her. As I stood there hugging her, I thought, "What kind of courage must it have taken for this little old lady not only to acknowledge her accountability but to accept responsibility for her actions?"

There I stood, an airline captain in uniform, with a braided cap and four stripes on each of my sleeves; I had the authority to have her arrested and sent to jail and she knew it!

Now, I've never been accused of being too thin. My picture, on the front cover, hints at that fact. I have been a weight lifter since I wrestled in high school at the age of seventeen; I also worked on a dairy farm. So although I was much older at this time, I still had a forty-eight-inch chest and eighteen-inch upper arms. I certainly wasn't small, but rather substantial and intimidating. What a terrifying experience it had to have been for her to confess to me what she had done.

But my heart had melted. Her courage, her humility, her bravery, and her willingness to accept responsibility for her actions had disarmed me and touched my heart. My irritation, my anger, and any feelings of resentment toward her had vanished.

In a world where so many seem to pride themselves on evading responsibility and denying any accountability for their actions, this little old lady stood out as a giant. Rather than dodge accountability, as she could have done simply by walking off the plane and saying nothing, she courageously chose to accept responsibility for her actions, despite knowing how adversely it might impact her life!

We talked for a few minutes, and I explained the extreme problem I would have faced if a fire had gotten started. She noted that she would "never put a lit cigarette down the paper towel waste basket," but I explained, "I am sure none of the others who caused aircraft fires ever expected to start a fire either; nonetheless, it has happened several times, and with tragic consequences." She guaranteed me that she would never smoke on an airplane again. I believed her; I commended her honesty and willingness to accept responsibility. I gave her another hug, and we both deplaned, happy to be safely on the ground and alive.

Remember, that this book is an exposé specifically of the W/W/H, not rank-and-file JWs. You will come to realize that the actions of this little old lady become very relevant to it. Her willingness to admit accountability and accept responsibility for her actions, even in the face of a most uncomfortable and stressful set of circumstances, paint her as a much stronger person than a look at her stature might suggest—a worthy example to be imitated, especially by the W/W/H..

REVIEW POINTS:

1. How and why was accepting responsibility a disarming quality in the case of the little old lady?

2. If she had not accepted the responsibility for her actions on this flight, what far greater problem might she have faced on another flight?

3. What lessons could the Watchtower/Witness/Hierarchy (W/W/H) learn from her worthy example? These will be considered as we continue.

The next chapter will highlight three situations that have to do with the abuse of authority by captains. Two of those situations ended in tragedy. Why? Could those tragedies have been avoided? How? Stay aboard and read on, to note the lessons presented therein!

Are you who are members of the W/W/H, (especially its upper echelon) also ready to listen, learn and apply the gripping lessons to come? I sincerely hope and pray so.

CHAPTER 2

ABUSE OF AUTHORITY: WHAT CAN BE DONE ABOUT IT?

- Why do many with authority *abuse* it?
- What is CRM and how does it work?
- Could applying airline CRM concepts help others in authority? How about the W/W/H?
- ❖ Flying: tragedies and lessons from the past.

You may never have flown before. You may never even have wanted to fly as a passenger, let alone as a pilot in command. However, understanding how a competent airline captain exercises authority, makes decisions, and applies crew resource management (CRM) concepts will help you greatly in seeing why these matters are being introduced in this *exposé*.

Just as these concepts rescued airline crews from a *lethal mentality* that saved the lives of countless passengers, the same concepts can prove to be helpful in correcting wrongs by other hierarchies, including those of the W/W/H. But to be of benefit to any hierarchy, CRM concepts must be learned and applied and, finally, practiced by everyone involved.

So what is CRM? The initials originally stood for "cockpit resource management," and then later, as it was appreciated that the same concepts could help virtually every hierarchical organization, the name was changed to "crew resource management." This will be elaborated on later in great detail, with explanations of the logistics involved in teaching CRM concepts. This would call for a change in thinking and mode of operation; how could superiors as well as underlings be taught these in an understandable and beneficial way?

Among the things that need to be learned by the captain of a jet airliner is the importance of choosing to rely on others in decision making;

there are air traffic controllers, weather briefers, airline dispatchers, and fellow crew members on the flight deck and in the cabin. Other hierarchies must also learn to tap into the experience and input of others, including underlings, not ignoring them because they are not part of the inner circle. If this is not done, the "superiors" may, sooner or later, experience disasters that could have been avoided.

However, from the time I got hired by United Airlines in 1966, it would be fourteen more years until CRM concepts would be learned and have a real impact on flight crew mentality and procedures. In the meantime, problems would continue, and along with them, more tragedies.

❖ For starters, consider three different but true situations.

I entered United's three-month new hire program on June 27, 1966, to receive training to become a flight engineer on the DC-6 (a four-engine prop-driven airliner that carried about sixty-five people—a dinosaur compared to modern airline jets). Shortly after I started my training, an instructor emphasized to us a key point from United's *Flight Operations Manual,* outlining standard operational policies and procedures, commonly referred to as (SOPs)

He called our attention to the first page, first paragraph, and first sentence of that manual, which gave this directive: *"No rule or regulation will ever be an excuse for the exercise of good judgment!"*

Now, that statement made a lasting impression on me because application of those words has literally saved my life on numerous occasions, not only as a captain for United, but also when flying my own airplanes.

During the discussion that followed the reading of the above noted directive, emphasis was placed on the need to get input from all possible sources, then for the captain to use his or her best judgment in making a final decision.

I am going to relate three actual accounts that pertain to this. The first involved me as a brand new flight engineer, the junior man on the flight deck. The other two did not involve me, thankfully. However, they both resulted in fatalities. The details were clearly presented to us and discussed during our biannual flight crew proficiency checks.

❖ First Account: Bad judgment brings embarrassment

It was my first trip to Chicago as a United Airlines flight engineer on the DC-6. I had only been out of school for a week, definitely a new kid. At that time, O'Hare was the busiest airport in the United States and was very intimidating to me because of my lack of experience. The gate that we had parked at inbound, was very close to the runway we would be using for our outbound flight.

Shortly after we started taxing outbound, we were on the runway apron for runway 4-Left, and I, as the flight engineer, had completed the checks for all four engines. There were four planes ahead of us for takeoff on that runway; the morning rush hour at O'Hare was starting, and the tower controller was batting planes out quickly.

In an effort to prove myself a sharp flight engineer, I started *reading* the "Before Takeoff Checklist": Questions from the flight engineer (second officer), with responses from the copilot (first officer) for each item checked, in order to be ready for takeoff when cleared by the tower controller.

The captain, who was unknown to me prior to this trip, was noticeably irritated by my seeming presumptuousness. I was taking the initiative by starting to read the before takeoff checklist. He barked at me, "I'll tell you when I want the checklist read!" Needless to say, I was embarrassed; I closed my mouth and kept it that way.

This was my first lesson in what had become an insidious cultural work ethic mentality that, many times, was considered normal and acceptable by airline captains during the 1960s and 1970s. The captain was the undisputed authority, and *everyone else* onboard was an underling and was not allowed to forget it. Sadly, all too often, this was the mode of operation by airline captains, until 1980, when crew resource management (CRM) concepts came into existence.

As the copilot switched the radio frequency to monitor O'Hare Tower, we heard the controller say, "United 236 cleared into position on Runway 4-Left; be ready for *an immediate!*"

In other words, "You will be cleared for takeoff as soon as the plane ahead of you lifts off the ground. I have another plane on a short final for landing!" This procedure is common at busy airports, to allow controllers to operate at peak performance and to keep aircraft traffic moving as efficiently and smoothly as possible. O'Hare's rush hour had definitely begun!

As the captain started taxing into position, on the runway, I could not keep quiet any longer, so I asked, "Sir... when do you want me to read the before takeoff checklist?"

"The... checklist? Oh, yeah, yeah. Now!" commanded the captain. As he continued taxing into position on the runway, the controller ordered, "United 236 cleared for an *immediate takeoff on runway 4-Left!*" We could see that an American jet was on a short final off our left side.

Our captain, having forgotten to call for the reading of the before takeoff checklist, had to hesitate on the runway, with engines at idle, while the copilot and I rushed as quickly as possible to try and complete the checklist.

However, the tower controller, noting we had stopped moving, cancelled our takeoff clearance and ordered us to *"get off the runway* on the apron just ahead—*immediately!"*

As we cleared the runway, the controller confirmed landing for the American jet on short final; he landed, with us clear of the runway. The incident was not extremely serious; it was more embarrassing than anything else, to the captain.

No doubt he had viewed me as being presumptuous, while I had viewed him as being rude and, not using good judgment in the proper exercise of his authority, as a captain should. Needless to say, I did not tell him what my views were. I submissively kept my mouth shut.

The captain never said a word about what had caused the problem. He took no responsibility for a situation that could have been easily avoided had he exercised good judgment and not operated in an exalted, authoritarian manner. I learned what I should *not* do when, many years later, I would become a captain.

The controller, of course, would not have allowed the jet on final to land on top of us. If we had not cleared the runway in time, he would have ordered American to "Go around," which, besides being irritating to their captain, would have cost them twenty more minutes in the air and wasted at least a thousand pounds of jet fuel.

As it turned out, we had to reposition behind four more planes that had moved up behind us when we had originally started onto the runway for takeoff. So our takeoff turned out to be about ten minutes later than it should have been, but at least no time or jet fuel ended up being wasted by the American jet for a go-around. Of course the whole problem could have been avoided if our captain had just used better judgment!

The controller had made the correct decision. To my own credit, even as a new kid, we could have been ready for takeoff if our captain had allowed the copilot and me to complete the checklist when I first started it. We did finish it, by order of the captain, before we were number one for takeoff; the second time around.

What's the lesson? Authority is one thing, but the abuse of authority or the tyranny of authority is quite another; it can lead to big problems that could adversely affect not just one person, but a whole airplane full of innocent passengers. It could lead and has led to major air disasters, but it could also bring great harm to members of any other type of hierarchical organization as well; including the W/W/H.

In the cockpit of an airliner, a stilted environment is an invite to serious problems, mistakes, and even tragedy, as the next two cases will illustrate. In both cases, innocent lives were unnecessarily lost.

❖ Second Account: The cost of bad judgment

On Nov. 11, 1965, United Airlines Flight 227, a Boeing 727, was scheduled from Denver, Colorado, to Salt Lake City, Utah, with a crew of six. It crashed on the approach. What could have prevented this accident from occurring in the first place? The answer is following standard operating procedures, or SOPs, as they are known.

United mandates that SOPs must be followed by its flight crews at all times. For example, the mandate requires that all approaches must be stabilized. You will shortly see why this is relevant.

A stabilized approach requires that as the aircraft passes the final approach fix for the runway in use (at Salt Lake City's airport on this flight that was 5.7 miles from the approach end of the runway), the following conditions or actions must have been taken with respect to the aircraft:

- Gear down or on the way down—three green lights.
- Wing flaps in the approach position.
- Aircraft speed within five to ten knots of the target approach speed.
- Engines spooled up in case a go-around is needed.
- Descent rate on target: 500–650 feet per minute (FPM), down and centered on the glide slope.
- The final descent checklist being completed.
- By one thousand feet above the runway, all items must be completed.
- At five hundred feet above the ground, confirm that the final landing flap setting is selected.

If any of these parameters is not set or becomes unstable during the approach, a go-around is mandatory.

Here's an illustration to demonstrate what's involved. Clench your right fist and rest it on your table or desk, as if you had your hand on the engine thrust levers. Look at a clock with a second hand, note the time, and move your hand forward about twelve inches; then count off seven seconds. That is how long it will take for jet engines, in the idle position, to spool up to full power. You will shortly see why I had you accomplish this action.

Concerning the ill-fated flight number 227, on November 11, 1965, the National Transportation Safety Board (NTSB) reported that the accident was "blamed entirely on bad judgment by the captain."

It is customary for the captain to share the flying with his or her copilot. The above noted segment, Denver to Salt Lake City, was being flown by the copilot, or first officer.

WHAT WENT WRONG?

From the Accident Report of the NTSB, or the Civil Aeronautics Board as it was then known (Civil Aeronautics Board, 1966): "Flight 227 passed the *outer marker,* 5.7 miles from the runway threshold at approximately 8,200 feet (MSL), over 2,000 feet *above* a normal glide slope." A mandatory go-around was called for at that point, no questions asked. There was plenty of time and fuel to accomplish it. But that go-around did not occur. Why not?

The report continues, "One minute prior to the impact the plane passed 6,300 feet (MSL) but it was still, at that time, *1,300 feet* above what is a normal glide slope and its descent rate was *2,300* FPM (four times normal). The copilot started to move the thrust levers (throttles) forward, to spool-up the engines, but the captain brushed his hand aside and said, '*Not yet.*'" The captain took over flying the aircraft.

The report goes on to say, "Just *30 seconds* prior to impact, the plane was 1,000 feet above the ground and 1.25 miles from the runway. The captain indicated in post-crash interviews that, *at this point he moved the thrust levers to the takeoff power position,* but the engines *did not respond properly.* However, the testimonies of the *Copilot, Flight Engineer* as well as the *flight data recorder* make clear that the attempt to add power occurred only about *10 seconds* before impact." The captain had denied responsibility and hidden the truth.

With engine spool-up taking a full seven seconds, is it not clear to you that a catastrophe was inevitable? It happened. Back to the report: "The aircraft struck the ground 335 feet short of the runway; the descent rate had been 2,300 FPM (three times the safe descent rate). "The plane impacted the ground with a vertical acceleration force of *14.7 G's!*"

To have that in perspective and understand just how severe a jolt that was, keep in mind that 14.7 G's, if applied to a person who weighed one hundred and fifty pounds, would be the equivalent of jumping off the top of a building and hitting the ground with the same force that would exist if that person weighed 2,205 pounds. Scary, isn't it? It is truly a wonder that there were only forty-three fatalities rather than 100 percent, the whole plane full, including the crew.

I remember in basic flight officer school when I started with United, the point was driven home: "If anything about a landing approach looks bad, is outside the SOP perimeters, or becomes unstable at any time during the approach, you must pour the coals to the engines and get your ass out of there! We don't want a repeat of the Salt Lake City accident."

That crash occurred just seven months before I reported to United's Flight Training Center in Denver in 1966, to begin my training. That accident had been and was being discussed at great length in school.

Some noteworthy points:

- At the outer marker, it was obvious that what had become mandatory and what good judgment demanded was a go-around. It should have been executed immediately.

- Nothing—not embarrassment, not ego, not tyranny of authority, not any attempt to keep schedule—or even show your copilot that you can fly better than he can, is, or could have been, an excuse for not exercising good judgment.

- The cost of bad judgment in this case: Of the ninety-one souls onboard, there were forty-three fatalities.

ABUSE OF AUTHORITY: WHAT CAN BE DONE ABOUT IT?

- The whole disaster could easily have been made improbable by following SOPs coupled with good judgment.

- Was the captain telling the truth when he stated, at the post-crash debriefing, that he "applied power 30 seconds prior to impact, but the engines failed to respond properly"? No! It was only ten seconds.

- Was the captain willing to acknowledge accountability and accept responsibility? *No!*

- The truthful air data recorder and two other cockpit crew members set matters straight.

❖ Third Account: Bad judgment brings another disaster -

The date was December 28, 1978; the place, Portland, Oregon. United Flight 173 had taken off from Denver, Colorado, at 12:47 Mountain Standard Time, headed to Portland. The flight started its approach to Runway 28L at 17:09 Pacific Standard Time; then the problems began. What went wrong and why?

The website AirDisaster.Com (www.airdisaster.com) provides details about the investigation of that United Airlines Flight 173. The following facts are yielded from the NTSB report.

"When the Captain lowered the Landing gear at his Copilot's request (Copilot was flying) the gear extended more rapidly than normal; followed by a thump...the aircraft yawed to the right... the flight attendants and passengers felt a severe jolt." A bracket had broken, but the gear was down and locked with three green lights. The plane could have been safely landed at any time, with no problem.

But rather than switching to tower control for the landing clearance, the captain advised approach control that "they had a gear problem and would stay with him at 5,000 feet."

Their instructions were revised by approach control to "turn left to a heading of 230° and maintain 5,000 feet." These instructions were acknowledged and complied with.

The time was 17:14 Pacific Standard Time. One hour and one minute later, the plane crashed into a wooded but populated area of suburban Portland, about six miles east, southeast of the airport. The flight engineer and nine passengers perished. How could the captain have put off his landing for over one hour, allowing all of the engines to run out of fuel?

What could have been done? What changes could be made, so that this kind of tragedy would never happen again?

Under the heading, "Crew Resource Management," the National Transportation Safety Board (NTSB) Report continued:

In many airline accidents investigated by the Safety Board in the 1960s and 1970s, the Board noticed a culture and work environment ethic in the cockpit which, rather than facilitating safe flying, may well have *contributed to many accidents that have occurred.*

The Board observed that *some captains* treated their fellow cockpit crew members as underlings [children] who should speak only when spoken to. This *intimidating atmosphere* really helped cause accidents because critical information was not communicated among cockpit crew members.

Is it not obvious that an atmosphere of intimidation or tyranny of authority and/or authoritarianism can result in a hesitancy to speak up? Do you remember my experience at O'Hare as a new hire in 1966?

Emphasizing the severe dangers of an intimidating atmosphere posed by such a warped mentality, the report continued, "It is obvious that the First Officer knew the aircraft was low on fuel, but, he failed to express his concerns, convincingly enough, to the captain…"

Actually, there were really several times when the copilot *and* flight engineer, (named Sandy) had warned about the fuel shortage. The complete cockpit voice recording that we heard at a proficiency check made that point perfectly clear. Even after Sandy told the captain, "I am getting several low-fuel pressure lights for the engines," the captain still delayed his turn toward the runway.

The captain's final words to Sandy, just before the last engine flamed out, were, "Sandy, you've got to keep those engines running!" Sandy's final words were, "Yes, sir," but it was not possible. The engines all flamed out; the fuel was all gone. Sandy had emphasized the low fuel status to the captain, even more times than the copilot had; sadly, Sandy perished, the only crew-member fatality.

The first news reports, after the accident, indicated how lucky they all were, in that there was no fire. Of course not, because there was no fuel left in any tank!

"As a result of this accident and others, the concept of (CRM)—'Crew Resource Management,' was born in 1980, with valuable input from NASA." It brought a change in thinking: Application of CRM concepts, training and practice, along with other sound workable procedures, would save countless lives. It has turned out to be so.

- CRM concepts and training can also serve as a model for any organization that has a hierarchy, including even a religious one such as the W/W/H. Abuse of authority is never acceptable; it rather invites tragedy.

The NTSB further reported:

The Safety Board issued recommendations to the FAA and the airline industry covering methods that encourage *teamwork;* the captain still is the leader, but, *relies more on the other crew members* for vital safety-of-flight tasks; he also *shares duties* and *asks for information* and help from other crew members. United Airlines was one of the first airlines to adopt these lifesaving concepts which are now almost universally used, by major airlines.

The value of CRM training was clearly demonstrated just nine years later. On July 19, 1989, a United Airlines DC-10 experienced a catastrophic engine failure over Iowa that destroyed the aircraft's hydraulic systems, rendering it virtually uncontrollable; CRM training *to the rescue!*

True, more than 100 people perished, but almost 200 passengers survived this emergency, a situation for which no pilots in the world had ever been trained to deal with.

This raises some important questions:

1. How could that crew possibly have known what to do? How could they have been ready for a disaster that they had never before encountered or been trained for?

2. How is this relevant to the way in which the W/W/H has used fraudulent prophecies (for the time of the end) to keep its members ready for and expecting that end at any moment?

The following basic concepts and the logistical details explaining CRM come from my own experience as well as from points noted in the "Crew Resource Management" article at *Wikipedia*. The following is what the article points out:

"CRM has a goal to foster a climate or cultural ethic where the *freedom to respectfully question authority* is *encouraged.* It is true that the impetus of CRM is enhanced situational awareness, self-awareness, leadership, assertiveness, decision making, flexibility, adaptability, event and mission analysis and *communication.* It recognizes that when there is a discrepancy between what *is happening* and what *should be happening,* an error is likely already occurring." (italics added).

This can be an apprehensive problem for many organizations, particularly any with traditional hierarchies, [that would include religious hierarchies]. Appropriate communication techniques must be taught to supervisors and their subordinates, supposed underlings, so that supervisors understand that the questioning of authority need not be threatening, and subordinates understand the correct way to question orders and develop the courage to speak up and advocate a more preferred choice of action, if it seems called for.

> ➢ Do you see how these concepts could render invalid the absolute and unconditional obedience, even total control demanded by religious hierarchies having a sect-like or cult-mode of operation?

> ❖ How do you think CRM concepts were taught and learned?

Did you notice in the above paragraphs that "communication techniques must be taught to supervisors as well as their subordinates…with the goal that the authority can be questioned without them feeling threatened"? How could this be accomplished? One way is by playacting.

In my class of thirty pilots (ten groups, each consisting of a captain, copilot, and flight engineer), we were given different scenarios involving aircraft emergencies that had occurred in the past. The purpose of this training was to help us learn how to find the best possible solutions to the problems presented and to discern how they could best be handled.

The role of each pilot rotated, so that captains got to be copilots or flight engineers, flight engineers could be captains, and so forth. We did many of these drills, and we were given notes for our discussions, telling us what particular feelings we should portray, what actions we were to advocate, and why we were taking those positions.

One scenario in particular stands out in my mind. For this one, although I was actually a copilot at the time, I was playing the part of the captain. Our problem: We were inbound into Boise, Idaho. There had been freezing rain the night before, and only one east/west runway would be open. Our weather briefing report when we departed Denver had said that one runway was due to be opened shortly, (before we arrived), after sanding of the runway was completed.

The plane landing just ahead of us was a DC-10, and while trying to stop, it had slid off the runway and was lodged halfway down the runway with its nose gear stuck in a snow bank; the tail and back part of the plane were obstructing over half the runway.

We had enough fuel to hold for forty-five minutes plus another thirty minutes as a reserve. The DC-10, which had been ahead of us by only ten minutes, was not going to be able to be moved until all the passengers had deplaned. The estimate was at least an hour and a half until the runway would be reopened. So what would be the choices?

Our cheat sheets told us how to feel about each other and why. Mine said, "Your copilot is a hot shot ex-fighter pilot from the navy and is used to having a tail hook to stop; the flight engineer is new and very inexperienced—his previous flying was all in small private aircraft."

It also said that "I, as the captain, wanted to plan on landing on the runway numbers and expected that I could stop before we reached the point where the disabled DC-10 was stuck."

The copilot's sheet said, "Your captain thinks he knows it all, is obsessed with perfect landings; he always uses up one-third of the runway before the plane's wheels touch the runway."

The flight engineer's cheat sheet said, "The captain won't be able to stop before he runs into the DC-10, so the engineer's choice was to advocate that we should try to make it back to Denver even though it would take nearly every drop of fuel we had."

WHAT SHOULD WE DO?

When I got back home, after this school, I presented this same problem about the disabled DC-10 in Boise to my wife; she was, even then, quite familiar with airline procedures, due to helping me study during the last month of new hire school. So I asked her, "What would you have recommended as the solution for a safe landing?" She thought for a few seconds and then replied, "I'd just land on a taxiway; that way, the DC-10 wouldn't be a problem at all."

Guess what the actual decision was for this real problem that had happened earlier to another carrier? That's right—*it had landed successfully on the taxiway.*

The lesson: Sometimes making a good decision takes input from one with less experience, but who is not hampered by conventional wisdom, viewpoint, or supposed legalities such as, in this case, "You can't land on a taxiway!"

Want to bet? That's what's great about being the captain—you can do just about anything, *in an emergency,* including what is normally illegal, if good judgment requires it; this is especially so if no metal gets bent and nobody gets hurt!

Kudos for my wife for coming up with the correct and best decision possible for that emergency and she came up with in it in just a few seconds! This was a problem that we, *three professional crew members,* had discussed the pros and cons of for fifteen to twenty minutes. None of us had even considered landing on the taxiway.

The point: the captain should be happy for all the input he or she can get *before* making crucial decisions. Don't sell any viewpoint by someone else short just because they have less experience—fitting *recognition is due* for the less experienced ones in our midst.

Captains or others in authority should ask themselves: "What does *good judgment* dictate?" Use your head. Don't be so proud, arrogant, or inflated with self-importance that you refuse to listen to others, even underlings, so that as a result you make an unreasonable decision or worse yet, one that turns out to be tragic, simply because you chose to ignore valuable and perhaps unwanted and unsolicited input from others.

More than one person in authority has learned to his or her chagrin that an underling had better judgment than he or she did. A captain or any other person in authority may be surprised at the benefits and insights that become available by taking the time to not just hear, but really listen to the suggestions others might have.

Note the following thought-provoking questions:

- If members of an airline crew can be ready for a life-threatening situation they have never experienced or been trained for, could an individual or group in a different venue do the same? How about the W/W/H?

- Is it necessary for the W/W/H to trick its adherents into believing the end of the world is imminent for the believers to be ready for it, if and whenever it does finally come?

- Is uttering false prophecies for over a one hundred and forty-year period of time really a better choice; or does the cry of "wolf" become meaningless in the end and cause far more harm than any possible good to believers of said prophecies?

These points will be covered thoroughly by the time you reach the end of this book. You have been getting, and will keep getting, more clues by means of the flying lessons yet to come.

The successful handling of the accident in Iowa is tremendous proof of the value of CRM concepts; but, they are not just for the airlines. These same concepts could greatly benefit persons or organizations controlled by any kind of hierarchy that professes the right to exercise authority or control over others.

This book, is an exposé of the W/W/H, and will make it clear that the application of CRM concepts could change the culture of it or any hierarchy from one of intimidation, intolerance, and repression to one of freedom of thought and speech, both guaranteed in our country. Independent thinking, suggestions, and yes, input from others, including underlings, are rights which were many times championed by Witness legal corporations in the past for themselves. So why deny the same rights or freedom of speech to their own adherents?

Supposedly this denial of free speech for any rank-and-file Witnesses who may disagree with the W/W/H is under the guise of promoting unity in the organization, while in fact, it is promoting and enabling the abuse of authority. The W/W/H in reality is demanding uniformity, absolute obedience, and really total control (sect-like and cult-like traits)—not unity.

You, the reader, are urged to check out all quotes and references contained in this book, not just to establish the accuracy of the quotes and statements but to understand fully the context that these quotes and statements come from. (My quotes have had to conform to United States copyright laws, so it has not been possible for me to quote as much material as I would have preferred to.)

The W/W/H loves to scream "Unfair!" when quotes are made that expose it, or it may label said quotes as incomplete or half-truths. You will see when you look them up for yourself that they are accurate, completely fair, honest, and in context.

If you feel hesitant to look up the quotes because of the hierarchy's demands not to do so, you should ask yourself, "Would I have listened to Jesus in the first century or would I have been hesitant and as a result followed the counsel of the scribes and Pharisees who threatened expulsion from the local synagogue for those who professed Jesus?"

The Pharisees did everything possible, including the use of tyranny of authority, to frighten the common people away from listening to Jesus and learning the truth about the abuses they were guilty of practicing; the W/W/H does the same trick when it is in danger of being exposed.

Do you recall Jesus' statement to the army officer who struck him? John 18:23 states, "'If I said something wrong,' Jesus replied, '*testify* as to *what is wrong. But if* I spoke the *truth, why* did you *strike me?*'"

(NIV; italics added) The NWT version uses the words, "spoke wrongly" and "why…hit me?"

Likewise, after you have read the quotes that I have provided from Watchtower publications, and if you see I have spoken the truth, should you not continue reading and benefit from the chapters to come?

POINTS TO CONSIDER:

1. Has the W/W/H practiced tyranny of authority? Who is it imitating?

2. Those in authority, such as the W/W/H, "need to understand that the questioning of authority need not be threatening, and subordinates must understand the correct way to question orders." (*Wikipedia*, "Crew Resource Management")

3. Will this hierarchy ever learn from CRM Concepts? Only time will tell. If their past history is a barometer of actions to come... don't hold your breath.

4. Has the W/W/H displayed sect-like or cult-like traits? Do you think that God would want any Christian to allow his or her own mind and conscience to become enslaved to another person or even a religious hierarchy with such traits?

5. Up-coming chapters show that the W/W/H does not want and will not tolerate counsel, let alone criticism, from those that the hierarchy considers underlings. Rank-and-file Witnesses are not considered worthy of giving counsel to the upper-echelon hierarchy.

6. You have seen from this chapter that such a mentality from the higher-ups in a hierarchal system is an invitation to harmful and dangerous decisions being made.

Obviously whenever there is an abuse of authority, there is the likelihood that someone who has been adversely affected will start talking about those abuses. Enter the "whistle-blower." There have been many from times past, as well as the present; but whether the whistle-blower was with a secular business, government, or even a religious organization, there is a tendency on the part of those being exposed to become belligerent. Nobody wants to be exposed for wrong-doing. What has the pattern been, by those being exposed? And what has happened to the courageous ones who blew the whistle?

Chapter 3

WHISTLE-BLOWERS PAST AND PRESENT: THE THREAT OF EXPOSURE

- How have religious hierarchies often reacted to their wrongs being exposed?
- A better way to deal with exposure.
- If one is afraid to examine one's religious hierarchy's errors, who really has the problem?
- ❖ Flying: Perception and negative panic.

A Whistle-blower is said to be a person who informs on someone engaged in an illicit or illegal activity.

Ralph Nader is credited as being the one to have coined the phrase, "whistle-blower," in the early 1970s. Many times the whistle-blower is an insider, or on other occasions, an investigative reporter or some other concerned party. In any case, the wrongdoer is the one exposed for his or her wrongs.

Although this term is not used in the Bible, there were prophets and others who exposed wrongdoers; most were insiders in the Jewish nation. Their actions were the same as those of a modern-day whistle-blower.

Consider two examples of whistle-blowers from ancient times, and note the opposite reactions by the wrong-doers, after being exposed.

When the prophet Nathan confronted King David over the matter of Bathsheba, it was an *exposé;* tragedy followed it (2 Sam. 12:1–15).

In this case, the prophet Nathan reached King David's heart, so that the king humbly acknowledged his accountability and accepted responsibility for his sin. He did, however, have to pay the price for all his sins, which included death for his and Bathsheba's child and devastating consequences for himself, Bathsheba, and others. What had happened?

King David attempted to cover up his sin of adultery with Bathsheba in several ways. First, he had Uriah, Bathsheba's husband, brought back home from the war and even got him drunk, hoping he would go to his own home, have sex with Bathsheba, and then later, after the child's birth, assume the child born to be his own (2 Sam. 11:8–27 and 12:7–15). But Uriah declined to go home. What then?

When that deception failed, King David had Joab (his general) arrange for what would appear to be the accidental death of Uriah, a casualty of war. Of course, several other set-up soldiers also died with Uriah, in order to complete the deception and to give it an air of legitimacy. But King David wasn't finished with his deception. One lie usually leads to more lies; one deception to more deceptions, and that was exactly what happened.

After Uriah's death, David took Bathsheba as another of his own wives to hide his sins of adultery, stealing another man's wife, and arranging for the death of Uriah and others. David kept these deceptions alive and unexposed for at least nine months until after the birth of his illegitimate son and the confrontation about his sin by the prophet Nathan (2 Sam. 11:26, 27).

David's acknowledgment of accountability and admission of sin resulted in God "letting his sin pass by;" although the law prescribed death for his sin, he was not executed (2 Sam. 12:13, 14). However, both he and Bathsheba did suffer the anguish of losing their son, and David did have calamity and the violation of his other wives come upon him and them. His wrongdoing did have far-reaching consequences that harmed or killed many innocent victims who had not been a party to his sins.

Notice the differences in this second example:

- When Jesus chastised the scribes and Pharisees for their tyranny of authority, hypocrisy, and greed, it was also an exposé (Matt. 23:13).

- An exposé usually involves a report revealed or exposed by an insider of an organization, revealing shocking, unexpected and/or unknown information. Of course, an exposé is of little value to persons who need the information but refuse, for whatever reason, to learn from it.

The Pharisees of Jesus' day were the most authoritarian, hypocritical, and greedy part of the Jewish hierarchy; they made it a point to evade accountability and dodge responsibility for their wrongs, which Jesus was exposing.

They went to the ultimate limit to try to wiggle out of this exposure, by even orchestrating the death of the only perfect whistle-blower the world has ever known. They pressured the Roman governor, Pontius Pilate, to get his soldiers to do their dirty work for them; they arranged for the death of Jesus, the Son of God.

Did anyone benefit from this exposé by Jesus? Yes, many common people did, but how about the scribes and Pharisees? In addition to the abovementioned negative qualities, they were also callous, devious, and ruthless. But did any of them have a humble attitude and exercise faith in Jesus? Yes, but only a small minority. Notice two of them.

One was Joseph from Arimathea, a wealthy man, a Pharisee and a member of the Sanhedrin (Jewish Supreme Court). He was a "secret disciple" of Jesus, who refused to vote in favor of the actions taken by the Jewish hierarchy against Jesus (Matt. 27:57–60, Luke 23:50–53, John 19:38–42).

Another prominent man was Nicodemus, also a Pharisee, a teacher of Israel and called, "a ruler of the Jews." He also was a member of the Sanhedrin. He was the one who came to Jesus secretly at night and asked what Jesus meant by the expression, to be "born again" (John 3:1–3).

Nicodemus boldly spoke up in favor of Jesus in front of the ones who bitterly hated him and sought his death. He also assisted Joseph of Arimathea in preparing Jesus' body for burial (John 3:1–15, John 7:45–53, John 19:39, 40).

So here were two prominent, courageous men. Both were Pharisees and both secret disciples of Jesus. Both were willing to stand up, by word and deed, against the religious hierarchy of the Jews who were, at that time, still considered to be God's special people, his favored nation.

The Jewish nation, according to the Bible, was God's chosen nation. Scholars date the nation's exodus from Egypt to be anywhere from 1200 BCE to 1550 BCE. But "rabbinical Judaism favors the date 1313 BCE" (*Wikipedia*). So from 1313 BCE until Jesus' death, (traditionally thought to have occurred in 33 CE), is a total of 1,346 years. Was the record of that Israelite nation *exemplary?* No, it was outrageous!

During that time, the nation had a total of forty-one different kings, but only six are reported in scripture to have "done what was right in God's eyes." That represents only 14.6 percent of all of their kings as good. Not an enviable record, is it?

The fact that those six kings had "done what was right in God's eyes" did not mean they were perfect, but the good outweighed the bad for those few kings. That leaves 85.4 percent of the kings in the category of bad, deceptive, and/or worse—a large majority (1 Samuel 10:1 through to 2 Kings 24:20).

The combined total of all the years during which the Jews were ruled by their good kings was only 181 years. That represents only 13.4 percent of years that were considered good, out of the 1,346 years, leaving 86.6 percent of the years to fall into the category again of bad, deceptive, and/or worse.

When we think of Jesus' actions as a whistle-blower in the first century, why do you think many were hesitant to put faith in him or perhaps even to listen to him? Let's see what the scribes and Pharisees did to keep their wrongs hidden, especially after Jesus' exposure of their hypocrisy and deception.

Do you recall the man who, according to the Bible, had been born blind and was cured by Jesus when he was an adult (John 9:1–34)? How did his parents feel when the Pharisees questioned them about it? They were afraid to talk about how he was cured, because as John 9:22 says, the Pharisees had determined that anyone "who acknowledged that Jesus was the Messiah…would be put out of the Synagogue" (NIV). The NWT version says, "Confessed him" rather than "acknowledged" and "expelled" rather than "put out."

There were two great loves that the Pharisees were especially noted for, namely, money and power exerted over the lives of their followers (Luke 16:14, Matt. 23:13–39). That mode of operation tends to bring out many undesirable traits in persons or organizations, such as lying, deception, and hypocrisy. That affected the Pharisees of Jesus' day, and has also affected modern religious hierarchies, such as the W/W/H.

If you are a person who has read the Bible extensively, think of what you know to be stated there about the Israelite nation during the 1,346 years just referred to. Many different whistle-blowers, such as the major and minor prophets in addition to Nathan and Jesus Christ, exposed the many wrongs of God's own people. With only a couple of exceptions, they all condemned the Israelite nation. This included both the northern Kingdom of Israel and the southern Kingdom of Judah.

The reason for this condemnation was that these kingdoms had turned their backs on God and had become thoroughly corrupt. (This included the kings, priests, princes, judges, and even some of their prophets.) Because the common people usually followed the bad example of these leaders, they had to pay the price right along with them and ended up suffering the same consequences; they become apostates.

What were the consequences for their apostasy? Their beloved temple and their capital city, Jerusalem, were both destroyed at least twice by foreign nations, the Babylonians and the Romans. Here are some scriptures to check out on these points: 2 Ki. 17:13; 21:2, 6; 23:7, 8, 26; 24:4; plus Isa. 1:4; Jer. 2:8; 3:21; 5:3; Ezek. 2:3; Hosea 8:7; 11:12, and

Amos 7:10, 17. There are many more, but these are enough for you to get an idea about their corrupt practices.

What is the point?

- Religious hierarchies, especially ones with sect-like or cult-like modes of operation, invariably state that they are "the only ones on earth that have the 'truth;' they are therefore God's special people and all other religious groups deceive their followers and thus must be avoided."

- Both kingdoms of the Jewish nation, north and south, were so corrupt and apostate that they were eventually subdued and in time destroyed, with God's permission and at his direction.

- As you can see, for any religious hierarchy today to claim that it is God's only group of people and therefore that it must be trusted and obeyed implicitly is clearly ludicrous. The facts belie such claims by the Jews or by any others, including the W/W/H.

- The actions of the W/W/H, coupled with the definitions given by the dictionary for a sect (and cult) plus C. T. Russell's definition of a sect (which includes the earmarks of a cult, as quoted in the Introduction), blow the whistle on them.

The excessive control and manipulation applied by the W/W/H leadership on its members, as covered in great detail in this book, clearly exposes the organization's sect-like and cult-like traits.

A scriptural account that praises some first-century Christians for checking up on the truthfulness of the Apostle Paul will be helpful, in view of the fact that the W/W/H condemns anyone who checks up on it. That scriptural account is found at Acts 17:11, "Now the Berean Jews were of more noble character than those in Thessalonica, for they received the message with great eagerness and *examined the Scriptures* every day to see if what Paul said was *true*" (NIV; italics added). The NWT version says, "whether these things were so" rather than "was true."

> ➤ Should not these words strike a responsive chord in the hearts of the members of the W/W/H? To allow and even encourage examination of whether or not they are speaking and teaching the truth would show them to be imitating the Apostle Paul.

However, to suppress examination of any sort would be imitating the sect-like traits defined by C. T. Russell. Two of the earmarks that he noted that were typical of a sect and/or a cult were the following:

- Must ignore individual thought

- Must avoid personal investigation

> ➤ By condemning and disfellowshipping any members who question or blow the whistle on its failed prophecies or who refuse to believe its dogma any longer, is not the W/W/H acting exactly in the same fashion as did the Pharisees of Jesus' day?

The harm done to innocent and/or unwary believers can be and has been physical, emotional, spiritual, yes even financial damage. This can become extremely devastating to victims, especially children, who have been manipulated and coerced into early baptism and who then are held accountable for the rest of their lives for enormous and complex problems that they never could have imagined. (See chapters 5, 8 and 10)

Do you recognize what these facts reveal?

The majority of organizations and people who have lived on this earth, God's people or not, a religious hierarchy or not, political and business leaders or not, and including ourselves, have made decisions and/or engaged in conduct that would sometimes be considered good, but which has also, at times, maybe even many times, turned out to be bad, deceptive, or worse.

- The W/W/H is no exception in this matter. Its unwillingness to acknowledge accountability (its members being the leaders of JWs) and to accept responsibility for its wrongs paints its members as imitators of the Pharisees rather than of King David. Their displaying sect-like and cult-like traits, clearly puts them in the position of opposing God.

Do you recall the little old lady from chapter one? Do you think the outcome for her would have been different had she denied her wrongdoing? What if she had been exposed by two other passengers who, in effect, "blew the whistle" on her, rather than her coming forth on her own?

There can be no question that her acknowledgment of accountability and acceptance of responsibility actually saved her from a far more unpleasant outcome than the one she actually faced. Rather than going to jail, facing a felony charge and all that went with it, she went home for the night.

Throughout human history, has not deception often been used anytime persons, whether business leaders, politicians, a religious hierarchy, or anyone else for that matter, are in danger of being exposed for their wrongdoing? It always seems to be just too big a pill for them to swallow.

Consider the Bible accounts of Adam and Eve (Gen. 3:12, 13) or of Cain and Able (Gen. 4:6–9). Since the dawn of recorded history, lying and deception have been the norm countless times, (as it was in the above mentioned biblical cases) to avoid and hide from exposure of wrongdoing. As a result, truth and honesty have been cast aside.

Sometimes it has been just one person who had the courage to buck the prevailing religious hierarchy. Consider these three from more recent times, the 1300s to 1553 CE.

Although not whistle-blowers in exactly the same way as the prophet Nathan or Jesus Christ, nonetheless, they were found guilty of supposed crimes against the religious hierarchy of their day, for which they suffered dire consequences.

- John Wycliffe (c. 1328–1384): Bible translator, condemned for errors and heresies by religious leaders, especially the Archbishop of Canterbury.

- William Tyndale (1492–1536): Translated the Bible into English. The members of the religious hierarchy of his day turned out to be the ones responsible for his arrest. He was tried for heresy and was choked, impaled, and burnt at the stake in 1536.

- Michael Servetus (1511–1553): Accused of heresy for his teachings, which were in opposition to the religious hierarchy of his day, especially those of John Calvin and his cronies. Servetus was railroaded through a mock trial and put to death by being burned alive at the stake.

Can you even imagine living in such a world?

What did the last two have in common? They were both violently tortured to death, being burned at the stake, and that at the instigation of the exposed religious hierarchies. Have things changed, or does the same mentality exist in our day?

Let's step forward to our times to see if the same lethal mentality and abuse by religious hierarchies still exist. Here are three examples of recognized cult leaders accused and/or convicted of wrongdoing. In these cases, the news media functioned, at least in part, as the whistle-blowers.

There were Jim Jones (1978), David Koresh (1993), and Warren Jeffs (2011). What do you remember about them?

Jim Jones was called "The Mad Messiah" and was involved with the television ministries known as the Peoples Temple in 1980. For his followers, the end came with mass suicide deaths in Jonestown, Guyana,

South America. Was he really the Messiah? Why did people put their faith in him? Why did his followers not sense fraud and escape before it was too late?

A *Wikipedia* article (Jim Jones) points out that "November 18, 1978 brought *mass suicide deaths to 909* Temple members as well as the killings of *five other people* at a nearby airstrip. *Over 200 children* were murdered at Jonestown, *almost all* of whom were *forcibly* made to ingest cyanide by *their elite Temple members.*"

- Would you call that spiritual abuse, along with deception and a cult-like mentality, including excessive control? I would too!

- Imagine if you, as a parent, had been an enabler.

- Do you think those "elite Temple members" were serving God's interests or their own?

David Koresh (whose birth name was Vernon Wayne Howell) was the leader of the Branch Davidians from Waco, Texas, in 1993. He, like many cult leaders before him, managed to hoodwink many. A fire at his compound brought death to eighty-two of his unsuspecting followers; over one-third of them were innocent children.

Koresh claimed to be the "Son of God," but what has history proved to be the reality? Was he not, in fact, a deceptive fraud, guilty of duping others and bringing grief and mourning to countless family members related to those believers who had followed him and ended up paying the ultimate price?

In 2011, there was fifty-five-year-old Warren Jeffs, the head of a polygamist camp, who sexually abused minor girls; he was also a member of the Fundamentalist Church of Jesus Christ of Latter-Day Saints. Among the official titles Jeffs held were "President and Prophet, Seer and Revelator" and "President of the Priesthood." Those religious titles did not make him innocent; nor did they prove him to be a true representative of God. He and many of his associates are now in prison, leaving behind countless victims of their wrongdoing.

Do you think money was a major factor in the seizing of power over the lives of others by each of these three men? Who do you think bore the financial load for these three men and their expensive enterprises? Was it not their misguided, deceived, and defrauded believers?

Does common sense indicate that things would be any different for the W/W/H? That organization has property, branch offices, factories for printing operations, assembly halls, and more, all over the world, worth many billions of dollars. It boasts the largest construction company in the world. Who paid for all of these things?

Can you even begin to imagine what the costs would be just to maintain such facilities, in addition to the cost of building them? What about the millions of hours of free time and labor provided by the members of the organization? They, of course, believe they are giving it all to Jehovah God.

> Do you think that the Watchtower Bible and Tract Society of Pennsylvania, New York and/or any of its subsidiary corporations anywhere in the world make any checks out to Jehovah God? Does God need man-made money? No! Huge greedy corporations do. The massive efforts the W/W/H has expended to operate as well as to cover up its massive moneymaking schemes will be covered in later chapters.

Why do you think that virtually all individuals, groups, and/or corporations involved in deception and wrongdoing continually deny guilt, whether before a court of law under oath, or to the press, or to their victims? Could it be because of pride, arrogance, fear of reprisals, and fear of losing followers, money, and influence over other people's lives? Whatever it is or was that has afflicted the minds of such deceivers, the bottom line is that they have never admitted a specific fault; they have done everything possible to hide accountability and refused to accept any responsibility.

When the activities of Warren Jeffs were being exposed by the news media, no doubt many rational people wondered, "How could his followers have believed in him and stayed associated with his organization, following his demands?"

There are at least three categories of players in these wrongs. First were the perpetrators, Warren Jeffs and his cohorts; second were the enablers of the wrongs, the minor girls' mothers (who were also victims); and third were the minor girls themselves (the targets of the sexual abuse).

Is it not possible that some of these players may have been unwitting accomplices? Could it be that some enablers as well as victims sincerely believed with all their hearts that they were doing what was right, maybe even God's will, despite the opposite being obvious to most other people? Would that make the wrong a right? Would it excuse the perpetrator's guilt? Think of King David and Bathsheba, mentioned earlier. Is it possible that at that time and in that culture, Bathsheba may have sincerely believed that she had no choice but to submit to King David's advances? After all, he was the authority figure—the king! Could she have believed that she had no right even to question his demands?

Can it also be that many who are or were at one time in association with Jehovah's Witnesses feel the same way? Is it likely that they have believed that they had no choice but to do whatever their hierarchy said and demanded? I recall one elder of Jehovah's Witnesses who told me that "even if we know that the hierarchy is/or was doing what is/or was wrong, we have no choice. We must believe and follow them, because after all, they are Jehovah's organization. Jehovah will correct them if they are wrong."

I asked him, "Would you have followed King Manasseh in the matter of child sacrifice, if you had been an Israelite?" He would not answer, for obvious reasons; his reasoning was definitely faulty. It would not be workable or sensible in any other venue, including flying a plane. But when a cult-like organization has a stranglehold on its members, as has been the case with many religious hierarchies, there seems to be no limit to the abuse and long-term damage that these organizations can foist and have foisted upon countless numbers of their believers, past or present.

This book has been written for the benefit of all who find themselves in such situations. I have been in that same boat myself. I have been an unwitting enabler as well as a victim of spiritual abuse during my nearly sixty years in association with Jehovah's Witnesses. I am deeply sorry for any hurt that I may have caused to others. I, too, have suffered as a victim. I am hopeful that this book will reach many who have had such harm foisted on them, providing encouragement and comfort, perhaps even the where-with-all needed to help them escape the harm. (Chapter fourteen) I am aware that many present JWs are plagued with serious reservations and are looking for a means and the support needed to escape.

Why do you think that normally rational people who are and/or were outsiders in relation to these different groups could see that they were destructive sects or cults, yet many of the persons who were insiders in the organization, both enablers and victims, failed to realize the danger they were facing? There is a term used to describe why the followers of a sect or cult will stay with their organizations and stay in submission, as followers, even though common sense may be telling them to get out. That term is "cognitive dissonance." What does that term mean, and how does it work? What can we learn from the bad experiences others have had because of it?

From Wikipedia comes this explanation: "'Cognitive dissonance' is a mental discomfort that comes about because one holds conflicting cognitions; in other words, one's ideas, beliefs, values or emotional reactions, inside one's head and heart are putting up a fight with opposing negative feelings such as surprise, dread, guilt, anger, disbelief or embarrassment; actually a state of dissonance has developed—a clash of ideas and beliefs" (*Wikipedia*).

The term "cognitive dissonance" itself was coined by Leon Festinger in his 1956 book, entitled *When Prophecy Fails*.

Cognitive dissonance would be similar to the way a person feels who wants to quit smoking for health reasons, maybe even to save his or her life, but at the same time, the person may want the pleasure felt from smoking. Which decision will the person make? Will he or she fight against the urge, or will the person give up trying to quit, choosing instead to remain a smoker?

The view of cognitive dissonance comes about when one is biased toward a certain decision, or viewpoint, even though other factors favor an alternative. For example, in this illustration, the person convinces himself that he or she is the exception and cancer won't get them. Or such person may feel and argue, "I am going to die from something, sometime, anyway—it may as well be cancer."

At what point does one get ones head on straight and consciously make the decision to get out of a situation that could be death-dealing? For those who have decided to stay with a destructive sect or cult such as those controlled by cult leaders Jim Jones, David Koresh, or Warren Jeffs, or who have chosen to stay with any organization displaying sect-like or cult-like traits, would not these victims have been far better off to have gotten out before it was too late? Better yet to have avoided the organization from the start.

Does this not also help you see how a mother could allow her minor daughter(s) to be sexually assaulted and abused by a fifty-five-year-old man, even if he claims to be a "Prophet, Seer or Revelator?" Is it not clear that the mothers are being manipulated and abused, just as was the case with their minor daughter(s)?

Think of the enormous damage done to the innocent mothers and children who were victimized by such selfish, perverted, and twisted leaders. How do you think the enabling mothers will feel if and when they finally wake up? How will they view their allowance of that abuse of their minor daughter(s) at that time?

Do you remember the six earmarks that C. T. Russell gave in his definition of a religious sect? These apply with even greater force to a cult.

When anyone gives up his or her own mind, allows another (person or group) to do the thinking for him or her and then decide for that person what is truth or error—when one accepts another's decisions without question, ignores individual thought, refuses to investigate, and allows one's conscience to be enslaved by another—that person is definitely headed for disaster.

Persons who are willing to put up with cognitive dissonance in a religious setting are by their own choice and/or course of action proclaiming that they themselves are members of a sect or a cult, even if they deny that such a possibility exists, perhaps to their dying breath.

Remember that the definition of a cult (Introduction before Chapter one), is: "a religious group, exploitative toward its members." It is usually regarded by *others* as dangerous and imposing excessive control over its members.

Because of cognitive dissonance, there is no way that sect or cult *followers* can possibly see themselves accurately or objectively. Because of their personal involvement, they have become mentally handicapped. They need help from someone else, one who can see what the problem is and provide needed help, the same way a seriously injured person needs the help of a doctor.

The W/W/H has created the same situation for its believers. Their problem is not one of being imperfect and just making a mistake. Rather, it is a problem *caused* because they have always refused to acknowledge accountability and take responsibility for errors. Many present and former members have been injured and handicapped and are in need of outside help; that is why I have written this book.

The W/W/H has always blamed some unnamed individual, believers in general, or anyone else they can dump the blame on for their errors, but they have never been willing to take the blame as the governing body or as the "faithful and discreet slave" for their errors. Yet they are the ones who are *responsible* because of erroneous teachings and draconian policies foisted on their members and published by them.

- Why is that, do you think? Why won't they accept blame for their wrongs?

- Why did the Pharisees not accept blame for their wrongs, after being exposed by Jesus, and then make needed changes?

- Are honesty and integrity the most important things to the W/W/H, or is protecting its position, money, and power, while hiding wrongdoing, the bigger issues?

Two scriptures may prove helpful as you continue reading. Rom. 3:4 says, "… Let God be true, and *every human* being *a liar*" (NIV; italics added). The NWT version says, "though" rather than "and."

Rom. 12:2 says, "Then *you* will be able to *test and approve* what God's will is—his good, pleasing and perfect will" (NIV; italics added). The NWT version says, "making your mind over," and "prove to yourselves" rather than "test and approve" and "his good pleasure."

Please note that the onus is on us—the readers. We are not instructed to let someone else (in sect-like or cult-like style) state, prove, or demand what *we* should believe. We should be able to prove it to ourselves. Do you notice how C. T. Russell's words, from 1911, keep coming back to haunt today's W/W/H?

The real questions facing abusers, enablers, and victims alike, are the following:

- Have the W/W/H and perhaps others continued committing the same wrongs, over and over again? Facts will be detailed in later chapters.

- Will this hierarchy and its enablers be willing, like King David, to acknowledge accountability and accept responsibility for their errors and make needed changes?

- Or will they continue to imitate the Pharisees (or other abusive religious clergy) who, in their case, silenced the perfect whistle-blower of that time, God's Son?

- Will the enablers and victims alike be willing and able to recognize that they have both been abused, deceived, and manipulated? Will they *choose* to leave the abusive situation, where they have been trapped, or will they allow cognitive dissonance to keep them captive?

How will they choose to react, whether Witnesses or people of another religious faith, if they find themselves in any of these roles? This may require standing up against a religious hierarchy or other authoritarian figures that may violently fight against them. But spiritual abuse, like physical or sexual abuse, must not be allowed to continue; that would be an outrageous wrong!

Have you wondered why members of an abusive sect such as Warren Jeffs' polygamist camp, a known and recognized cult, have continued to be a part of it? Why could not the mothers and children (enablers and victims) see and shake the problem of cognitive dissonance? What was missing?

Sometimes even when it seems that it should be so easy to see and discern the wrong being foisted on a victim, he or she is many times still unable to discern it. Why is that?

Flying: A flying lesson will assist understanding.

- ❖ An essential element in learning to fly an airplane and in earning even a private pilot certificate involves training perceptive powers while inside the cockpit, especially for instrument flying. Seeing the need for such training will enhance your understanding of why the victims of sects and cults, or other perpetrators who wield excessive control, just don't seem to get it.

Let's analyze the logistics involved in this process. It is required that a person learning to become a private pilot must do some instrument flying, learning the basics of such flying. When under the hood or in a flight simulator, nothing can be seen outside the cockpit. The student must fly depending entirely on the flight instruments on the panel. His understanding and interpretation, of what those flight instruments are telling him or her, is far more difficult than it sounds. It is impossible to fly this way safely without training and practice, practice, practice!

The requirement of getting even a minimum amount of instrument training is to enable the student at least to fly straight and level and to safely make climbs, turns, and descents in clouds. With such training, the student may, even in an emergency, be able to fly an instrument approach in moderately bad weather with restricted visibility, to successfully make a safe landing at an airport rather than getting into a panic and crashing into a house or building.

Sounds like a good plan, doesn't it? Additionally, learning perception through training can help thwart cognitive dissonance in a religious venue, which can be just as deadly or even more so.

I recall when I was a student pilot and had about five hours of instrument training (practice under the hood), my instructor asked me, "Do you think you could stay level and fly right side up in clouds, if you could not understand what your flight instruments were telling you?" I thought for a second and then confidently replied, "I think so." We were five thousand feet above the ground, and with my hood in place, I could not see the smirk on my instructor's face.

"Good," he said, and then he pulled my hood down so that all I could see was my lap—no flight instruments and nothing outside the cockpit. "Just fly straight and level," he ordered. A minute went by; I was flying by the seat of my pants, as they say. I could feel no sensations or changes that seemed out of line with flying straight and level.

He asked me, "How are you doing now?"

I was becoming suspicious, so I replied with a little less confidence, "I think…I am OK."

"Fine," he replied, and a few more seconds crept by. "How about now?" he asked.

I was really losing confidence fast, so I hesitatingly replied, "I think…I am still OK…I am not sure…!"

He lifted my hood up far enough for me to see all of my flight instruments but nothing outside the plane. I was horrified—we were in a spiral at two thousand feet above the ground and descending at nearly two thousand feet per minute. A crash was only seconds away!

Needless to say, I reacted immediately, pulled the plane out of its spiral, leveled the wings, and started a climb—*Whew!* After over ten thousand hours of flying and nearly fifty years of experience as a pilot, I can still remember that experience in living color. Are you sweating now too?

My instructor noted, with a chuckle, "I think you've got the point. If you are in instrument meteorological conditions, but you are not qualified to fly instruments (perceive what they are telling you), you will have only about a minute and a half to live."

Obviously, he would not have let me crash; he could easily have taken over at any time, and he would have if I had ignored the warnings that my flight instruments were giving me. And as for me, I learned a lesson that I have never forgotten. Mission accomplished.

Even though the "fly-by-the-seat-of your-pants" feeling may be telling a pilot everything is OK, that feeling must be ignored and dismissed in favor of the truthful flight instruments presentation. Otherwise confusion, such as occurs with cognitive dissonance, could not just ruin the pilot's day but could bring an end to his or her life.

One more point involving training is noteworthy. To earn an instrument rating on a pilot certificate requires a minimum of forty hours of instrument flight training. But usually it takes a little longer, and even then, the pilot, although instrument rated, is a beginner, by no means really proficient at flying real-life instrument approaches to the lowest minimums (i.e., weather with extremely low visibility at the airport). More practice leads to greater proficiency.

This same principle, involving the need to learn perception, also applies in religious issues we face and the choices we make. If a person can and will do his or her own thinking and use good judgment, the person may well never succumb to a sect-like or cult-like mentality which others may be trying to foist on him. Or if he or she is already a victim, the person may be helped to break free.

A very relevant scripture comes to mind: 1 Tim. 4:7, which says, "…; rather, *train yourself* to be godly" (NIV; italics added). The NWT version says, "training yourself" and "godly devotion" rather than "train yourself" and "be godly."

Unlike pilot training, which requires you to be under a hood with a flight instructor sitting next to you, godly devotion can be learned through effort expended by you. Note that the scripture just quoted, addressed to the young man Timothy and written by the Apostle Paul, says, "train yourself" and "be training yourself." Would it say that, if this training was impossible to accomplish? I don't think so either.

Is it not obvious that if any person or organization with a sect-like or cult-like mentality tries to seize your right to make your own personal or religious decisions, they are clearly overstepping their bounds? If those with such a mentality presume to be your masters while you are dealt with as an underling (or a child) and are forbidden to ask questions or to investigate, how will you train your own perceptive powers? Why should anyone tolerate such conduct by a religious hierarchy?

I am ashamed of the fact that it took me nearly six decades to break free of the spiritual abuse and sect-like bullying foisted on me by the

W/W/H since I was nine years old. Such a sect-like mode of operation can have a stranglehold on one that is very difficult to overcome. Practical suggestions for dealing with this situation will be provided in chapter 14.

I wonder why it took me so long to clearly see what the W/W/H with its Watchtower printing propaganda machine had been foisting on me and my family. Cognitive dissonance victimized all of us for a considerable time. Chapter 5 chronicles how I finally managed to get and keep my blinders off.

Sadly, many millions of present day JWs (including some of my own family members) are still flying by the seat of their pants; they appear to be unable to see and hence are totally unaware of the extreme control that the W/W/H has been foisting on them and others for years.

This situation is truly just as dangerous as literally flying an aircraft, in instrument meteorological conditions, without the skill to discern what the flight instruments are telling the pilot. Fatal consequences are waiting in the wings for all such adherents; that fact pains me.

What does this tell us?

- It takes proficiency to accomplish virtually everything of value that we may attempt to do; that means practice, practice, practice, and lots of it! That is true of what one learns in the secular work venue as well as in the religious thought and teaching venue.

- How qualified do you think you could become in flying a plane if your instructor did all the flying and practicing, when you were the one who was paying for lessons to train you?

- The instructor cannot take the flight check with the FAA for you and then expect that the FAA will issue you the instrument rating, right?

- Likewise, becoming a mature adult takes time and practice. Along the way, mistakes will be made, and one is expected to learn from them; they are part of one's training to become an adult. No one can either grow up or think for you, can they?

- However, if a person does not want to learn or refuses to learn when perhaps lifesaving information is presented, that person will likely suffer for the uninformed choice won't he or she?

A very relevant scripture comes to mind from Heb. 5:14, which says, "But solid food is for the *mature,* who *by constant use* have *trained themselves* to distinguish good from evil" (NIV; italics added). The NWT: "through use…perceptive powers trained…right and wrong…constant use…distinguish…good and evil."

This scripture, along with the one noted two pages before this one (1 Tim. 4:7), make it clear that we have to train ourselves. It definitely is not the right of the W/W/H (or any other) to do it for us. As you continue reading, you will see value in recalling these scriptures and the points made by Mr. Russell about a sect or cult. These very earmarks have become an ever increasing part of the W/W/H's mentality and its policies.

Do you discern the similarity, in comparing the lethal mentality of some airline captains during the 1960s and 1970s, to that of the sect-like or cult-like traits displayed by the W/W/H? Underlings are treated like immature children!

How safe do you think airline flying would be today if the concepts of CRM had not been taught, learned, and practiced by all airline crew members? Do you think it will be possible for the W/W/H to continue to display the destructive traits of a sect or cult without eventually suffering the very same death-dealing consequences that have often come to other groups because of that mentality?

Recall that the Pharisees handled dissenters by expelling them from the synagogue. This same type of threat hangs over the head of any one of Jehovah's Witnesses who dares to be a whistle-blower by exposing failed prophecies, double-talk, deception, or other wrongdoing on the part of the W/W/H. (See chapters 9, 10)

Active Witnesses are even warned against checking out the Internet, unless of course they look at the official W/W/H site (www.jw.org), which is controlled and monitored by the upper echelon hierarchy.

You, the reader, are urged to check all references contained in this book, both in detail and in context.

If you feel it would be disloyal to do so, you are not alone; you may even feel incensed at the mere suggestion, by a whistle-blower such as me, stating that the W/W/H has been dishonest. Due to that, you may not choose to investigate. If you make that decision, you may later wish that you hadn't. I felt that way also, and it took me many decades to finally succeed in taking off my blinders and, eventually, in keeping them off. I am so glad that I finally did. I pray that you will too.

A scriptural proverb that may be of great value to you, comes from King Solomon, who is considered to have been one of the wisest men ever to have lived on earth. Note his words recorded at Prov. 4:7, "Wisdom is the prime thing. *Acquire wisdom;* and with all that you acquire, *acquire understanding*" (NWT, italics added). The NIV says, "Get wisdom and understanding" and "Though it costs all you have."

Obviously, the choice is yours. You have been endowed with a conscience, free will, and the ability to think, reason, and understand. How will you use these God-given gifts?

As one who has served, in the past, as one of Jehovah's Witnesses for nearly sixty years and one who is very well qualified to author this exposé, I ask, "Don't you owe it to yourself to make an honest and thorough investigation?" No one can do that for you. Each of us must do it for himself or herself, but the rewards can be enormous.

❖ A Flight lesson: Beware of negative panic. It can have *deadly consequences* that you may not realize.

In 1966, while I was still a flight engineer on the DC-6, an in-flight emergency occurred in the cabin of one of the other DC-6s. A curtain closed off the flight attendants' galley from the main cabin; the coffee maker was on, and its base was very hot. When the flight attendant took a tray full of coffees to the first class passengers, she walked through the two curtains on her way out of the galley. When one of them swung back into the galley, it landed against the coffee maker's hot plate. It didn't take long before the curtain caught fire.

The flight attendant, seeing fire climbing the curtain, set her tray on a passenger's fold-down table and then quickly grabbed the closest fire extinguisher and extinguished the fire. While this was all happening, a male passenger sitting in the aisle seat of the first row behind the bulkhead—just three feet from the fire—was reading a newspaper. And as the fire started climbing the curtain toward the ceiling, he just kept *moving his newspaper up higher* so that he could not see the obvious fire.

After the fire was out, the flight attendant asked this man, "Why didn't you tell me the curtain was on fire?"

He said, "What fire?" And then he passed out.

Our flight instructor who related the tale of this emergency at my next proficiency check pointed out that this type of problem is called "negative panic." It can happen to any person who just will not admit to himself or herself that a life-threatening emergency is occurring. The person experiencing this can become so paralyzed with fear that he will do nothing, not even to help himself. Some passengers have died during a survivable aircraft fire because even though they were not hurt or handicapped, they refused to get up out of their seats and get off the burning aircraft. They stayed put and died in their seats unnecessarily.

This real in-flight emergency is relevant to our discussion because negative panic can become like cognitive dissonance, where the obviously right decision, to get off the burning aircraft, is not made. Negative panic, in such a case, can become the number one enemy; it can have fatal consequences. The same is true in a religious venue.

If one really becomes aware that he or she is in a life-threatening situation, religiously, the person must be willing to make the right decision. He or she must get out of that death-dealing situation. Remember the case of Jim Jones in Guyana, South America, and of David Koresh in Waco, Texas? Both situations spelled death for their loyal, although misguided, followers.

Getting away from a potentially death-dealing environment must become the number one priority if survival is to become a reality.

Recall the scriptures quoted earlier in this chapter: Rom. 3:4, where we are admonished to let God be true even if it makes every man a liar, and Rom.12:2, to test and prove to yourself what is God's will for you.

- What will you do, if you are an active Witness? I hope that this chapter has helped you to choose to think for yourself and pay attention to the whistle-blowers; there have been many from times past, and there are many in the present.

- If so, you will likely continue reading with benefit. That will be true of you even if you are not affiliated with the Witnesses. Remember, the counsel to Christians is to let God be true, even if it makes every man a liar.

- Negative panic, in the guise of fear of what others may think, must not stop you from reacting to what you become aware of as reality. *Choose to think!*

REVIEW POINTS:

1. What has been the track record in the past for many religious hierarchies, when their wrongs have been exposed?

2. What quality did King David demonstrate that separated him from the scribes and Pharisees?

3. Do you think that God considers it acceptable when the W/W/H (or others for that matter) follows the example of the scribes and Pharisees in trying to silence whistle-blowers in this time period?

4. A person may find it difficult, if not impossible, to continue living with inconsistencies in his or her life. Cognitive dissonance, like negative panic, can prove to be fatal. What choices do you think a person faced with such inconsistencies should make?

Although we have covered some negative traits of W/W/H from the past, it would be unfair to ignore the fact that there have been some good things that I have experienced from having been one of Jehovah's Witnesses in the past.

Let's check them out and see what some of these are that have been beneficial for me and my family. The next chapter will address the good...

Chapter 4

JEHOVAH'S WITNESSES: "THE GOOD..."

- How can Bible study help us, besides religiously?
- How can something that looked so good bring such major disappointments? What has gone wrong?
- Is there a cost to a life of strict conformity or belief?
- Are good deeds negated by hypocrisy?

If you are a senior citizen, you already know that life is filled with uncertainty. By the time you reach your seventies, you can look back on both good decisions, such as whom you *chose* to marry, or on bad decisions, perhaps whom you *did* marry. I myself picked the perfect wife!

There are not too many perfect marriages; however, some members of couples commendably seem to have made better choices in picking a mate than others. Decisions involving picking a marriage mate can have long-term consequences that can impact happiness and contentment, or sorrow and grief! The same is true with regard to religious choices and decisions.

Other decisions or events in life are out of our realm of personal choice, some perhaps foisted on us by others or some brought about by force of circumstances or maybe as a result of deception and excessive control by a religious hierarchy with sect-like or cult-like traits. As noted earlier, the W/W/H has consistently displayed such traits throughout its history.

There is a word involving the mode of operation of others that may dramatically affect our decisions, good or bad. This is the word "hypocrisy," defined by *Webster's Revised Dictionary (1913)* as, "a feigning to be what one is not... a false appearance of virtue or religion... a deceitful show of a good character, in morals or religion... a counterfeiting of religion."

Another relevant word to this discussion is "agenda" - defined by Wiktionary (4/6/2013) as, "A temporally organized plan for matters to be attended to... Derived terms: hidden agenda." [i.e. kept secret]

A recent conviction involving Gerald Arthur ("Jerry") Sandusky shows how an agenda on the part of an individual can turn what at first looks like a very laudable course of conduct into a web of lying, hypocrisy, and deception that brings enormous damage to others, especially when minor children are involved.

Mr. Sandusky, a former college football coach, founded a charity in 1977 called The Second Mile as a group foster home dedicated to helping troubled boys. It turned out to be more than a nonprofit charity serving underprivileged and at risk youth in the State of Pennsylvania. It served as a front for Mr. Sandusky to meet his victims. You may recall that he was a serial child molester, yet he consistently denied any wrongdoing.

In the fall of 2012, he was found guilty on forty-five of the forty-eight charges against him of child molestation. It is likely he will spend the rest of his life in prison.

- Do you think Mr. Sandusky's noteworthy accomplishments and record as a college football coach or the fact that he is the author of several books related to his football coaching career or that he founded a charity with laudable goals would excuse his conduct as a child molester? Would his good conduct allow one to overlook his pedophilia desires that became actual sexual abuse of many young boys over a period of fifteen years?

- Likewise, would the good done by a religious hierarchy excuse bad, deceptive, or worse conduct that has caused untold damage to countless numbers of adults as well as to children?

Obviously, just having an agenda does not automatically mean that the agenda is bad. But sometimes it is, as was seen in the Sandusky situation.

The W/W/H has done many noteworthy things that have indeed turned out to be good and have come under the heading of being worthy, laudable, and commendable works.

But think back to the account about King David, mentioned in the previous chapter. Did the fact that he, as a youth, stood up against Goliath and killed him (1 Sam. 17:32–51) excuse his deception, adultery, and ordering the murder of innocent men or his covering up of his capitol crimes when he later became the king? Of course not; remember, it was his acknowledgment of accountability and acceptance of responsibility for his wrongdoing and his repentant attitude that brought God's forgiveness and saved him from execution.

A little background information will prove to be helpful here. The following points are taken from the Witness book, *Jehovah's Witnesses Proclaimers of God's Kingdom* (WTB &TS 1993, p. 718–723).

"In 1870 Charles Taze Russell and a group from Pittsburgh and Allegheny, Pennsylvania, U.S.A., began a systematic study of the Bible." In 1931, "The name *Jehovah's Witnesses* [was] adopted by resolution at a convention in Columbus, Ohio on July 26, and thereafter at conventions around the earth." That organization was growing, and as with kids, growth brings many changes. Some turn out to be good. Others, in time, become recognized as not so good, maybe even bad… deceptive…and worse.

That book also discloses that the year 1943 saw the introduction of the Course in Theocratic Ministry (later called the Theocratic Ministry School). It is conducted in all congregations of Jehovah's Witnesses, and at first, it provided training in public speaking for men and boys. Later, girls and women were urged to join.

If you think about how comfortable or uncomfortable you are in talking before a group of others, especially persons you don't know, you can see that such training could be a confidence builder for nearly all activities involving interaction with others. It can help and has helped many overcome timidity and shyness, including myself.

Starting on September 1, 1953, an extensive program of training Jehovah's Witnesses in house-to-house preaching got under way. You no doubt recognize that the above mentioned school paved the way for this activity and greatly enhanced it. Was there an agenda involved? Likely so, but at the same time, such training proved helpful to me in just plain growing up and learning to deal with and be relaxed around others, especially those older than myself. It may well have made it easier for me to get hired by United Airlines in 1966. I was relaxed and did not feel intimidated during my employment interview.

The following will help explain in what way being associated with Jehovah's Witnesses served as a benefit to my family and me.

The Bible is recognized by millions of people around the world as a must read book for a good education. I would readily agree with that. Its outstanding counsel, principles, and especially Jesus' Sermon on the Mount (Matt. 5–7) can help people of any language group, culture, or ethnic background, in many ways.

The Hindu leader, Mohandas Gandhi, is reported to have once said, If *all* people living on this earth lived by and applied the teachings of that *sermon,* we could solve nearly all of the major problems of the world. If you have never read The Sermon on the Mount, I recommend that you take the time to do so. It only takes about twenty minutes; you will learn much and be glad you did.

Whatever you may personally think about Jehovah's Witnesses, they are well known as Bible readers, and most of them are very well qualified to help you find any scripture you may be looking for, even if you can only remember a couple of words from the verse in question. Of course there are people of other religious groups who can do likewise; but it is the rule with Witnesses, not the exception.

That ability to know the Bible well and be able to do research to find what one is looking for, even if used in other venues, can help one solve many other problems in life, especially relating to personal relationships.

Having the ability to do research can be of great help in many ways besides just religiously; that has been the experience of my wife and me. For example, we have considerable experience as paralegals, having been able to handle a number of legal issues, including district court appearances, *pro se* (on our own, without needing an attorney).

Children, too, learn many practical skills, such as how to sit still at meetings, how to make comments or give answers in their own words, how to talk to complete strangers, and how to prepare and deliver Bible talks. Such instruction and training as a youngster eventually enabled me to give lectures with ease to tens of thousands of people at large Witness conventions.

Such training can have a telling effect on a person's future, for the better. Of course, all of these things, normal activities for Witness families, come with an agenda. These people are in fact trained and required to proselytize in recruiter-like fashion. There is no question that such activity requires effort and work on the part of the parents as well as their children. So there is an upside as well as a downside to this. But such training can yield rewards, according to the efforts expended by both the parents and their children.

There have been some very helpful books published by the W/W/H, covering information and counsel for parents trying to raise their children successfully. Note these examples, which are all published and copyrighted by the Watchtower Bible and Tract Society of PA or NY, for the benefit of Jehovah's Witnesses and interested people the world over:

- *Family Happiness—How to Find It* (1980): Covers how to find and live a rewarding life, as well as necessary points on how to communicate as a family; very helpful.

- *Learn From the Great Teacher* (2003): For children, to help them be on guard and protect themselves from sexual predators and learn meaningful lessons from the Bible.

- *Life—How Did it Get Here? By Evolution or by Creation?* (1985): Delves into how life came to be on this earth. The opposite side of the evolution coin; very well documented with scientific facts.

- *Listening to the Great Teacher* (1971): For young people. It covers Jesus' wise sayings and how to apply them to oneself with benefit.

- *My Book of Bible Stories* (2004): Discusses every major event recorded in the Bible, in chronological order. It was especially written with young children in mind, and it is easy to understand. The chronological order helps adults also.

- *Questions Young People Ask—Answers That Work* (1989): Written for adolescents, especially older teenagers and it expands on previous books for youths.

- *Your Youth—Getting the Best Out of It* (1976): Written for teenagers; includes tasteful ways for parents to discuss sex (with older children) in a clean and dignified way, and more.

This is not a complete list, but it will give you a good idea of some of the literature and counsel that has been provided by the leadership of Jehovah's Witnesses, which has proved to be very helpful to both Witnesses and non-Witnesses the world over.

What parent has not anguished over an unexpected question? Have you heard about the young boy who asked his mother, "Mommy, where did I come from?" As she scrambled for the right words to say, she thought to herself, "Isn't he a little young for this kind of question?" Nonetheless, she started with an explanation, wondering all the time, "How much does my child already know?" When she had finished with her somewhat awkward attempt at an explanation, which went completely over his head, he replied with a quizzical look on his face, "Oh, I thought I came from Ohio."

If you have already had an experience like this occur in your family, you understand what it is like to face such a situation. A couple of the abovementioned books cover practical ways that you as a parent can speak with your children, boys or girls, in a tasteful and dignified way, about sex and many other subjects dreaded by parents. Such material is accurate, straightforward, honest, truthful, and tastefully presented. And no, it doesn't involve a stork!

Certainly, such helpful provisions provided by the leadership of Jehovah's Witnesses cannot be faulted. For that matter, virtually every religious organization in existence has some good and strong points to recommend it. Some of them provide orphanages, hospitals, and homes for unwed mothers and the homeless, and so on. Many very good things are provided by other religious groups and not just by the Witnesses.

Some religious organizations provide food pantries and/or warehouses with provisions for those in need, some with strings attached and some without. Either way, many organizations and individuals, from virtually all religious organizations, and many with no religious association at all, do endeavor to do good things for others. No fault is to be found with such honest and selfless giving. There are others, like doctors, civil engineers, and even well-known entertainers, sports figures, and others who have generously lent a hand to help people in poorer nations, some even for extended periods of time. Such action is nothing but good and commendable.

The Witness leadership has encouraged Witnesses, who could do so, to volunteer and help when disaster strikes, sometimes in the United States or even the other end of the world. Usually all of the costs for travel are covered by the individual volunteer and not by the Watchtower organization.

The Witnesses' governing body has made available funds that have helped Witnesses, and sometimes non-Witnesses, faced with such tragedies. The primary emphasis is on helping Witnesses in distress. But on more than one occasion, for example with a family that is not a Witness family but is living next to a Kingdom Hall as a neighbor, that family is given help at the same time as the Witnesses at that hall are given help. Certainly both the Witnesses and non-Witnesses in such cases are grateful for the help that has been offered without cost to the individuals involved. There can be no valid complaints about such voluntary giving and serving.

I would be remiss if I failed to mention something else that the leadership of Jehovah's Witnesses has done, which has benefited the Witness hierarchy primarily, but which has also secured freedoms for other religious groups in the United States and the world over. Although there is a downside to its actions, the W/W/H has fought many court battles to secure freedoms such as freedom of religion, freedom of speech, and freedom of the press.

The Witness *Proclaimers* book, (WTB&TS 1993, p. 678) in the chapter entitled, "Defending and Legally Establishing The Good News," discloses that the Watch Tower Society felt it necessary to establish a *legal department,* in Magdeburg, Germany in the year 1926 then later in the United States. The book goes on to point out, that the Society's legal department, fought many court cases through several courts, obtaining, defining and guaranteeing freedoms not just for the *Witnesses* organization, but for all U.S. citizens, with 138 of such cases being presented to the U.S. Supreme Court. (WTB&TS 1993, p. 679)

The downside is that while the W/W/H has demanded and secured these freedoms for itself, as a religious organization, it has denied these very same freedoms to its own membership, under the guise of maintaining unity in the congregation. Chapters 9, 10, and 11 go into specific details on these matters and the hypocrisy involved.

I recall the day when my oldest son came home from school and advised us that in Social Studies that day, an attorney had come to the school and talked to the class about the Witnesses. He noted that the attorney had said, "Jehovah's Witnesses have done more to secure religious freedoms in the United States than any other religious group." But the downside tempers the joy over its victories in court, doesn't it?

Some good experiences my family and I have enjoyed, in association with Jehovah's Witnesses in the past, have involved visiting faraway places ranging from St. Petersburg, Russia, in the east, to Christchurch, New Zealand, and Sydney, Australia, in the southwest, covering about three quarters of the world.

There were, of course, other advantages which benefited me, from my association with Jehovah's Witnesses such as learning to be well organized, and not procrastinating. That helped me to be a better worker which in turn sharpened my skills as I grew to adulthood. Of course, Witnesses are not the only ones who teach such beneficial skills and work ethic.

But, with five meetings a week, most of Jehovah's Witnesses lead very busy lives. Whether at school or work, caring for the house or learning a trade, doing the normal things that are a part of everyday life for everybody, there must be added the very time-consuming activities of being active as one of Jehovah's Witnesses. A person must be very well organized to care for all of the things that are expected and/or required of him or her.

For elders and ministerial servants in congregations, there is far more time and expense involved; preparing talks, traveling to other congregations sometimes hours away, and delivering talks on Sunday. It can amount to an enormous amount of time, energy, and money. All this travel expense falls on the person who has this "privilege" of volunteering free labor, not on the Watchtower Society.

Since both time (an average of seven hundred and twenty hours per month) and money are limited commodities, the time and money used to care for all the activities and demands that descend upon one who opts to become associated with Jehovah's Witnesses is enormous. That time and money must be stolen from some other place; where does it come from?

It is taken from the family, so they have to bear the loss too. This can turn out to be a costly mistake; I know because I made that mistake.

Had I known how great those costs would eventually turn out to be to my entire family, I would have chosen not to commit myself and them to that kind of a cost. Broken promises and deception have ruled and harmed millions of believers. For the W/W/H, the good has not outweighed the bad (chapter 6).

Consider this point: If a thief, gangster, drug pusher, pedophile, or other wrongdoer helps needy people and contributes liberally to worthy charities, does that excuse or wash away his or her wrong, illegal, or even hurtful activities? Would it be considered acceptable if that person was an authority figure—perhaps a politician, doctor, religious leader, or a school or professional team coach (remember Jerry Sandusky)?

Who, in any nation or culture (except for the perpetrators of wrongs themselves) would think such authority figures should be excused despite violating or molesting minor children, boys or girls? The obvious answer is no one.

Suppose we changed the players, and they were not just minor children but also adults who were harmed by an individual, a corporation, or a religious hierarchy. This harm could be and has become more difficult to deal with, for many, as they got older. Would you think that such harm should be excused because the victims were adults? I don't either.

Don't we have courts to unravel such sticky problems and hand out just punishment and justice? Later chapters in this book will discuss in detail how these questions are relevant to the leadership of Jehovah's Witnesses. Chapters nine, ten, and twelve will prove to be very enlightening on these points.

Jesus' words as recorded in Matt. 23:1–36 (discussed in more detail later), helps in understanding the matter at hand. The Pharisees were singled out specifically for condemnation by Jesus. Was everything that they did bad and corrupt? No, of course not; they were teachers in the nation of Israel and members of the Jewish Supreme Court.

But in your reading of that chapter of the Bible, you will notice that the one thing Jesus ripped into them for, more than any other, was their hypocrisy. That was what really shot them down and condemned them. As the thirty-third verse of that chapter says, "You snakes! You brood of vipers! How will you escape being condemned to *hell*?" (NIV; italics added) The NWT version uses the word, "*Ge·hen′na?*" instead of "hell" (italics added).

The term "*Ge·hen′na*" is described by the W/W/H as, "utter destruction...hence with no resurrection to life as a soul being possible" (WTB&TS vol. 1, 1988, p. 906). In other words, total destruction with no chance of ever living again, anywhere.

The fact that Matthew chapter 23 uses the word, "hypocrites," as applying to the Pharisees more than to any other group in the whole Bible makes it clear that no matter how a person views that word, it will lead to the most adverse judgment any human can receive. In view of the fact that some good deeds, as practiced by the Pharisees, did not get them off the hook from this judgment, makes it clear that all individuals and organizations should be free of hypocrisy, in order to steer far clear of such an adverse judgment! The W/W/H would do well to take to heart this strong warning and make needed changes soon, before it becomes too late and hence impossible, to do so.

REVIEW POINTS:

1. What are some of the good works done by the W/W/H and its members? Do those good works excuse the denial by the W/W/H of constitutional freedoms to those same members?

2. How is hypocrisy defined? Do those definitions fit the W/W/H and its mode of operation toward its members?

3. In addition to the very real costs of day-to-day activities facing Jehovah's Witnesses, what other costs are added that can be devastating for parents and their children?

4. Is it possible that the desire for wealth, power, and control over the lives of others has played a large part in the decisions made by the W/W/H?

5. Does the end justify the means? Where would you draw the line?

How do you think one would be likely to feel if he or she has spent a whole lifetime doing the bidding of the W/W/H, and not one of that organization's promises or prophecies during *their lifetime* had come true, in fact none of their prophecies for, in reality, a 131 year period of time had come true - not even one?

These matters will come to light in my life story, covered in the next chapter. How did I come to grips with them?

Chapter 5

MY LIFE: A MIXED BAG!

- How did trusted adults use deception and coercion in an effort to push me into baptism?
- Was I the exception, at that time, or was it the norm to manipulate the thinking of minors?
- Did the Watchtower/Witness/Hierarchy (W/W/H) continue to use such tactics?
- If you had been hurt, deceived, and manipulated by that hierarchy, would you feel, "It's not that big a deal?"

I had been baptized as an infant (of course, I was too young to remember that event) and raised as a Catholic, the religion of my father, until I was four years old. Then my mother began teaching my siblings and me the beliefs of Jehovah's Witnesses. We were exposed to both sets of teachings until one eventful summer.

It was the year 1950, and the place, Yankee Stadium, New York City, for an eight-day international convention sponsored by the Watchtower Bible and Tract Society of New York, the mother corporation of Jehovah's Witnesses. I was pressured to get in line to be baptized by immersion in water. I was only nine years old, and I do not remember that baptism any more than when I was baptized, as an infant, by a Catholic priest. Was I *really* baptized?

I have tried to find someone, anyone, who would or could have seen me get baptized. Neither my two older brothers nor my mother nor anybody else has been able to confirm that I really was baptized then. I remember a line and thousands of people, none of whom I knew, but I do not remember ever getting changed into a bathing suit or getting baptized.

What was the motivation in an attempt to get me baptized? Was it my decision, or was it foisted upon me? What are the ramifications of baptism imposed on Witness children, especially minors, some as young as five years old? Neither I nor my two older brothers (aged thirteen and ten) had any way of knowing at those tender ages what would later be expected, demanded, and/or required of us if we were baptized as JWs or what the consequences would be if we later decided to leave the organization of the W/W/H.

I was told by my mother, "This system is going to end very soon; in fact you will never reach high school before Armageddon comes. Since you are old enough, if you don't get baptized, Jehovah's angels will be obligated to kill you, along with everyone else who is not a Witness." Where did she get that idea? From the W/W/H (the higher-up echelon) by means of its members' convention talks, presented with a stampede mentality, and through the publications read, believed, and acted upon by my mother.

Was this not, in reality, manipulation, coercion, deception, and actually child abuse against an unknowing, innocent, and unsuspecting nine-year-old child and his siblings? The W/W/H and my own mother had used my brothers and me, like pawns in a chess game, to further their agenda—an international convention with the largest mass baptism in history up to that point in time.

Chapter 8, entitled, "The Baptism Deception—for Youths: The Dark Side," and chapter 10, entitled, "Disfellowshipping: The Dark Side Leading to the Destruction of Families"; both give detailed attention to this fraudulent practice of child baptism.

The efforts to manipulate us kids and deceive our father had already been at work. My mother had told our dad that we just wanted to go on a camping trip to have fun with some friends. The year 1950 was long before cell phones. Once my siblings, my mother, and I had left in a car belonging to another Witness, there was no way my father could contact us. Like it or not, we were headed from Ypsilanti, Michigan, to an eight-day international convention of Jehovah's Witnesses in New York, over six hundred miles away.

Up to that point, nothing had been said to us kids about baptism; that was sprung on us—like a steel trap—after we got there. There had been no study about baptism and no explanation of the significance of it. Nor had there been any explanation of the negative ramifications that we would be subjected to if, later, we acted like normal stupid kids, broke a Witness rule, and as a result, found ourselves disfellowshipped and then shunned by our friends and family for the rest of our lives. Fear mentality had manipulated us—*Get baptized or die!*

Soon after we left home, the news media was reporting on an international convention of Jehovah's Witnesses in New York City and on a tent city nearby, where thousands of Witnesses, including us, were camping in tents on freshly mowed hay fields. But although the cat was out of the bag, there was absolutely nothing my father could do about it by then. He had been deceived, and his role as the family head had been usurped, contrary to Bible instruction (See 1 Cor. 11:3, regarding headship).

My father had figured out where we really were, what had happened to his family, and that deception had been used by my mother to get us there. When we got home, it became the beginning of the end for our family. Although my father had bought flowers that day for my mother, a war of words soon eclipsed any good intentions that may have been his motive for buying them. A bigger battle was brewing that would soon tear our family apart.

As Catholics, we kids customarily knelt down at our bedsides at night with our father and repeated together the "Our Father" prayer as well as the "Hail Mary" prayer. Our mother had convinced us that to repeat the "Hail Mary" prayer would be wrong and offensive to Jehovah, so all three of us boys refused to say that one. To this day, I can still remember my father nearly flying downstairs to the kitchen and demanding that my mother tell us to say the "Hail Mary" prayer. She refused, and my dad left home that night, very angry. Shortly after that event, my parents were divorced.

Why can I remember the above traumatic incident, which started the destruction of our family and stole my father from me, but I can't remember getting in the water and getting baptized? I don't know either, but I can't.

In those days, the 1950s, divorce in families was the exception and not the rule, as it is now. I can remember kids whispering behind my back, "He hasn't got a dad." It would be thirty-five years before I would learn the truth about what had really happened.

My mother had always told us, "Your father divorced me because of my religion; that is why we're poor and have the troubles we do." It was a half-truth, a term also used frequently by the W/W/H to refute all accusations against them by any who oppose them, especially when the accusations are correct and there are really no valid objections to them. Of course that means there is, in fact, an element of truth, perhaps even a very large element.

In reality, my father had started divorce proceedings, but on the day of the hearing with the judge, my father's attorney told the judge, "Mr. Staelens does not want to go through with this divorce; he wants to keep his family together." My mother, however, had decided that she would be happier and that we would all be better off, with the end of the world so close, to be rid of my father, so she filed a counterclaim for divorce, seeking custody of us kids. She obtained it.

Among Witnesses, only adultery is allowed as grounds for divorce with a possible remarriage, and such had not been the case here. Mother's reason for divorce was incompatibility. I learned the truth: she had gotten the divorce and had done so without proper scriptural grounds. While cleaning out an old filing cabinet for Mom, I unintentionally found all of the legal divorce papers that provided the unhappy truth of what my mother had done. What a shock it was!

After learning this truth about the divorce, twenty-four years after my father had died, I found myself plagued with anger and guilt. Why? Because he went to his grave, at the age of fifty, with me still believing that he had been responsible for the mess our family had faced. What a monstrous deception!

There was no possible way for me to apologize to him for the wrong belief that had been hammered into our heads. No way to correct the outrageous wrong against him, foisted on all of us by my mother and the W/W/H. Can you sense the feelings that I was experiencing? It had clearly been a case of child abuse!

Incidentally, the Watchtower Society's legal department had provided help and counsel for my mother with respect to how to get custody of us children. The laws of cause and effect began to play a part in the lives of all of us, and that continued for years. We children had our father ripped away from us by my mother, with the help of Watchtower attorneys. This was clearly a case of their manipulating all of us, including our mother, just like pawns. Our whole family had been victimized.

Sometime later, my brothers, sister, and I had a reunion in Phoenix, Arizona, and discussed the events of the divorce and the years from then until our father's death in 1961. I asked, "Do any of you ever remember a time when Dad bad-mouthed Mom?" The answer from each of us was an emphatic, "*No!*" Yet every time we went to see our father (three times a year, by court order), our mother would pump us up with hateful talk about him.

My oldest brother noted, "I think that Mom would have considered the electric chair too kind a punishment for Dad." Any time we did visit our father, he would ask, "How is your mother?" We would tell him, "Fine." He would reply, "That's good," and that was the end of the discussion. Which one of our parents, do you think, was acting as a true Christian should?

During the final years of our mother's life, our youngest brother took care of her in Phoenix, Arizona. But none of us was ever again really close to her. The laws of cause and effect were playing out. Those same laws are playing out now on the part of millions who in the past were active as Jehovah's Witnesses, but who can no longer stomach the record that the W/W/H has made of destroying families and of other serious wrongdoing.

As the years went by, of course, we all got older, grew up, moved away from our mother's influence, and started our own families. My two older brothers and my younger sister went to college shortly after high school. College education was highly discouraged by the W/W/H, and as a result, by my mother as well. After all, "The end is right around the corner, and a higher education is just a waste of time; it also shows a lack of faith and a distrust of God and his promises, including a disrespect for God's faithful organization," meaning the Witnesses, of course.

While I was still at home during my senior year in high school, and having bought into the W/W/H deception that the end was imminent, I started pioneering (that is, spending a hundred hours a month in the ministry of Jehovah's Witnesses, door-to-door canvassing, calling back on interested people, conducting Bible Studies, etc.). Really it was nothing less than hardcore proselytizing, and as always, with free volunteer labor from duped believers.

It would be many more years until I could and would see the need for any college education. Additionally, both as a child and even after I became an adult with my own family, I found myself being manipulated. I had become not just a victim but also an enabler, used and abused by the W/W/H.

Much more time would go by before I would fully comprehend how all-pervasive the deception, coercion, and tyranny of authority was that had been foisted on me and on countless others by the very ones who I had thought were righteous, holy, and clean—God's special people—Jehovah's Witnesses.

However, I was a young man, and I had the normal desires of any young man. Additionally, I worked the last two years of high school on a dairy farm. I was well built, having wrestled on the high school wrestling team. I even looked pretty cute—so my wife of fifty-three years tells me—so what happened? The mirror tells me I am an old man; what a nightmare this matter of getting old has become!

There is no denying that sex was on my mind as a teenager, but since sex out of wedlock would disgrace the congregation and my mother and likely get me disfellowshipped from the local congregation, we got married, in March of 1960, at the tender ages of nineteen for me and sixteen for my wife, Dale. Difficult to believe, isn't it?

While we thought we were in love, we were both dumb as posts. In no way were we, by any stretch of the imagination, ready for marriage, but we were ready for sex! As it has turned out, we made many adjustments and eventually grew up and survived and now have been married for over fifty-three years. This is quite unusual in this day and age.

There is an additional and embarrassing point that you will see the reason for later in the chapter on baptism. Although we did not have sex before marriage, we had engaged in what was customarily referred to as "heavy petting." This was also grounds for disfellowshipping (and still is) by the W/W/H. Judicial committees, in each congregation, handle such matters.

We were put on a guilt trip by an article we read in the *Watchtower* magazine, and as a result, we confessed our wickedness (which was really weakness) to our congregation servant. By that time, we had been married for four years and had two children. We were given stern counsel, but were not disfellowshipped. I believe, if the truth be known, that the same type of activity is even now common among many dating Witness youths and older ones, probably being the rule and not the exception.

This point will become relevant in chapter 8, "The Baptism Deception—for Youths: The Dark Side."

Remember, in 1950, as a nine-year-old child, I had been assured that the "system would end before I ever got into high school." But *that did not happen!* I had been deceived, and baptism (if it did occur) had been foisted upon me. I had spent years as a pioneer for the W/W/H and been getting along on minimum wage jobs ever since high school to support the JW ministry and my family. I had not gone to college, and I was reaping the results for having bought into the deception foisted upon me by the W/W/H and by my mother. It was definitely a very difficult time for us, economically.

In 1961, my father died at the age of fifty, as a result of a head injury. We were coming up on two years of marriage, and I had inherited thirteen thousand dollars from his estate. At that time, and after having struggled financially on minimum wage jobs, it seemed like we now had a fortune.

But in view of my continued indoctrination by the W/W/H leadership, I was still buying into the idea that the end was imminent. I believed that we should be doing everything possible in the ministry to help out in an area where no, or very few, Witnesses lived (called moving to "serve where the need was greater") and that I should be honing my skills as a recruiter.

So off to northern Michigan we moved, to carry on our ministry in Crawford County where no Witnesses lived. It was not necessary for me to work because we still had some inherited money left. I saw no need; after all, "the end was just so close!"

I had taken one flying lesson before we left southern Florida. I'd loved it, and so when we got to northern Michigan, I continued taking flying lessons regularly at the Gaylord Airport. I was leaning to fly!

My flight instructor had flown in Korea but had not been able to get a job with the airlines because when he was released by the military, pilots were "a dime a dozen." After a few hours of instruction, he allowed me to "solo" (fly the plane alone) for the first time. What a thrill it was! When I got back on the ground safely, I made a comment to him, "Maybe someday I'll be able to get a job flying for the airlines." His immediate response to me was, "Kid, you don't stand a snowball's chance in hell!" (Since he could not get a job flying for an airline, with all his thousands of hours of flying experience as a military pilot, who the hell did I think I was?)

It probably did sound totally impossible; however, five years later found me attending flight school as a new hire for United Airlines. Right place, right time, hurrah for me and my family! As the years flashed by, time had not run out, but my money had. The system still had not ended, so we moved back to Ft. Lauderdale, Florida, where I continued flying, at great cost to my family, in order to get my private pilot's license and then my commercial pilot's license with an instrument and multiengine rating.

By the fall of 1964, my total flying time was about two hundred and five hours. That is not much, and it was unheard of to be hired by any airline with so little flying time prior to this date.

During that time, our circuit servant (traveling minister) visited the congregation for his semiannual visit. While I was working with him in the door-to-door work, recruiting, I mentioned my concern that I was working for only minimum wage and that we had two children, aged one and two. "I don't know how we are going to make it or what to encourage my children to do for work as they get older," I queried.

To correct my "faulty thinking," he dogmatically said, "Jim, it won't be a problem for you because this system will end before your kids ever get into high school."

"Brother," I replied, "I was promised that same thing about myself, fourteen years ago when I was nine years old and they were pressuring me to get baptized in New York City."

He dropped the subject like a hot potato. However, there was going to be more, much more: coercion, promises, guarantees, deception, and as a last resort, bullying and threatening. Those came my way just one year later. How would I react when it occurred? Would I be able to get my blinders off and break free of spiritual abuse and control by the W/W/H?

I had applied for work with several airlines, and their reply was the same in each case: "You need more qualifications—either more education (at least some college) or more flying time." Attending Broward Junior College in Ft. Lauderdale would be less expensive than renting an airplane to get more flying time. So I made a captain's decision. I was going to get some college education after all. I enrolled in Broward Junior College in early 1965.

So here I was, working a forty-hour per week job. I was attending college on Monday, Wednesday, and Friday evenings. I was going to the Kingdom Hall for meetings on Tuesday, Thursday, and Sunday. Saturdays I would fly for an hour when I could afford it. I was also caring for all of the responsibilities I had in the congregation as the Bible study servant. Throw in preparing for meetings and going door-to-door, as is required by the W/W/H, and you can sense that I was one busy puppy. How long could I possibly keep up that pace?

I was burning the candle at both ends and in the middle; then along came November of 1965. A new circuit servant was visiting our congregation, Brother Patrick, a name I will never forget. A showdown was coming, and I knew it.

My wife and I agreed that I really had no other skill that could be used to earn a decent living. I was going to try for the airlines. She was willing to help me by keeping our household expenses to a minimum.

By this date, we had two children. For a guy on minimum wage, that, with the two of us, meant very strained finances. Our usual main meal at that time, five days a week, was macaroni and cheese. I still remember that it cost just seventeen cents a box. On Friday, payday, we splurged with beans and franks. We were definitely traveling through time in economy, if not poverty class. I was prepared mentally to rebel against the circuit servant if necessary. I needed that airline job!

It was no surprise when the circuit servant, Brother Patrick, took me aside during his visit and said, "Brother Staelens, I understand from the congregation servant that you are going to college and you are pursuing a flying career with the airlines. Is that right?"

"Yes," I replied.

"Why?" he demanded.

I continued, "Brother Patrick, I have two children and 'one in the oven,' due to be born in December. I am working for about minimum wage [I was a teletype operator for a large concrete company in south Florida], and I have no skill worth anything except, I know how to fly. I have to try to take care of my family!"

He shot back, "Do you know how the Society feels about college?"

"Yes," I replied.

"How do they feel?" he demanded, his voice raised an octave.

"They don't recommend it," I admitted, "but how am I going to care for my family?"

"You will never have time to get through flight school, before this system ends, let alone work for the airlines long enough to retire!" he countered.

"But I've been told that before, in fact all of my life, since 1950. Will you help me and my family out financially, if we can't make it?" I asked. He no doubt thought I was being a wise guy, but I was being pushed and had reached the point where I was not going to put up with it any longer!

"I can personally guarantee you that this system will end before you can even get hired, let alone get through flight school. I mean it," he promised, with all of the dogmatism and tyranny-of-authority he could muster. Actually, he made that worthless guarantee to me three times in a row. But I wasn't buying it, and he was becoming desperate.

Finally, he played his last card: "If you don't drop out of college and stop this nonsense of trying to get a job with the airlines, I'll have you removed as the Bible study servant in the congregation, and you will have no privileges at all!" (God forbid!) He was threatening me, and I was becoming more like a pit bull.

"You can do what you think you should, and I will do what I know I have to do, to take care of my family," I stated emphatically.

He was becoming furious with me, and he turned his back on me in a huff and recommended my removal to the branch office. To the credit of the brother in the branch office, his recommendation was rejected. About three weeks later, back came a letter from them, a copy of which was shared with me by the congregation servant.

The branch office wrote to Brother Patrick, "In your report, recommending Brother Staelens' removal, you say he doesn't miss any meetings, gets about the same number of hours in the ministry each month as the other servants do, and cares for his duties as the Bible Study Servant well. He seems to be a good example, so we refuse to remove him as a Servant, just because he is going to college and flying airplanes."

That slap on the wrist of the circuit servant was sufficient, and I had no more discussions with him about that matter. Six months later, I was hired by United Airlines and found myself on my way to Denver. I had never been west of the Mississippi River, but my dream was coming true! I flew, at United's expense, to Denver to attend their flight training center, as a new hire, for three months. I was of course deleted as a servant in Ft. Lauderdale. I was busier than I had ever been in my lifetime, but overjoyed and delighted that our sacrifices were finally paying off. *I was becoming an airline pilot!*

Forbes Magazine carried an article at about that same time, which named flying for an airline as the "sixth best job available in America." I don't know how it is listed now, but for the twenty-four years and seven months that I flew for United, it definitely was for me the best possible job I could have had, not just the best in America, but in the whole world.

It really was an excellent choice, the right choice of work for me, even from the viewpoint of one who was one of Jehovah's Witnesses. For now, I was "on top of the world" as an airline pilot, no pun intended.

I was enjoying "The Good," flying for United Airlines, and there would be much more to come. But along with that, there would also come, "The Bad, The Deceptive, and Worse." It would be true for me as a pilot and a father of seven children, but it would especially be because of my association with Jehovah's Witnesses. A major change in circumstances and viewpoint was coming.

The next twenty-five years seemed to flash by at lightning speed. A test of my honesty, integrity, and taking blame for bad decisions and wrongs was coming, more than once. How would I handle these problems when they came?

As our children came along and got older, I found myself becoming a strict, in fact overly strict, disciplinarian. After all, that was the way I was raised by my very authoritarian and sometimes tyrannical mother. We had reached the 1970s. Jimmy, our firstborn, was the one usually in trouble, but more than once, it was his brother Ed, our second son, who let his older brother take the hit in place of himself.

This one time, for example, my wife and daughter were away from the house, and I discovered that one of the two boys had done something I considered seriously wrong. I couldn't even tell you now what it was.

Each boy (about nine and ten years old at the time) denied that he was the guilty one. I had told my kids that no matter what they did, they must always tell the truth. "Even if you burn down the house," I told them, "you must not lie; you'll get a worse spanking for lying than for any other bad thing you could do."

In this case, I was sure it was Jimmy who was lying. So I made a decision; I took him up to the bedroom, took off my belt, and gave him a severe whipping on his bare butt, thirty-nine strokes. Your mouth has probably dropped open as well it should; that was way too severe a punishment!

In today's world, I would be sent to jail, and they would throw away the key. Nonetheless that was what I did, and I am thoroughly ashamed of myself for my grossly wrong conduct; (I believe it happened three or four times). These whippings were usually for lying. But these were just kids, my kids, not adults—where was my head? I have no answer. But the worst was yet to come.

When my wife Dale and our daughter Pam got back home, I told them what Jimmy had done and that I had given him a severe whipping of thirty-nine strokes with the belt. Pam exclaimed, "That wasn't Jimmy; it was Eddie!"

I was mortified. "*My God, what have I done!*" I gasped, as tears welled up in my eyes. I quickly took my leave in an attempt to regain composure and try to figure out what I could possibly do to rectify my horrific wrong.

I remember that a similar expression, "My God, what have *we* done!" was reported to have been said by one of the pilots of the *Enola Gay,* as he looked over his shoulder at the rapidly ascending mushroom cloud and witnessed the horrific devastation, after the plane had dropped the first atomic bomb on the civilian population of Hiroshima, Japan. The B-29 was in a high speed turn, trying to outrun the bomb's shock wave that was chasing them at the speed of sound and was only seconds away. There was no way on earth to change what had just happened. It was recorded in the aircraft log book and went down in history—the first time an atomic bomb had ever been dropped on a civilian population.

Although my actions were on a much smaller scale, and I know that the damage I had done to my son Jimmy pales in comparison to what happened to Hiroshima, my feelings were the same. I was Jimmy's father, and what I had done was inexcusable. I deserved to go to jail (or hell) for what I had done, and there was no way on earth that I could take it back, no way that I could change what I had done. How could I possibly make things right? I thought, I prayed, and I came to the only possible conclusion that would do.

Nobody, not my wife or anyone else, had any idea what was about to happen; I had only prayed to God. I went back into the house and found Jimmy. I told him, "Come upstairs with me," and we headed up the stairs again, to where he had gotten his severe whipping earlier. I slowly unbuckled my belt and took it off again.

Now that I think about it, I can only imagine what was going through his mind at that moment. Maybe, "My God, is he going to do it again?" I doubled the belt over; his eyes grew to the size of saucers as I snapped it and handed it to him. As I stripped down my pants to my bare butt, I said to him, "Jimmy, I whipped you earlier, and I was wrong. I am ashamed of myself and terribly sorry. You may whip my bare butt as long and as hard as you wish; I deserve it."

I lay down on the bed, in front of him with my bare butt exposed. He started to laugh, and then...he started to whip me. I know my severe whipping of him was far more hurtful than his whipping of me, but neither of us ever forgot that moment, and I promised myself that I would never again severely punish any of my children unless I had an admission of guilt or two witnesses to the wrong.

Although I used the belt, even after this incident, I began to try to moderate the use of it, and I did, in time, find a less appalling way to administer punishment that didn't involve the belt at all. I obviously had more growing up and maturing to do myself, in spite of my age. Bad habits are especially difficult to overcome.

But in this case, with Jimmy, it was a matter of taking responsibility for my wrong actions. I was the one who had severely wronged and hurt my own son, not just physically, but no doubt emotionally as well, and he had done absolutely nothing deserving of such punishment, which made my wrongdoing even far more objectionable.

I am in my seventies now, yet never have I ever heard of another parent doing what I did to correct such a wrong. I felt it was the only thing I could do, to try to make things as right as possible; there was no way I could turn the clock back and erase what I had done, and I knew it.

I have since then apologized to both of my sons, more than once, for my wrongdoing in the matter of severe whippings, and I have asked them both for forgiveness. I don't know of any other time that I administered severe whippings when some kind of discipline was not called for.

But nothing I can say or do now will excuse or erase the fact that I did, three or four times, administer severe whippings that would land me not at an airport, but in jail, in today's world—and rightly so. But alas, time was still one-directional; like a jet airliner in the air, you can only travel forward.

Parents, like politicians, business leaders, clergy, or any other persons in authority must be willing to take responsibility for their actions. Otherwise—and especially if they demand honesty and accountability from others such ones will in fact be guilty of hypocrisy and a miscarriage of justice.

My reason for telling on myself will become apparent in chapter 6, "Over Thirty Failed Prophecies During 131 Years: Grave Disappointments," and in chapter 8, entitled, "The Baptism Deception—for Youths: The Dark Side." You will find this account about my son and me to be very relevant as you read coming chapters.

The calendar was racing toward 1975; there were only a couple of years yet to go. The year, 1975, had been published and prophesied by the W/W/H as the certain date when six thousand years of human history would be up and the foretold "Millennium" was expected to start.

Anticipation was red hot about that year, and continued promises by the W/W/H kept fanning the flames of expectation. They had said that it was more of a probability than just a possibility that the end would come then. They had checked and double-checked the chronology, and there was no doubt in their minds. (See relevant quotes in the next chapter.)

I had bought into their dogma, and my life showed it. We were a very busy family. I had taken my blinders off to get the job with United (1966), but I put them back on and kept them until 2006 (for another forty years). Recall cognitive dissonance?

We were calling on people, conducting Bible studies, and vigorously studying; after all, the time by now was extremely short. I had bought into it again. I still had not really caught on to the fact that over thirty times, the W/W/H had falsely prophesied the end of the world.

The year 1975 did turn out to be a traumatic and tragic year for us, but it was not because the system ended. Instead, 1975 saw the death of our twenty-two-month-old son, Ronald, as the result of an accident while he was in an infant seat on a bike. Any parents who have lost a child can relate to the extreme heartache, the what-ifs, the denial, the anger, the "I wish it had been me instead of him" feelings. But no matter how much I wished it, I simply could not turn the clock back. Time would continue to march straight ahead.

I would have that same feeling, wishing I could turn the clock back again, just three years later. The year 1975 had come and gone without the end of the world, and the W/W/H was in damage control mode yet again; the organization had become quite experienced at this, through more than thirty previously failed prophecies. The hierarchy would simply dump the blame for any, and all false prophecies on personal Witness expectations. *The W/W/H could not possibly be at fault.*

The governing body has never in its modern-day history admitted fault; the fact that members of this body are the ones who did the bogus chronology and foisted their dogmatic false prophecies on millions doesn't seem to matter from their viewpoint. (See chapters nine and twelve for further information on their evasion of responsibility for their wrongs as well as for the things they have said to shift their accountability and responsibility elsewhere.)

The year 1978 saw an airline strike by the pilots. Flying for United was a dream come true for me, and I was unwilling to jeopardize that dream by going on strike as the Union leadership had ordered. I bought into the faulty promises of the leadership of United Airlines instead, and so I worked.

That decision and the resulting emotional trauma resulted from the fact that they had lied to me and deceived me. It had happened to me before with the W/W/H, and now it was happening again in the venue of secular work. I was sorry, but time was still one-directional; there was no way I could turn the clock back. In reality, both those who had worked and those who had gone on strike had become pawns in the hands of United's leaders and the union's leaders.

As time continued its forward march, I remained very busy and found myself over halfway through a normal lifetime. What had happened to the W/W/H's promises that this system would end before I entered high school or before I could finish flight school? Or before my two older sons, who are now in their fifties, entered high school?

The guarantees by the W/W/H had all fallen by the wayside, as had their thirty-plus failed prophecies for when the end of this system would occur. But I was gaining more experience as a Witness teacher, and I was considered good at it. That, added to the fact that my job as an airline pilot provided me with an average of over fifteen days a month off work, was a huge lure for the W/W/H to use me more and more to satisfy their agendas. And I, unfortunately, was ignorantly willing to capitulate to their dictates and sect-like manipulation.

Thirteen years later, January of 1991 would find me retired at the age of fifty; I was taking early retirement. After all, the time for the end must be close by now! We started pioneering again, expecting to finish out the end of this system doing all we could to help others "learn the truth."

Our early retirement years were not all peaches and cream, any more than the first thirty-one years of marriage had been. We were still traveling a bumpy road and experiencing the frustration and anguish that many parents before us have had to endure and deal with as their children struggled to make the transition from dependent children, through all the adolescent years, to become adults with families of their own.

Those first few years of retirement saw us traveling to far-flung places such as St. Petersburg, Russia, Jamaica, New Zealand, and Australia, doing missionary work and making friends along the way. We were enjoying the experience of meeting and working with others who viewed things as we did, although, of course, false hopes had been foisted on all of us by the W/W/H.

Little did we know that in just six short years, those "golden years of early retirement" were going to turn into the "crappy brown years" of old age and all the maladies that come with that time of life. It is truly a blessing that young people don't know about such things when they are young. And of course, we were still buying into the W/W/H's line: *"The end is imminent."* They still had us shackled by their sect-like and cult-like mentality and actions.

The memorable date was March 8, 1997, actually my wife's birthday. It had not been a happy one, and it was definitely going to get worse—a lot worse. My stepfather in Phoenix had died, and we were on a jet, headed back to Denver, then on to Alamosa, Colorado, to get home.

My wife and I were enjoying First Class service, and the plane had just started descending from thirty-one thousand feet. I was in distress, experiencing a headache that was rapidly getting worse. Dale asked me, "Are you OK?"

"Not really," I replied. "I feel like someone buried an axe in the middle of my head, and my arms feel like they weigh a hundred pounds each!"

She was noticeably worried, and asked, "Do you want to tell the captain?"

"Heavens, no," I replied. "If he asks the Center (ATC) for preferential treatment to land, he'll be making out paper work for the rest of the month. I'll just check with the gate agent after we land." We were headed for Denver International Airport. When I had flown to Denver six years earlier, I had flown into Stapleton Airport, so I didn't know where the First Aid station was located at Denver International.

After we deplaned, I asked the gate agent for directions to First Aid; she asked why, and after I told her, she ordered, "Just sit down there and don't move. I'll call the paramedics."

About two minutes later, they wheeled up in a fancy electric cart. They asked a couple of questions as one started taking my blood pressure while the other started unbuttoning my shirt. "Open your mouth," ordered the first one, after which, she sprayed nitroglycerine under my tongue from a spray bottle. "You should be having a stroke with your blood pressure at this level!" she noted.

Dale and I looked at each other; we were both starting to get more than just a little worried. Something was radically wrong. Electrodes were being hooked up to my chest in preparation to take an EKG. Meanwhile, the passengers in the boarding area kept their eyes glued in my direction, no doubt wondering what was going on.

The one who had hooked up the electrodes nodded to his companion as he unhooked the electrodes and said to me, "You're having a heart attack— *right now*—you're in the middle of a heart attack." In seconds, an ambulance was racing toward the gate; our destination had changed from Alamosa, Colorado, to the University Hospital in Denver.

The beginning of catastrophic changes was set in motion that night; they would have far-reaching consequences which neither of us could even begin to imagine.

At the hospital, the doctors found that one of my arteries was nearly completely blocked; that was what was causing my severe headache.

The heart attack was causing the heavy arms. First things first: I needed a stint implanted in that artery. During the operation, they lost me, and I died "clinically" for a couple of minutes. But they managed to get my ticker working again. The good and the bad!

Four days later, March 12th, turned out to be the date of my bypass surgery as well as our thirty-seventh wedding anniversary. It would be many years before we could again enjoy our anniversary date; there were just too many unhappy memories due to the trauma, heartaches, and postoperative problems that would make me wish that I had not survived that operation at all.

Several days later, after I recovered sufficiently to travel, I found myself being wheeled by friends to their car, then to the plane for Alamosa. I remember that as I walked with help and a great deal of difficulty out of the Alamosa terminal, I burst into tears, uncontrollably sobbing. The world I had lived in before the night of March 8th had ended. I couldn't figure out what was wrong with me. The aftermath of the heart attack and bypass surgery was overwhelming.

I had flown well over five million miles and had handled many life-threatening emergencies, with the "steely eyes" of a veteran airline captain, "calm, cool, and collected," and now I started crying, uncontrollably, over spilled milk or even things of less consequence. What had this operation done to me? I found myself on an emotional roller coaster, with an out of control feeling that was as foreign to me as a thirteen dollar bill. As time went on, things went from bad to worse for me and my family.

I recall my wife asking me one night, with an exasperated voice, "What is wrong with you?" From a man of steel, I seemed to have turned into a bowl of Jell-O!

"I know you can't understand how I feel," I noted. "But I...I feel like I am on a plane spinning toward the ground with no yoke in front of me, no way to stop what is happening—no way to avoid disaster!" She couldn't understand. No one did.

My life, which for over thirty years had been well structured, organized, reasonable, and well under control, now seemed to be totally out of control. I had no idea where to start to get things right side up. My life was reaching a meltdown.

We had just gotten home from a meeting at the Kingdom Hall. I had given a talk that night that had made me sound like good old normal Jim to almost everyone, but...not to my wife. Dale knew that something was terribly wrong.

As we later walked through the doorway at home, she demanded, in an unkind voice, "I want to know where my husband from thirty-seven years ago has gone!"

It was not a good night for me, and this became the last straw. I was angered by her attitude, and a sickening dread, a black cloud had enveloped me. I retorted, "That bastard died on March 8th, 1997. I have his body, I have his fingerprints, I have his wife, and I have his money...but *I am not that guy. Don't you get it, he's dead!"*

I could take no more. I wanted to die! I stormed out of the house. It was about ten o'clock in the evening, and I started walking. I walked nearly half a mile. I remember that it was a starry night, and I could hear coyotes howling in the distance. I dropped to my knees, sobbing, and the sobbing turned into praying. I had reached the end of my rope.

I loved my wife and children, but...my life had become totally out of control, from my viewpoint. I could see no way out. I poured out my heart to Jehovah God, begged him to bless and take care of my family, and began entreating him with all my heart just to let me go to sleep and not wake up. I did not want to be alive when the sun came up in the morning, and I remember specifically praying for this night to see the end of my life on earth.

I remember telling him I was sorry and heartbroken for all the wrongs I had been guilty of, the difficulty I had brought upon my wife, and the severe discipline I had meted out to my older sons when they were young. I told him that I understood my situation; I knew I was not deserving of a resurrection, but I entreated him again to care for my wife and kids—but then my prayer was interrupted.

An animal brushed up against my body—I was startled—it was Utah, my dog! He had tracked me down and found me somehow, my faithful and, at that moment, much needed companion, part Rottweiler and part Black Lab. He was a large, muscular dog, and he wasn't chasing coyotes! He had not left the house with me. I didn't know, and at that moment didn't care, how he had found me, but I felt a calm settling down, and my apprehension was evaporating.

Utah just curled up next to me and stayed there, probably thinking "Isn't my master supposed to be in the house instead of out here with the coyotes?" Confusing, huh? I finished my prayer and drifted off to sleep.

When the sun came up in the morning, I was still alive, and Utah was still alive—the coyotes had not gotten either one of us. I decided that perhaps Utah had been sent by "someone" and that maybe…maybe I had better re-evaluate my situation and try harder to find a solution to take better care of myself and my family.

I had made things worse for my family, not better; likely they were home wondering what on earth had happened to me or even if I was still alive. It had been a trying night for all of us, except Utah; he had done just fine.

Dale and I were still on slippery ground, and I had a long way to go in trying to get right side up. The problem was more mine than hers, and it was likely a number of negative things that were at work in my head. I was still taking some high-powered medications because of my heart attack, and there is no question that my emotional makeup had gotten a makeover. I was wrestling not with another schoolmate on the high school wrestling team but with major changes in my own viewpoint on a number of issues. My feelings had changed, and I was struggling to understand just why.

On one occasion, when I was on a fairly even keel, I had dropped or spilled something and had started crying. I made the comment to Dale, "How in the world could I have handled all of the emergencies that I did—dealing with the death of a passenger on my plane, in spite of my mouth-to-mouth resuscitation efforts? I even survived a plane crash—I had handled all these things professionally—I was cool as a cucumber, and now I burst into tears over the smallest things. My emotions are a wreck!"

Dale commented with a chuckle, "Now you can have more empathy for me." There is an element of truth in that; I do seem to have more empathy for others since my own heartbreaking problems than I did before. But that did not give me the skills that I desperately needed.

Remember CRM? Those concepts had to be taught, learned, applied, and practiced; we had airline professionals to do the teaching and directing for the pilots. Now I needed professional help. Dale knew it, but I was trying desperately to work things out for myself without getting any outside help. Pride needed to be set aside, but it hadn't been—yet.

That was a mistake, and it took us longer to work things out because of my reluctance to get professional help. Dale had left me on three different occasions because she just couldn't see me making the changes that were called for. Each time, she moved in with one of our kids, and each time, I would see the need to make some changes, but…

I was always stopping short of what was really needed. Old and especially bad habits are hard to break. When Dale left for the third time, I actually figured, "Three times and out!" I thought I just could not make it work. I had an appointment with my doctor for some blood tests, and while there, I told him that Dale had left me again and that I believed it was all over for us. How could she keep on forgiving my irrational behavior? I was a lost cause.

He thought for a moment and said, "Jim, my ex-wife wasn't much of a wife, but she is a really good shrink. I want you to go see her; I think she can help you and Dale." So I reluctantly set up an appointment. After two sessions, I began to feel like there *might* possibly be some hope for Dale and me to get back together.

She asked me, "Do you think your wife would be willing to come back home and come to these sessions with you?" I doubted it, but I was willing to give it a try.

When I called Dale and told her that I was seeing a "shrink," she couldn't believe it. Number one, I was getting professional help at the suggestion of Dr. Linden, our family doctor, whom Dale knew and respected. Number two, I was actually getting help from a *woman* shrink; maybe there was some possibility of success!

Dale came back and went to a session with me. Julie, my shrink, was kind and also very discerning. She made the comment, "Your problem is not impossible to solve; you're going through the same things you would experience when a child dies."

I couldn't understand; how she could have found out about the death of our son, Ronald? I hadn't told her about his tragic accident and death years before. So I replied, "We did have our son, Ronald, die, but that was back in 1975. I don't see how that could have any bearing on our problems now, over twenty-two years after his death."

She said, "I am not talking about your son. It's you that I am talking about. The Jim Staelens that was here before the heart attack *is dead*. He's gone, and he's not coming back!"

Julie continued, "When your son Ronald died, you no doubt went through feelings of anger, resentment, denial, and a ton of what-ifs, didn't you?" We were both nodding our heads in agreement. She continued, "You both survived that ordeal, and you can survive this one too. You both have to allow time and put forth the effort needed to help each other heal mentally and emotionally, but it is survivable."

It made sense to both of us, and for the first time since the heart attack, real progress was being made. We both had changes to make, but make them we did, and we have been together ever since without ever having come close to either of us leaving again. Our marriage, now in its fifty-third year, is the strongest it has ever been, and we are both grateful for Julie's help. Just reading the Bible and prayer had not gotten it done—I, in fact both of us, needed *professional* help.

We had found a solution for our marriage problems, but other issues were confronting me first of all, and then they became issues for Dale also to wrestle with. They involved the issue of religion and Jehovah's Witnesses, specifically.

The W/W/H's broken promises, failed guarantees, and 131-year history of over thirty false prophecies guaranteeing the world's end had all been dogmatically and authoritatively put forth. But not one of those prophecies, not even for 1975, had come true. I was struggling to overcome cognitive dissonance.

Here I was now, an old man. I had not only gotten through flight school, but I had flown for United Airlines for a total of twenty-four years and seven months and had retired as a captain. As of 1997, over six years of retirement had gone by. (And that number now is twenty-two years!)

I had never in my wildest imagination dreamed that I would reach old age without the end occurring first, and I know of countless other active Witnesses as well as ex-Witnesses close to my age who were given similar guarantees and promises. Many have died. Others have grown old dealing now with grave disappointments over the same continuous failures by the W/W/H. Countless numbers of others had already caught on to the organization's deception and had abandoned it ahead of me. Why had it taken me so long to catch on? We had been captured and were victims of cognitive dissonance.

Ask yourself how long, for example, you would have worked at a job, getting promised a paycheck but not getting even one? How many months, how many years would you have continued laboring for a company, with only empty promises, but no pay, to show for that work?

At that time, I believed that the W/W/H had only uttered false prophecies for seven different dates. But as described in chapter six, it has actually been over thirty failed prophecies—prophecies found in the hierarchy's own literature.

I have not only grown old, but I have died clinically once. It was becoming indelibly clear that the mathematical odds of my living to see the end of the world before I died in the normal timeframe were somewhere between poor and nil.

If that had been your experience over a period of nearly sixty years, would you be likely to believe more promises of the same type? When would you say, "Enough is enough—I no longer believe *any promises* made by you. You are like the little boy in Aesop's fable, who cried '*wolf!*' just to watch everyone fly into a panic"

It is a fact that not one of the failed prophecies concerning specific dates or events, promised and published by the Watchtower Bible and Tract Society, was given by God. They were all false prophecies, given by the W/W/H. None of that hierarchy's failures was the fault of expectations by rank-and-file Witnesses. The prophecies had all been given in sect-like and cult-like fashion, meaning that they must be believed by sect members. If whistle-blowers brought up questions or doubts concerning their failures, they were to be disfellowshipped and shunned by all, including close family members, perhaps for the rest of their lives.

That sounds like the mode of operation used by the Pharisees of Jesus' day doesn't it? Dissenters were to be "expelled from the Synagogue." The Pharisees' view was, "They must be shut up! (Perhaps even kill them.) Don't let them expose us!"

The modern-day W/W/H has chosen to imitate the Pharisees of Jesus' day rather than to imitate King David's reaction when exposed by the prophet Nathan.

Several years ago, I took off my blinders for the last time. I stepped down as an elder, stopped going door-to-door, ceased going to meetings at the Kingdom Hall, and refused to accept any further sect-like and cult-like indoctrination. I would take no more. My view: "Stop trying to force-feed me, your figurative, (Jim Jones' *cyanide-laced), soft drink."

The fact that millions of former active Witnesses have abandoned ship in order to survive provides proof that the W/W/H is "reaping what it has sown." Its ship is sinking.

Many have left because they view the current W/W/H *Titanic*-like organization to be as useless as the crippled *Titanic* of 1912. They have felt the need to escape that organization to save their lives spiritually and to get out of the vacuum they have been living in; it is not survivable but is death-dealing. The only survivors of the *Titanic* disaster were those who abandoned that ship before it sank. Would you have tried to escape back then, if it were possible?

If you are presently involved with the W/W/H, will you see the need to escape its failing organization, filled as it is, not with water, but with tyranny of authority, dogmatism, and deception? Will you stay onboard or is it time to *abandon ship?* You must decide for yourself.

REVIEW POINTS:

1. Is the deception and manipulation of minors by their parents and the W/W/H not a clear case of child abuse?

2. Have parents and many others served as enablers in the organization's deception and abuse of its members?

3. Has the W/W/H continued to use the same tactics to manipulate adults and children over the past years, from the 1880s up to, and including now?

4. Has the W/W/H exhibited sect-like and cult-like traits, dominating by fear in an effort to keep its victims enslaved?

5. Is it not past time to leave and survive, while you are still able to do so?

The next chapter will get into the issue of false prophecies, over thirty of them.

How could so many have been duped for so long? It's time to think, reason, and investigate!

Chapter 6

OVER THIRTY FAILED PROPHECIES, DURING 131 YEARS: GRAVE DISAPPOINTMENTS

- Whom does the dictionary define as a prophet?
- A dubious record held by the W/W/H, involving prophecies about the end of the world.
- If someone utters a prophecy that fails, who should take the hit for the failure?
- Double-talk and a clever, deceptive cover-up.
- Pointed Questions for active Witnesses.

"It" started over 1,969 years ago, the first time being 44 CE. "It" has happened over two hundred times since then, with one of the most recently projected times said to be 2047 CE, just thirty-four years from now. What is "It"? It is predictions, promises, and prophecies foretelling something that the Bible says it is impossible for humans to know in advance, namely, the date (times or seasons) when the world will end.

According to some, "It" refers to the end of our planet, earth; to others, "It" refers to the end of the present political, religious, and economic systems of things.

The W/W/H holds a dubious distinction. It has prophesied and published, by means of the Watchtower Bible and Tract Society, its mother corporation, more different dates stating when the end of the world and/or events relating to that end will occur than any other person or group in history has published. But the one thing that all of the two hundred-plus dates and prophecies hold in common is that they have all failed and have proven to be false prophecies.

Why haven't humans been able to figure out the right date? The reason is simple, because, according to the Bible, humans cannot know and never will know in advance the date of the world's end.

Under the subtitle, "The Day and Hour Unknown," in the NIV translation, Matt. 24:36 clearly states, "But about that day or hour no one knows, not even the angels in heaven, nor the Son, but only the Father." The NWT version reads basically the same.

Again, under the subtitle, "Jesus Taken Up into Heaven," the NIV says in Acts 1:7, "He [Jesus] said to them: 'It is not for you to know the times or dates the Father has set by his own authority.'" The NWT version says, "does not belong to you...times or seasons" (or, in a footnote, "appointed times") and "placed in his own jurisdiction."

The W/W/H is aware of this fact. After first referring to the two above quoted scriptures, the *Watchtower* magazine pointedly says, "It is impossible for us to figure out the world's end in advance" (*Watchtower*, March 15, 1980, p. 18). That was not news to them, as you will see; it was known long before.

Have not money and power been at the heart of all such attempts to predict the date of the end of the world? The facts included below and throughout this book will bear testimony to the real motives pressuring religious hierarchies to deceive their members with false prophecies.

The W/W/H asserts that since it has not named a specific day and date for the end, or ordered believers to flee to the mountains, it can justify prophesying a month and/or year for the end and/or events related to that end. Is that not still a contradiction of what Jesus said would be the case? Why has the hierarchy done it?

Note the following definitions from *Webster's Revised Unabridged Dictionary (1913):*

1. Promise: A declaration... which binds one person to another... to give assurance... binding declaration
2. Prophecy: (sē) A declaration of something to come... interpretation of Scripture.
3. Prediction: The act of foretelling, that which is foretold; prophecy

4. Prophesy: (sī) verb. To foretell... predict; to make declaration of events to come.
5. Prophet: One who prophesies or foretells events

Note: The definitions above do not require that the one(s) making the prophecy be or claim to be inspired by God.

The book, *Jehovah's Witnesses Proclaimers of God's Kingdom* (WTB&TS 1993), contains selected points about the modern-day history of Jehovah's Witnesses, covering the years 1870–1993. The foreword asserts, "No one knows the modern-day Witness history better than they do."

While many beliefs about the significance of the dates for the end of the world originally proposed by the W/W/H have since been abandoned and/or modified as the prophecies failed, millions of believers have still put faith in their prophecies. But all of those prophecies turned out to be false, bringing grave disappointments, frustration, and economic harm to deceived and heartbroken believers.

A common misconception presented by it has been the belief that this system would end after 6,000 years of human existence and they believed that specific date would be in the year 1873 (WTB&TS 1993, p. 631).

➢ Why do you think the hierarchy has changed its prophesied date for the end, and/or events related to it, from 1844 to 1873, to 1874, then to 1878, and so on?

➢ Is it not obvious that the change was mandatory, because the first date and others later prophesied all became failures—false prophecies?

Keep these points in mind as we consider the following thirty-plus failed prophecies, and please feel free to check any and all of the references; you can use a Witness library or CD, or you can do a web search for most dates listed, and many times, a web search engine will even pull up the book or magazine that is quoted or referenced here.

When the dates came and went without fulfillment, there were of course grave disappointments for those who trusted in them, because those people had made personal decisions based on the false prophecies. When the prophecies went unfulfilled, many of the rank-and-file believers experienced not just emotional loss but also financial loss. Also, each time a date failed, the W/W/H just named another date and kept on going with more lies and more deception.

Noting these dates—what was prophesied about them and how they turned out—can aid one in understanding why many hundreds of thousands, even millions, of long-time active Witnesses no longer exercise confidence in the W/W/H and refuse to associate with Jehovah's Witnesses in their Kingdom Halls. The organization tries to keep the actual number of those who have left under wraps.

Please note that the following dates and highlights come from *Jehovah's Witnesses Proclaimers of God's Kingdom* (WTB&TS 1993, chapter 28, pages 618–641) as well as other W/W/H/ publications. Specific quotes will be given with the page number in parentheses.

A summary follows of at least thirty prophesied but failed dates for the end and/or events associated with that end:

1. 1844: (In retrospect) "So the 2,300 years above mentioned indicate that Christ was due to leave the most high place—heaven itself—in 1844" (*Watchtower* 1880, p. 3; reprints, p. 115).

    ➢ Do you believe that Christ "left heaven" in 1844?

Note: The specific date, Oct. 22, 1844, was taught by the Millerites, led by William Miller, a sect of more than fifty thousand. They abandoned their material possessions and took to the hills, where they waited for the world to end in Armageddon. So the W/W/H latched on to the same year Miller had falsely prophesied, 36 year earlier.

2. 1873: "They had surely approached the dawn of the foretold Millennium" (WTB&TS 1993, p. 631).

3. 1874: "A greater Jubilee for all the earth had begun…1874…the times of restitution of all things had arrived" (WTB&TS 1993, p. 631).

4. 1878: "[Jesus] assumes power as heavenly king…they [Witnesses]… given…heavenly reward at that time" (WTB&TS 1993, p. 632).

   ➢ 1878: Was the first date they prophesied for what is commonly referred to as the rapture.

5. 1881: "by the fall of 1881, the door of opportunity to become a member of [the] bride…will close" (*Watchtower* January, 1881).

   ➢ There have been many dates given since then for when this would happen. The most recent was an admission that "nobody knows" when; that is a true statement!

   ➢ Who was really inspiring their failed prophecies?

6. 1889: "In this volume we offer a chain of testimony on the subject of God's appointed times and seasons, each link of which we consider Scripturally strong…it is beyond the breadth and depth of human thought, and therefore cannot be of human origin" (Russell 1911, vol. 2, p. 15).

   ➢ Are they not saying that the origin of their chain of testimony is from God and not themselves?

7. 1892: "The date of the *close* of that 'battle' is *definitely marked* in the Scripture as *October, 1914*. It is already in progress, its beginning dating from October, 1874" (*Watchtower* January 15, 1892, p. 22; italics added).

   ➢ Do you believe that Armageddon was in progress starting in October 1874 and finished by October 1914?

- ➤ Was this stated as a possibility or dogmatically as a fact? Did you notice the words *"definitely marked* in Scripture?"

- ➤ Since it was stated as a fact *"definitely marked* in Scripture," was it not clearly a prophecy, not by God, but by the W/W/H?

8. 1897: "Our Lord…now present since October, 1874 A.D" (Russell 1897, Millennial Dawn Vol. 4, p. 621).

  - ➤ Active Witnesses are well aware of the fact that their W/W/H now names the autumn of 1914 as the date when Jesus came to earth, invisibly, to begin his presence as king.

9. 1902: "In view of the strong Bible evidence…we consider it an established truth that the final end of the kingdoms of this world… will be accomplished by the end of A.D. 1914" (WTB&TS 1902, p. 99).

  - ➤ Did that turn out to be true? No!

10. 1914: "It is around October, 1914; maybe later…we are looking for…(1) The termination of the Gentile times—Gentile Supremacy in the world—and…(2) the inauguration of Messiah's Kingdom in the world" (*Watchtower* October 15, 1913, p. 307).

11. 1914: "The war [World War I] will proceed and will eventuate in no glorious victory for any nation, but in the horrible mutilation and impoverishment of all. Next will follow the Armageddon of anarchy" (*The New York Times*, October 5, 1914, p. 8) [Provided by the W/W/H]; (italics added).

12. 1914: Would include the "glorification…to share in…Heavenly Kingdom with Christ" (WTB&TS 1993, p. 635).

  - ➤ These paragraphs include the W/W/H's efforts at damage control over this prophecy that also failed, as was the case for all previous failures.

- ➢ The organization admitted that "failed expectations and failed millennial promises led to a dramatic drop in meeting attendance" (WTB&TS 1993, p. 633).

- ➢ The year 1914 was the second date prophesied for what is commonly called the rapture.

13. 1916: "Battle of the Great Day of God Almighty *now in progress; and our faith, guiding our eyes of understanding through the Word should enable us to see the glorious outcome—Messiah's Kingdom*" (*Watchtower* September 1, 1916, Reprints p. 595; italics added).

14. 1917: "The Bible chronology herein presented shows that the six great 1,000 year days beginning with Adam are ended, and that the great 7th Day, the 1,000 years of *Christ's Reign, began in 1873*" (WTB&TS 1888, 1917, p. ii; italics added).

- ➢ Do you believe that Jesus started reigning and the millennium began in 1873?

15. 1918: "The Spirit of 1918 will bring upon Christendom a spasm of anguish greater than…the Fall of 1914" (WTB&TS 1917 & 1918 ed. p. 62).

16. 1918: "Also in the year 1918, when *God destroys the churches wholesale* and the *church members by millions,* it shall be that any that escape shall come to the works of Pastor Russell to learn the meaning of the downfall of Christianity" (WTB&TS 1918, p. 485; italics added).

- ➢ Do you believe that God destroyed the churches wholesale and church members by the millions in 1918?

- ➢ Russell died on October 31, 1916, two years before that 1918 prophecy was given. Do you believe that any who escaped came to the works of Pastor Russell to learn more?

17. 1920: "Even the republics will disappear in 1920" (WTB&TS, 1918, p. 258).

    ➢ Do you believe that the republics disappeared in 1920?

18. 1920: The booklet *Millions Now Living May Never Die!* was published in 1920. There was a need to reignite a sense of urgency into the Watchtower followers, after the many failed prophecies that surrounded the year 1914 had become so obvious. What to do? A public discourse and a booklet should do the trick! So in February, 1918, came the talk, "*The World Has Ended: Millions Now Living May Never Die!*" and a booklet that declared that the earthly resurrection was scheduled for 1925. In March, the title was changed to the more compelling "*Will Never Die*" rather than "*May Never Die.*" Did their damage control work? Not very well - many left!

    ➢ Anyone old enough to read that booklet, then, would be over 102 years old by now. How many millions, do you think, are on earth that are that old now or are even ninety-three years old, if they were born in 1920?

19. 1922: "Even before 1925 the great crisis will be reached and probably passed...the year *1925 is even more distinctly* indicated by the Scriptures than 1914" (*Watchtower* September 1, 1922, p. 262; italics added).

    ➢ Do you believe that the great crisis was reached and passed before 1925?

20. 1923: "Our thought is, that 1925 is *definitely settled by the Scriptures.* As to Noah, the Christian now *has much more* upon which to base his faith than Noah had upon which to base his faith in a coming deluge" (*Watchtower* April 1, 1923, p. 106; italics added).

    ➢ Do you believe that you have more basis for faith in what the W/W/H said about 1925 than Noah had about the flood due to come in his day?

21. 1925: "The year 1925 is here...Christians have...*expected* that all members of the body of Christ will be *changed to heavenly glory*...[The third date prophesied for what is commonly called the rapture]. Christians *should not be so deeply concerned* about what *may transpire* this year that they fail to joyfully do what the Lord would have them do" (*Watchtower* January 1, 1925, p. 3; italics added).

   ➢ Did you notice the backpedalling of expectations regarding 1925?

22. 1925: "It is to be expected that Satan will try to inject into the minds of the consecrated, the thought that 1925 should see an end to the work" (*Watchtower* September 1, 1925, p. 262). The W/W/H had said the end would occur in 1925; they also had said that the faithful would be going to heaven, so there would be no more work on earth to do, would there?

23. 1925: "This year [1925] also was associated with expectations for [the] resurrection of faithful pre-Christian servants of God, with a view to their serving on earth as princely representatives of the heavenly kingdom… though mistaken, *they* eagerly shared it with others" (WTB&TS 1993, p. 632; see also WTB&TS 1920, p. 88).

24. 1925: "The year 1926 would therefore begin about October first, 1925. *We should, therefore expect* shortly after 1925 *to see* the *awakening of* Abel, Enoch, Noah, Abraham, Isaac, Jacob, Melchisedec, Job, Moses, Samuel, David, Isaiah, Jeremiah, Ezekiel, Daniel, John the Baptist, and others mentioned in the eleventh chapter of Hebrews" (WTB&TS 1924, pp. 224, 226; italics added).

   ➢ Do you believe that all of those faithful men of old were resurrected to life on earth in 1925, or shortly thereafter?

25. 1925: "Some *anticipated* that the work would end in 1925, but *the Lord did not state so.* The difficulty was that *the friends inflated their imaginations* beyond reason; and that when their imaginations burst

asunder, they were inclined to throw away everything" (*Watchtower* 1926 p. 232; italics added).

- If "the Lord did not state so," Why do you think that the W/W/H was so presumptuous as to "state so?"

- Why did some have such an anticipation or expectation? *Who had promised* the rank-and-file members that everything would be ended and they would go to heaven in 1925? A clue: *It was not God!*

- 1931: "There was a measure [large measure] of disappointment on the part of Jehovah's faithful ones on earth concerning the years 1917, 1918, and 1925, which disappointment lasted for a time… and *they also learned to quit fixing dates"* (WTB&TS 1931, p. 338; italics added). [Add thirteen other prophecies prior to 1917]

- Notice that they, the "faithful ones," learned they should not fix dates, but obviously the W/W/H did not learn that. How do we know? They just kept on doing what they had been doing since 1844; they just continued "fixing dates."

26. 1940: "The year 1940 is certain to be the most important year yet, because Armageddon [is] very near. It behooves all who love righteousness to put forth every effort to advertise the theocracy while the privileges are still open" (*Informant* 1940, p. 1; italics added).

- This was published seventy-three years ago! Does this not sound like the tactic of a used car salesman? "Put forth every effort to advertise…while the privileges are still open."

- Had they not previously prophesied that Armageddon would be here by 1874, 1914, 1916, 1918, and 1925? That is five different dates for Armageddon, with one more—1975—yet to come. All six of them have failed, without exception!

27. 1940: "The *Kingdom is here,* the King is enthroned, *Armageddon is just ahead.* The glorious reign of Christ that shall bring blessings to the world will immediately follow. *Therefore the great climax has been reached.* Tribulation has fallen upon those who stand by the Lord" (*The Messenger* 1940, p. 6; italics added).

28. 1941: "Receiving the gift, the marching children clasped it to them, not a toy or plaything for idle leisure, but the *Lord's provided instrument* for most effective work in the *remaining months before Armageddon*" (*Watchtower* September 15, 1941, p. 288; italics added).

29. 1941: "What the near future will bring and is already hastening to bring to them [the German people]—Armageddon, the battle of the great day of God Almighty." (*Consolation* October, 1941, p. 11; italics added) Seventy-two years ago!

30. 1968: "True, there have been those in times past who 'predicted *an end to the world',* even announcing a specific date. Yet *nothing happened…*They were [all] ***guilty of false prophesying.*** Why? What was missing…? Missing from such people were God's truths and evidence that he was using and guiding them" (*Awake!* October 8, 1968, p. 23; italics and emphasis added).

   ➢ This is the "pot calling the kettle, black." The W/W/H had stated twenty-nine prophecies before this date; all of which failed. Does this not clearly mark the W/W/H as being "guilty of false prophesying," by its own words? Gross hypocrisy!

   ➢ If there is any question in your mind, please look back at the beginning of this chapter and note the dictionary definition of the words, promise, prophecy (sē), predict, prophesy (sī) and prophet.

31. 1974: "Reports are heard of brothers *selling their homes and property* and planning to finish out the rest of their days in the old system in the pioneer service. *Certainly this is a fine way to spend the short*

time remaining before the wicked world's end" (*Kingdom Ministry* May, 1974, p. 3; italics added).

- ➤ This was *over thirty-eight years ago*—over half of a lifetime, and just sixteen months before the autumn of 1975. Has it been a "short time remaining?" Has it not been a very long time, and still the end has not come?

32. 1975: As referred to in *Jehovah's Witnesses Proclaimers of God's Kingdom* (WTB&TS 1993, p. 632), the millennial events start, and heavenly resurrection. The question is also asked, *"Did the beliefs of Jehovah's Witnesses on these matters prove to be correct?"* (p. 633; italics added) the question is unanswered, but the answer is obviously *no*.

- ➤ Did you notice that *the W/W/H does not ever admit* to having false beliefs or proclaiming false prophecies? Instead, it just dumps the fault on the "beliefs of Jehovah's Witnesses." Vague, isn't it? It is never the fault of the W/W/H; it is always the fault of believers—the victims!

The publication goes on to admit that because such prophecies were incorrect, meeting attendance dropped dramatically as it had in the past, when prophesied dates or events failed which led to serious disappointments. (WTB&TS 1993, p. 633)

Then, in discussing the disappointments over 1925, the publication says, *"They [referring to rank-and-file Witnesses] recognized that a mistake had been made but that in no respect had God's Word failed."* (WTB&TS 1993, p. 633; italics added)

- ➤ That is true; it was not God's word that had failed or prophesied 1925 for the end (and many other proclaimed false prophecies); it was the word of the W/W/H, (the so-called "faithful and discreet slave") which has *never accepted blame* for any of its blunders; do you recognize that fact?

Deut. 18:22 is a scripture that is extremely important to our discussion of the previous thirty-plus false prophecies: "If what a prophet proclaims in the name of the LORD does not take place or come true, that is a message the LORD *has not spoken.* That prophet has spoken presumptuously, so do not be alarmed" (NIV; italics added). The NWT version puts it this way: "When the prophet speaks in the name of Jehovah and the word *does not occur or come true*, that is the word that *Jehovah did not speak.* With presumptuousness the prophet spoke it" (italics added).

➢ Is it not clear that not a single prophetic statement made by the W/W/H and quoted from their hierarchy's own literature, in the over thirty examples just considered, came from God? The group speaking and publishing the prophecies, the W/W/H, had done so presumptuously.

➢ Do you recall that it has prophesied four different dates, 1878, 1914, 1925 and 1975, for the "heavenly resurrection," commonly referred to as the rapture? All of these predictions failed. Why? They were all false and fraudulent; they were not true.

Note also the following question: Do the previous quotes, with all of their revisions and contradictions over a period of 131 years, suggest to you that the writers of some of these articles either ignored or were unaware of what had previously been written?

Their history reminds me of the words of Sir Walter Scott (1808), from an epic poem about the Battle of Flodden Field in 1513. He wrote, "Oh what a tangled web we weave when first we practice to deceive." His warning: "The liar spins and weaves his own trap for himself, not realizing he has done so until he's caught in it; lies beget more lies, and that masking lies with more lies creates an ever-more-complex arrangement of falsehoods." This describes the web of lies and deception that the W/W/H has spun for itself.

Both by the scriptures as well as its own publications, the W/W/H stands indicted of deception, false prophecies, and gross wrongdoing.

It has deceived millions of trusting believers as well as harmed them emotionally and financially.

If it is not God who has spoken by the members of this hierarchy, who do you think it is who has directed or inspired their thinking, actions, and speaking?

Note that chapter 7, entitled, "Has the W/W/H claimed to be God's Prophet? Yes or No?" proves that this hierarchy, in addition to foretelling false prophecies, has claimed to be God's prophet.

For now, reviewing the definitions given on the third page of this chapter will help solidify in your mind that the thirty-plus examples just considered do in fact meet the definitions given by the dictionary for the words "promise," "prophecy," "predict," "prophesy," and "prophet."

Let's make a comparison between ancient Bible writers and the W/W/H, in the matter of honesty. The Witness book, *All Scripture Inspired of God and Beneficial* (WTB&TS 1990), makes this point about the honesty of Bible writers: "Throughout the Bible, *the unhesitating candor* of its writers is strong *proof of its reliability*" (p. 341; italics added).

Examples are then given of such people as Moses, Aaron, King David, Solomon, the Israelite nation, and the Christian writers such as the Apostle Peter. Then the above publication continues: "It builds confidence in the *Bible* as truth when we realize that its writers spared no one, *not even themselves*, in the interest of making a faithful record" (italics added).

Notice how the W/W/H leadership has transferred responsibility away from itself, the perpetrator, to the victims of its failed prophecies. The *Watchtower* (July 15, 1976, p. 441) noted that "If anyone has been disappointed...he should now concentrate on *adjusting his viewpoint,* seeing that it was not the word of God that *failed or deceived* him and brought disappointment, but that *his own understanding* was *based on wrong premises*" (italics added).

- ➤ Was it "his own understanding" that was "based on wrong premises," or was it the wrong premises foisted on him by the W/W/H?

- Who calculated the chronology and published the literature prophesying when the end would come?

- Who printed and taught these wrong premises and was responsible for the great disappointments experienced by Jehovah's Witnesses?

- Was this double-talk again an effort to transfer the blame for failed expectations, predictions, and prophecies away from the governing body and the W/W/H, the responsible ones, to the rank-and-file Witnesses, their victims, who were not responsible?

- Would this not be like a car manufacturer blaming its customers for a major faulty car component?

- ➤ If after experiencing serious disappointments, including the suffering of financial loss because of believing sect-like and cult-like indoctrination by the W/W/H, those who had experienced this became angered and talked about it, would that not be a normal reaction to deception?

Cause and effect were bound to play a part in what followed failed prophecies, and people did talk about it. With such a record of failed prophecies from 1844 to 1975, for 131 years, is it any wonder that a significant decrease in meeting attendance occurred after each and every failed prophecy?

There is no way that the W/W/H could escape reaping what it had sown. Untold hundreds of thousands/millions of Witnesses were injured mentally, emotionally, and financially by all of its failures. "As a result, some withdrew from the organization. Others, because they sought to subvert the faith of associates, were disfellowshipped…

disappointment over the date was a factor" (WTB&TS 1993, p. 633). A *major* factor!

> ➤ Does it make sense to you that the victims of failed prophecies should be "disfellowshipped?" Should it not be the ones responsible for their failures, their misrepresentation of God, and deception who should be disfellowshipped?

It is important to note, that not just *some* of the dates prophesied proved erroneous and failed, but that *100 percent of them* proved to be wrong and hence failed.

Will the W/W/H take to heart constructive criticism, or is this hierarchy only willing to give counsel and criticism and then punish any whistle-blowers who would dare to call attention to its failures?

As a retired airline captain, I ask, how long would United have kept me on the payroll if I had crashed on landing even 10 percent of the time, let alone 100 percent of the time? How long would any company stay in business if it consistently broke its promises and refused to accept responsibility for its errors and wrongs that hurt others?

> ➤ What does that say about the reliability, honesty, integrity, or faithfulness and discreetness of the W/W/H?

What if a father started telling his eight-year-old child that he was going to take him to Disney World on vacation next year and the man continued to tell that child the same thing, year after year, until this child grew to adulthood and moved away from home to start his own family? But the parent never did take him there. Would that child not view those statements as broken promises and his father as a habitual liar?

Suppose that the father in this illustration said concerning the trip to Disney World, "Our trip is immediately ahead of us, very soon, imminent; so close you can taste it," and this went on for years. Would the son still believe it? Or would he be inclined to leave home at eighteen years of age convinced that there never really was any intent, on the part of his father, to take him to Disney World?

Since 1975, for the past almost forty years, instead of prophesying specific dates for the end and/or events associated with it, the W/W/H has innumerable times used the very expressions noted in the paragraph above. Do you think its followers and believers have gotten sick and tired of its lying and deception, and as a result they are leaving?

You bet your booties, *they definitely are!* Even the stranglehold of cognitive dissonance can eventually be broken. Recall my own experiences, related in chapter 5. In recent years, there has been a massive departure of active and at one time loyal JWs from the W/W/H and its organization. Are you one of these? Do you know others who have left?

When I started writing this book, I thought there had been only seven failed prophecies from the W/W/H. The average active Witness today probably could not list more than three. But now I am aware of and have documented in this book over thirty, and I am sure that even that is not the total number of fraudulent prophecies. Did you have any idea that there have been so many failed prophecies from the W/W/H? Why are so many coming to light?

The answer to this question is clearly stated in Luke 8:17. "For there is *nothing hidden* that will not be disclosed, and nothing *concealed* that will not be known or brought out into the open" (NIV; italics added). The NWT version says, "concealed…manifest" instead of "hidden… come into the open."

Consider some quotes from 1950 to the present.

The article, "Who Will Share in the Final Witness?" (*Watchtower* January 15, 1950, pp.27, 28), says, "Share in the glorious treasure of *giving the final witness now*…feed on the fruits of victory. **The time is short**…This old world has been weighed in the balances and found wanting, its **days are numbered**, its **hours are numbered**, as God knows its final hour" (italics and emphasis added). This article was published sixty-three years ago!

- Was the time short? No! Sixty-three years is a lifetime. Has that proven to be a true prophecy? No, it was a deception, a fraud—it failed!

- Does it sound like a used car salesman making his pitch again? Yes!

The article, "A Completely New World for This Globe" (*Watchtower* June 1, 1950, p. 171), says, *"The time is short. Those who do not inform themselves* and who do not now choose the new world which the true Higher Powers [at that time, they were believed to be Jehovah God and Jesus Christ] will shortly establish *will never live to enter into its blessings and glories"* (italics added).

- What does the word "short" mean? In general usage, a small length in space or time, definitely not a long period. Does the above quotation qualify in the matter of *accurately stating when the world will end?* No! Sixty-two years have gone by since then. Was it a true prophecy? No! It was a deception, as usual.

Briefly, have a look at a few more random examples.

The article, "Where Are We According to God's Timetable?" (*Watchtower* May 1, 1967, pp. 259–262) says:

"Ours is *a most critical generation.* Bible chronology and prophecies agree on this fact. We who live today *stand at the threshold of Armageddon"* (italics added).

- The meaning of "threshold," according to the *Webster's Revised Unabridged Dictionary (1913):* 1. a piece of timber, which lies under a door, especially of a dwelling house, church temple, or the like; the doorsill; hence, entrance; gate; door."

- ➢ How long would you stand at the threshold of a door without going into the house or going someplace else? Minutes? Hours? Days? These words were written forty-five years ago.

- ➢ Has the W/W/H misunderstood the meaning of words like "soon," or is it trying to stampede followers by deception?

Consider this example; with regard to a stampede mentality, the *Watchtower* (December 15, 1971, pp. 753–754) *asserted* that the end is *"ominously near"* and we are standing at the "portals" of God's righteous new order. "Ominous" gives the impression that trouble is about to occur or imminent.

- ➢ Forty-one years have gone by since then; was it really "ominously near" or at "the portals?" Was it a true prophecy? No! It was a deception, yet again.

The article, "The Last Days—A Time of Harvest" (*Watchtower* January 1, 1988, p. 18), says "The harvest work is urgent for a second reason. ***Soon*** it will be completed…" (italics and emphasis added).

- ➢ That was twenty-four years ago.

The inside page of any *Watchtower* magazine, (10/15/2012 is an example) entitled "The Purpose of this Magazine," says, "The Watchtower is to honor Jehovah God…It comforts people with the good news that God's Kingdom, which is a real government in heaven, will ***soon*** bring an end to all wickedness and transform the earth into a paradise" (italics and emphasis added).

- ➢ That has been the basic statement of purpose for decades, noted in all copies of the *Watchtower*.

- ➢ Webster (1913) defines "soon" to mean "in a short time—promptly; quickly."

JIM STAELENS

> ➤ The fact that the W/W/H has been using that word and words with similar meanings for over a hundred years shows deceptive intentions with hundreds if not thousands more false prophecies.

The *Watchtower* (January 15, 1974, p. 58) also adds a note about truthfulness: "What about truthfulness? *Do we really respect the truth,* or are we willing to *twist the truth a little bit* to get out of an inconvenient circumstance…*A liar…is serving the Devil*" (italics added).

> ➤ From the quotes we have considered up to now, do you think that the W/W/H has respect for the truth?

> ➤ Has not the hierarchy been willing to "twist the truth a little bit?" Really, even more than a "little bit"—more accurately, one would say, a great deal.

> ➤ Given the hierarchy's own words, whom do the facts seem to indicate that it is serving?

To close out this chapter on failed prophecies, there are two scriptures, in addition to the ones we considered earlier, that make it clear that neither the W/W/H nor any other group or person will ever be able to correctly predict, in advance, when the end will come. Note the following scripture verses. First of all, please note what Matt. 24:44 says: "So you must be ready, because the Son of Man will come at an hour **when you do not expect him**" (NIV; italics and emphasis added). The NWT version says, "On this account YOU too prove yourselves ready, because at an hour that YOU **do not think to be it,** the Son of man is coming" (NWT; italics and emphasis added).

To thinking Bible readers, the proviso in the Bible book of Second Peter is important. After referring to the last days and the flood of Noah's day (chapter 3:1–7), it makes the following point at 2 Peter 3:8, "But do not forget this one thing, dear friends: With the Lord a day is like a thousand years, and a thousand years like a day" (NIV; the NWT version says basically the same).

In view of these very clear scriptures, what arrogance is manifested by a person, or a religious hierarchy, who professes to be following Jesus Christ, to assert that they have discovered when the end of this system will arrive!

Of course, that does not mean just the W/W/H has done so; others have done likewise, just not as often. The W/W/H holds the record for publishing more such prophecies than any other person, group, or entity in history. So what does it say when we recognize that all of its prophecies have been false?

REVIEW POINTS:

1. How many different dates and events have been prophesied for the end of the world and/or events connected with that end by the W/W/H? Why did all of those prophecies fail?

2. Why do you think the W/W/H has kept changing to different dates for the same events, such as when Armageddon or the rapture will occur?

3. Considering the above quotes, do you believe that the W/W/H has published *prophecies* conforming to the English dictionary definition of that word?

4. Have you, if a present or past Witness or related to any such person, been adversely affected because of false dates or events that have been prophesied by the W/W/H? Have its false prophecies created problems and cost you or any family members in a financial way?

5. Who is accountable for such failures? Do you think the hierarchy should be held responsible for these hardships, including financial loss it has caused for its unsuspecting believers and/or other victims?

6. Has the W/W/H admitted fault for errors and false prophecies, or has it passed the buck? Why do you think it has hidden from and refused to take responsibility for its flagrant errors and false prophecies when it has admitted that the Bible "writers spared no one, not even themselves?" (WTB&TS 1990, p. 341)

Let's consider how this hierarchy's procedures of deception and passing the buck would or would not work in any other kind of venue—flying, for example:

If an individual is not a pilot but wants other people to believe that he or she really is a pilot, perhaps hoping to get a job with the airlines, what might the person do to convince others of something that is not true? What might be done to deceive others? Just stating that the person is a pilot does not make it true.

Would the person just wishing he or she was a pilot make it true, a reality? Would the person telling others over and over again that he or she is a pilot guarantee truthfulness? Would shouting loudly that the person is a qualified pilot prove anything? The obvious answer to all these questions is—*No!*

What would be the best way, for a flight manager representing the airlines, to learn the truth about how qualified this would-be pilot is? The manager would put the person in the cockpit of a plane or simulator with a flight instructor and find out, for sure, how good, bad, qualified, or not this person really was. The truth would quickly come to light; it could not be hidden for long. That is exactly how it is done.

United's "New Hire Program" was three months long; its purpose was to separate those who thought or claimed that they were qualified from those who really were. At the time I got hired in 1966, 20 percent of the new students washed out (failed) within those first three months.

The fact is that airline pilots—captains, copilots, and flight engineers (for jets that require one)—are the most frequently tested group of professionals that I know of. Twice a year, every year for their entire career, they are all given a "flight proficiency check" (in a plane or a simulator). If they can't pass, it is the end of their job. That is not true of doctors, lawyers, politicians, or any other professional group that I am aware of. And it is certainly not true of religious leaders.

Do you discern the point of this information? You may be aware of the fact than many others have been duped and deceived by religious leaders. If one wants to avoid being a victim, as others have been, he or she must be willing to do thorough research in order to separate truth from falsehood. Lying and deception can be identified if one puts forth effort to look at all available resources.

But is it not clear that, in the case of the W/W/H, it has shown it has no intention of starting to tell the truth now? Its web of deception is too massive and yet its members continue to claim to be God's prophet. Are they in truth his prophet? Yes or no—what are the facts? Chapter 7 will clearly address this matter.

CHAPTER 7

HAS THE W/W/H CLAIMED TO BE GOD'S PROPHET? YES, OR NO?

- There is a saying… "There are none so blind as those who will not see." Why is that the case?
- What, besides age, can help one become mature?
- ❖ Flying: Of course you can, if you learn… but how?

Early in chapter six, I covered the definitions of five words: "promise," "prophecy" (sē) ("a prediction"), "predict," "prophesy" (sī) ("to predict"), and "prophet." Such authoritative definitions make it clear that the W/W/H has in fact uttered and published more than thirty prophecies dealing with the end of the world and/or events associated with that end. These documented predictions from 1844 to 1975 all proved to be false prophecies.

On occasion, when confronted with its past published false prophecies, the W/W/H has claimed that it never actually said, "Thus sayeth the Lord" or "Thus sayeth Jehovah," and therefore that it never actually claimed to be God's prophet. What are the facts? What has the hierarchy really claimed, in its own publications about itself? God's prophet? Yes or no? Please note the following seven specific points:

First, if we step back in time to when Charles Taze Russell was the founder of the Witness organization and the former of Zion's Watch Tower Bible Tract Society, what will we learn? Double-talk and deception were already at work. Recall prophecy number six from chapter 6, for the date 1889. In *Studies in the Scriptures* (WTB&TS vol. 2, 1911, p. 15), Russell claimed that "the chain of testimony in his book…is *beyond* the breadth and depth of human thought, and therefore ***cannot be of human origin***" (italics and emphasis added).

> ➢ Was Russell claiming that the testimony in his book was from God? Yes or no?

Second, *The Watchtower* (October 1, 1919, p. 297) makes this dogmatic statement: "This was the test—the coming down of fire; and the fulfillment *exactly on time* has proved that *Pastor Russell* was **one of God's great reformers** and **prophets**" (italics and emphasis added).

> Does the *Watchtower* specifically and dogmatically state that Pastor Russell was one of God's prophets? Yes or no?

The point about "the coming down of fire" was likely in reference to the experience of Elijah the prophet involving his contest with the Baal worshipers infecting the nation of Israel (1 Ki. 18:20–40). The specific verse that this comment appears to be referencing is 1 Ki. 18:38, "Then the fire of the LORD fell and burned up the sacrifice, the wood, the stones and the soil, and also licked up the water in the trench" (NIV). The NWT version says, "At that the fire of Jehovah came falling…"

> Was the context of this scripture discussing Pastor Russell, or has it been taken out of context? Was it not, in fact, only discussing Elijah and events facing the Israelite nation?

Third, stepping closer to our own day, note this comment: The article "Down with the Old—Up with the New!" (*Watchtower* January 15, 1959, pp. 39–41) says, "For an answer, people should listen to the plain preaching by *the remnant* [those of Jehovah's Witnesses who claim they will rule with Jesus in heaven] prefigured by Jeremiah…*Who made them a prophet* to speak with authority that they claim? Well who *made Jeremiah a prophet?*" (italics added)

The reader is expected to believe that God made Jeremiah and the remnant his prophets by personal appointment. According to the Bible, that was true of Jeremiah but not of Russell or the remnant. Their claim is false—deceptive!

However, if you will look back, you will see that already, by 1959, the W/W/H had to its credit over twenty-nine false prophecies (1844 to 1941) about the end and/or events connected with that end, with more to come.

> Does the hierarchy's consistent record of failed prophecies (more than any other individual, group, or religious organization over the past 1,968 years) identify it as a true prophet? Yes or no?

> Do you recall the scripture from Deut. 18:22 quoted in chapter six? Does it not say that when what a prophet speaks does not come true, the prophet has spoken presumptuously and what he has prophesied is not a word from God?

Fourth, the *Watchtower* (October 1, 1964, p. 601), under the subtopic, "Prophecies Proclaimed Earth Wide Today," says, "Those who do not read can hear, for God has on earth today ***a prophet-like organization***, just as he did in the days of the early Christian congregation" (italics and emphasis added).

> That *Watchtower* issue is asserting that one should believe that the W/W/H is serving as a prophet, as the "early Christian congregation" did.

> The bullets above apply here also. What is this hierarchy's record in this matter? Has it spoken presumptuously in what has prophesied? Do the facts show it is really God's prophet?

Fifth, note the *Watchtower* (August 1, 1971, p. 466), which first quotes Amos 3:7, which says, "The Sovereign Lord Jehovah will not do a thing unless he has revealed his confidential matter to his servants *the prophets*" (NWT; italics added). The NIV says, "LORD" rather than "Jehovah."

Then, this same issue of the *Watchtower* (August 1, 1971,) continues, "In this century who has been ***correctly informed*** about the future? the clergy? the political leaders? the economic heads? ***Or*** has it been ***the Witnesses of Jehovah?***" (italics and emphasis added)

> Of course the W/W/H is hoping the reader, of this magazine, will believe that it, through *Watchtower* publications has been

keeping JWs, and others, correctly informed about the future, as God's prophet. As you know by now, that is not true.

Sixth, note this quote from the Watchtower (January 15, 1977, p. 40): "...do you put your faith and confidence in the speculations of...human advisers?...these opinions...are not what Jehovah has revealed **by *the mouth of his prophets*** concerning the near future." The article continues, "Jehovah's Christian witnesses [really the W/W/H] have been ***most active in telling others*** what the Bible says about inescapable ***coming events***" (italics and emphasis added).

> ➤ Active in telling—Yes! Accurate in telling—No!

> ➤ All of the previous four bullets apply to this quote as well, especially since this was published just sixteen months after their last failed prophecy for the end to occur in the autumn of 1975.

Seventh, let's consider one more pointed quote from the Watchtower (October 15, 1980, p. 17). "Thus, God gives his humble servants *special knowledge* that others do not have...to herald...the warning of this system's approaching end" (italics added). That was published thirty-two years ago—half a lifetime.

> ➤ By asserting that it has "special knowledge that others do not have," is not the W/W/H claiming that it is inspired by God?

> ➤ These are just seven examples from the hierarchy's literature. I could provide many more; however, is it not perfectly clear that it, since the time of C. T. Russell, ***has claimed to be God's prophet?***

> ➤ In light of its failed prophecies, thoroughly documented in chapter 6, is it not perfectly clear that the W/W/H has proven itself to be a false prophet and hence, clearly not a true prophet of God?

Regarding the first bullet point at the beginning of this chapter, there are several reasons why a person may not see something, even if his or her life is at stake. A person could be blind (making physical sight an impossibility). A person could be too far away and out of sight of what he or she needs to see, and so be unable to see it. Or a person could just be unwilling to look at and see what he or she needs to see, that is, the person flatly refuses to see. These are the ones referred to in the phrase, "none so blind as those who will not see." This is inexcusable.

Seeing involves more than just physical sight; it requires being able to correctly interpret what the importance is of what a person is looking at. Discernment is needed. That is true of things you are "seeing" in this book. Such seeing, "discernment," does not come about automatically. An illustration can make this point.

You will recall from chapter five, about my own pilot training, how pilots learn to fly through clouds. Even though it is impossible for them to see outside their airplane, they can fly without crashing or getting lost. That procedure is referred to as instrument flying ("flying IFR," by instrument flight rules). A pilot does not need to "see" outside the airplane until just before landing, but he or she does need to "see," perceive, and understand what the flight instruments inside the airplane are saying. The pilot must be able to interpret and respond to what those flight instruments indicate must be done to stay right side up and to land safely. This ability is not inherent; it must be taught, learned, and practiced for hours. Remember my experience while getting trained for IFR, under the hood?

> ➤ A real-life flying experience will help you to understand even better. My wife and I were headed from Alamosa, Colorado, to Great Falls, Montana, in our own plane, at twelve thousand feet above mean sea level. I was giving my wife Dale some flying experience, and we could see that in about two minutes, we were going to be "in the soup" (flying through clouds). She said to me, "You had better take over; we're about to go IFR." (Yes, she did understand what that means—to enter instrument meteorological conditions in an airplane.)

My response, "No, I think you need some real IFR practice." Although she is often a "What-iffer," she kept her hands on the yoke and continued flying; the autopilot was disengaged.

Pilots who are able to fly IFR are able to do so only because they have practiced instrument flying for at least forty hours; in other words, it is through practice that they have become proficient at flying IFR, and they have passed an FAA written exam as well as an in-flight test to demonstrate proficiency. They have an "Instrument Rating."

As a captain, I was IFR qualified and rated for this flight; I had filed and received an IFR clearance from air traffic control, and we were flying that clearance in the same way that I had done countless times while working for United Airlines.

So I patiently (though I'm not always as patient as I should be) accomplished my purpose: I pointed to the air-speed indicator, the attitude indicator (also called the "artificial horizon"), the altimeter, the rate-of-climb indicator (IVSI), and the course-deviation indicator of the GPS. I pointed to them one at a time, starting in the upper left corner of the panel and working my way around to all of the flight instruments. Of course I was ready to take control of the plane, if it became necessary.

"The trick," I noted, "is to keep scanning all of the flight instruments—don't fixate on just one. If you see something getting off from where it should be, start making an adjustment, but keep your scan going." She listened, she understood, she learned, and she responded. "Good job!" I reassured her.

I continued with my rationale for wanting her to get some real IFR experience. "Many people have died, needlessly, because the pilot flying was not IFR qualified and found himself 'in the soup' or perhaps flying over water at night, which can present conditions that make it impossible to have enough cues from the ground to stay right side up." I further noted, "If anything were to happen to me, which I don't expect to be the case, it would be great if you had the confidence and ability to just keep going and get safely on the ground, even if we're "in the soup."'"

Continuing, I said, "John F. Kennedy, Jr., was not instrument qualified or rated, and that fact became a major factor in the plane crash that occurred on July 16, 1999, that cost him and others their lives." Dale understood and kept flying, practicing, and learning.

By the time we got to Provo, Utah, our fuel stop, she was flying like an airline captain…well, not quite, but you get the idea. She was doing very well, well enough that she was able to stay on her altitude, stay on course, stay right side up, and all that other good stuff, *while* flying through clouds where it is impossible to see anything outside the plane in reference to your position in space.

The point is simple: It takes time, desire, work, and a teacher in order to learn something new and get good at it. It could be said, *you are becoming mature as a pilot.* In Dale's case, she was not preparing for an IFR rating; she was just adding to her experience. She already was very capable; she could take off, climb to cruise altitude, follow the GPS course, and land safely *in good weather.*

This added training was to just give her an edge, a little extra margin of safety, and the ability to take over in instrument meteorological weather conditions if it became necessary, and then successfully to land at an airport rather than losing control of the plane and crashing.

Of course, anyone in the cockpit of a small plane, if he or she has vision, can see the flight instruments. But if the pilot chooses not to look at those instruments and really see the flight panel, or if the pilot does not really understand what he or she is seeing or is not able to respond to what the flight instruments are saying to do, if the person is flying under instrument meteorological conditions, he or she will have a very short time (about a minute and a half) to live. Recall my experience from chapter 5; flying by the seat of your pants just won't work.

Recall the scripture that I quoted in chapter three, Heb. 5:14. Solid food is for mature, persons who become trained by constant use of their faculties (NIV). The NWT version says that solid food is for mature people, because they constantly use their perceptive powers, so they are able to distinguish right from wrong.

Be willing and able to really see, understand, distinguish, and perceive the points coming up in this chapter, indeed throughout this book. It will be essential if you are to benefit from what you read. Obviously a person does not have to learn something he or she does not want to learn. Even if the person has the information available to see, if he or she flatly "will not see" what is presented, the person may turn out to be like the proverbial ostrich and "hide his head in the sand." In such a case, the fault for not understanding—perhaps a very important new point—is clearly the person's own.

Of course, I am well aware of the fact that an ostrich does not literally bury its head in the sand to hide. The ostrich can run at 45 mph, and its feet can be used, kangaroo style, to fight an enemy, even a full-grown lion, with deadly consequences for the lion. If an ostrich chooses neither to run nor fight, it may simply lay its head on the ground and try to look like a pile of sand, camouflage style, trying to avoid an enemy.

Some of Jehovah's Witnesses, whether among the hierarchy, the abusers, enablers, or even the victims (rank-and-file Witnesses), who are still associated with their organization, may have very serious reservations about staying and may choose to fade into the background, ostrich style, rather than to fight or run from what has become, for them, a very abusive situation. Real practical solutions, to help one to escape from spiritual abuse and cope with the aftermath, will be covered in chapter fourteen of this book.

The book, *Reasoning from the Scriptures,* a Witness publication, presents double-talk for the W/W/H's definitions on the subjects of *prophecy* and *false prophets*. Under the subject, "Prophecy," note this definition that is provided: "An inspired message; a revelation of the divine will and purpose. Prophecy may be a prediction of something to come, inspired moral teaching, or an expression of divine command or judgment" (WTB&TS 1989, p. 295).

Remember the previous dictionary definition? Prophecy is "a prediction; the faculty or practice of prophesying."

The first heading in the abovementioned book chapter asks, "What *predictions* recorded in the Bible have already been *fulfilled?*" (WTB&TS 1989, P. 296) (italics added) Notice that the word "predictions" is used as a synonym for "prophecies." This is their choice of words.

Notice that both of these definitions involve a prediction of something to come. Whether or not the one giving the prophecy claims to be inspired by God or not is irrelevant. Yet as you have seen, the W/W/H has indeed claimed, on several occasions over many years of time, that it is truly God's prophet.

The obvious difference in examples above, from Witness literature, is that dogmatism is exerted whereas a complete or accurate definition from a recognized authority—a dictionary is conspicuously missing.

Now consider the subject of "False Prophets" (WTB&TS 1989, p. 132). From the book comes the following definition: "Individuals and organizations proclaiming messages that they attribute to a superhuman source but that do not originate with the true God and are not in harmony with his revealed will."

Please note that in the *Reasoning* book, neither of the definitions given by the W/W/H lists a reference as an authority for the definition. The hierarchy simply considers its definitions to be acceptable because the members of its governing body, the ones responsible for the publishing, copyrighting, and printing of their book, have said so. But their statement is dogmatic and deceptive and not accurate.

If I told you that an "airplane" is defined as "a light framework with fabric stretched over it, attached to a string for flying in the wind," would my definition be correct? Should it be considered "authoritative" just because I, as a retired airline captain, said so? Absolutely not!

You no doubt recognize that the definition I just gave was that of a kite and not an airplane. My stating the definition authoritatively, dogmatically, or loudly or printing it on the page of a book or magazine would not change the fact that the definition I presented for an airplane was wrong. After all, I did not provide an authoritative definition.

Remember again the dictionary definition of "prophet" (chapter 6): "One who prophesies or foretells events." That same dictionary defines "false" as: "Uttering falsehood... given to *deceit*... untrue; *treacherous... designed to deceive*; counterfeit; *hypocritical*" (italics added).

So by dictionary definition, a "false prophet" would be one who *"predicts events"*, but whose prediction is not according to the truth or fact, it is *"designed to deceive, hypocritical."* (italics added)

Does this definition not clearly identify the W/W/H as a false prophet?

From 1873, when the organization started, until 2013, that makes one hundred and forty years of "predictions" (prophecies) involving the "end," as well as associated events. All have come under an authoritative definition of "false prophecies," being *"designed to deceive, hypocritical."*

In view of the above facts, can anyone truthfully deny that the W/W/H has identified itself, by what it has said and done as well as by its own literature, to be a false prophet, regardless of any specious reasoning and double-talk to distort the facts?

Reasoning from the Scriptures (WTB&TS 1989, p. 133) makes this comment: "True prophets speak in the name of God, but merely claiming to represent him *is not enough."* Below this comment, reference is made to Deut. 18:18-20, which says, in verse 20: "However, the prophet who *presumes* to speak in my name *a word that I have not commanded him* to speak or who speaks in the name of other gods, *that prophet must die*" (NWT; italics added). The NIV says, "is to be put to death."

The W/W/H has never claimed to be divinely inspired, as Bible writers were. That leaves room for that hierarchy to utter false prophecies with impunity—right? *Wrong!*

Note this quote from the *Watchtower* (October 15, 1980, p. 17): "Because he is a God of love, he reveals enough of these details to those who serve him loyally that they can be ***properly informed***, up-built and *protected*" (italics and emphasis added). Then Amos 3:7 (quoted earlier) is referred to, where it says that "the Sovereign LORD will do nothing without revealing his plans to his prophets" (NIV). The NWT version says, "his confidential matters…" Then the abovementioned *Watchtower* (p. 17) makes the point that God will give his servants a special knowledge that others will not have.

Lest there be any doubt about whether or not the W/W/H refers to itself as a prophet, note this quote from the article "They Shall Know that a Prophet Was among Them" (*Watchtower* April 1, 1972, p. 197). It says, "So, *does* Jehovah have a prophet to help them, to warn them of dangers…things to come?" (italics added) The subtopic, "Identifying the Prophet" continues: "Affirmative…*He had a "prophet" to warn them*. This "prophet"…was the small group…known as International Bible Students; today…*Jehovah's Christian Witnesses.*"

Of course it was the W/W/H, not rank-and-file Witnesses, that was responsible for all of the above noted published and failed prophecies. Is it not indelibly clear and obvious that the hierarchy has many times claimed to be "God's Prophet" and to have been given the ability to speak in God's name with "special knowledge that others do not have?"

Is not the hierarchy also clearly and dogmatically asserting that "Jehovah…has revealed his confidential matters to it; the W/W/H, as his prophet?"

But, if its bold, dogmatic, and presumptuous statements asserting that it is God's prophet were true, then how on earth could it have prophesied and published over thirty false and failed prophecies, from 1844 to 1975? Not even this hierarchy would likely have the audacity to assert that it was God's fault that all of its prophecies failed, would it? Clearly it is the fault of the W/W/H, because even though it has claimed to be God's prophet, it has instead *proven* itself to have been a false prophet; not just once, but over and over again!

REVIEW POINTS:

1. Has the W/W/H prophesied? Yes or no? What do you think?

2. Have its predictions come true? Yes or no? What has been proven?

3. Has the W/W/H repeatedly claimed to be God's prophet? What do you believe now? Is it Yes or no?

4. What have the last two chapters shown?

5. As the old proverb goes, "Deceive me once; shame on you (the deceiver). Deceive me twice (or more)—shame on me!"

You likely remember from your science classes in school that some insects go through a process in their life cycle called "metamorphosis." A not so pretty insect will change completely into a beautiful butterfly. A tadpole will turn into a frog. In all cases, the finished transformation looks absolutely nothing like its beginning form. So what does that have to do with our discussion here regarding the W/W/H?

The book, *Jehovah's Witnesses Proclaimers of God's Kingdom* (WTB&TS 1993, pp. 44, 45), explains that from the years 1870 to 1875, C. T. Russell and others got together to study the Bible; although Russell formed the group and was in charge, they all provided input. But as time went on, changes started to occur; they were similar to the process of metamorphosis. That has occurred with the human race since the dawn of civilization. Some individuals have emerged from the transformation as leaders; others have become tyrants (e.g., Nimrod mentioned in the Bible at Gen. 10:8 or Hitler, a more recent historical example during World War II).

The W/W/H has proven to be no exception to this process in the course of human events. Why and how? In 1887, Lord Acton, a historian and moralist, expressed his opinion in a letter to Bishop Mandell Creighton, in which he wrote, "Power tends to corrupt, and absolute power corrupts absolutely."

As we learned earlier, in 1911, C. T. Russell wrote about the earmarks of a religious sect or cult. In time, the organization he had founded morphed into the same type of organization with the same kind of traits.

Can you really see, discern, and comprehend the magnitude of what you have learned? Can you see the deliberate deception on the part of the W/W/H? In view of the web of deceit it has woven, can you see why it has been unwilling to change? How does that make you feel?

What do these lessons from history teach us? That there has never been even one person (other than Jesus Christ) or organization that has it all together so that they would be qualified to dictate to others. Of course the Bible says that Jesus was perfect, but even so, he did not choose to dictate to others; rather, he lovingly entreated them to follow him. 1 Pet. 2:21, 22 says, in effect, we should follow his example because he did not commit sin nor was there any deception in his mouth.

If you check any concordance under the words "corrupt," "corrupted," "corruptible," "deceive," "deceived," or "deception;" you will find these words most often referring to humans, including God's chosen people. An exception (Gen. 3:13) - "The serpent… deceived me…" NWT

The lesson is that imperfect humans can and do at times go bad; they can be deceived and can be corrupted. History has proven that to be true. So unless the W/W/H has convinced itself that its members are not human, it is no exception to this fact. It is not that it is faultless—it is just that it will *never admit fault*.

Is it not perfectly clear that there are major lessons and directives from the Bible, which we have considered in this chapter; lessons that the W/W/H has missed (or more accurately - has refused to see and acknowledge)? As Sir Walter Scott suggested, its "tangled web of deceit" has come back to haunt it.

We will consider another example of this in the next chapter. Although water baptism is practiced by many religious groups, what is the dark side of baptizing Witness youths? Has deception reigned in this area also?

Please stay seated for that next segment of our "flight."

Chapter 8

THE BAPTISM DECEPTION– FOR YOUTHS: THE DARK SIDE

- In what ways have W/W/H teachings about baptism been deceptive? Do they have an agenda; if so what could it be?
- What does the Bible really teach about baptism?
- What dark side about Witness baptism has trapped and harmed countless youths and their families?
- What ramifications, barren of reason, can become the reality for young ones who submit to baptism?
- ❖ If you were a passenger on an airliner, would you want to see a student pilot in the captain's seat?

First things first: how does the authoritative *Webster's Revised Unabridged Dictionary (1913)* define "baptism" and "Baptist?"

baptism: "the act of baptizing... by which he is *initiated into the visible church* of Christ... by immersion, sprinkling, or pouring, (italics added).

baptist: (Baptist) One who administers baptism... a denomination of Christians who *deny the validity of infant baptism... administered to believers alone...* by immersion." (italics added).

In view of the fact that this book is an exposé of claims made by the W/W/H, let's "cut to the chase." What does its organization say, in its own literature, about the matter of baptism? What is its definition? More important to Christians, let's see what the Bible really teaches about the subject of baptism.

Should youths, regardless of age, be baptized? What could become the long-term negative consequences if they are?

Because of the sensitivity of the following information, I urge you to please check all references, both in Watchtower publications and in the

Bible. Quotes involving statements by Tertullian and Augustus Neander or nearly any other reference can be checked using any good Internet search engine by typing in the name, question, or reference.

The W/W/H's definition of "baptism" does not agree with that from *Webster*. Their book, *Reasoning from the Scriptures* (WTB&TS 1989, p. 54), gives the following definition. Note the differences as compared to the dictionary: "Christian water baptism is an outward *symbol* that the one being baptized *has made* a *complete, unreserved,* and *unconditional dedication* through Jesus Christ to do the will of Jehovah God" (italics added).

> ➢ Do you believe that a child, six, eight, or ten years old, could possibly or realistically make a "complete, unreserved, and unconditional dedication" to God? I could not and did not when I was being pressured to be baptized at the age of nine.

Notice that *no authority* is listed for the hierarchy's definition. Why not? It's simply because, to do so *would expose* their deceptive baptism teaching. They just state their definition dogmatically, hoping, expecting, and demanding, in sect-like fashion, that their followers accept it.

It is a fact that there is not one single scripture in any Bible translation that says that baptism symbolizes one's "dedication to God." The hierarchy's definition is deceptive at best and fraudulent at worse. It is a fabrication. This chapter will clearly show its likely reasons and probable agenda.

Page 55 of the abovementioned *Reasoning* book (1989) contains the subtopic and question, "Was infant baptism practiced by first-century Christians?"

The first scripture listed is Matt. 28:19, 20. This is the place in the Bible where Jesus issued the command to "go make disciples...baptizing." Would it not be expected that if baptism really symbolized or involved making a dedication to God, this is the place where such instructions would be clearly given? But they are not; note what this verse actually says. (Italics are added in the following quotes.) "Go therefore and make *disciples* of all nations, *baptizing them* in the name of the Father and of the Son and of the Holy Spirit;" then verse 20 adds, "and *teaching them* to obey everything I have commanded you" (NIV). The NWT version says, "or make *learners*" (via a footnote) and "*teaching them* to observe."

Notice that there is nothing said there by Jesus about "dedication to God;" nor is such a thing said in any other translations. Nor did Jesus, as recorded in the Bible, give any command or teaching using the word, "dedication;" his command was clearly to make disciples (as in the NWT footnote: "learners").

The original Greek word, "disciples," used here in the Bible, is translated as "teach" in the King James Version. Thayer's *Greek-English Lexicon of the New Testament* (1977, # 3100, p. 386) says that it means: "1. *to be the disciple of one; to follow his precepts and instruction;* 2. *to make a disciple; to teach, instruct*" (italics in the original). In other words, a disciple is a pupil or learner or someone who is instructed.

That makes sense, doesn't it?

By the way, the exact quote from the *Authorized King James* version of the Bible, at Matt. 28:19, 20, says, "Go ye therefore, and *teach* all nations, *baptizing them* in the name of the Father, and of the Son and of the Holy Ghost: *Teaching them* to observe all things whatsoever I have commanded you" (italics added).

- Did you notice that the footnote in the *New World Translation* and the definition in the Greek-English Lexicon show the meaning of the Greek word "disciple" to be a "learner?" They do not say "dedicated one," do they?

- Would not the original biblical Greek use the word "dedicate" if what the W/W/H teaches about baptism "signifying dedication" was true?

What does that hierarchy's *New World Translation of the Holy Scriptures* say about the words "dedicate," "dedicated," and "dedication?"

The *Comprehensive Concordance* (WTB&TS 1973) of its translation, prepared by them, lists only nine scriptures in the entire translation that use the words "dedicate," "dedicated," and "dedication." Please check all nine of them;* the first one listed under "dedicate" is the only one that refers to "persons being dedicated" ("consecrated" in the NIV), and that one verse involves dedication to the pagan Canaanite god, Baal (* last page of this chapter).

The only instance of the use of "dedicate," (to a god) is Hos. 9:10 (NWT; italics and first brackets added), "...and they [apostate Israel] proceeded to *dedicate themselves* to the shameful thing, and they came to be disgusting like [the thing of] their love" (second brackets theirs). The NIV says, "*Consecrated themselves*...shameful idol...vile as the thing they loved."

None of the other verses in the *New World Translation*, under "dedicate," "dedicated," or "dedication," refer to a person as "making a dedication to God."

> ➤ If Christian baptism really symbolizes a "dedication to God," why does the Bible not clearly state that to be the case? Why does the only reference to persons being "dedicated," in the hierarchy's own Bible, involve being dedicated "to the shameful thing," the god Baal?

There is additional very strong evidence against the definition of baptism as "dedication to God." Do you recall the events leading up to the baptism of the Ethiopian eunuch, noted at Acts 8:27–36? Search the account thoroughly, and you will find absolutely no mention of his making "a complete, unreserved, and unconditional dedication to God," either before or after his baptism.

Very specifically, the account records the question by the Ethiopian to Philip, as recorded at Acts 8:36, "Look here is water. What *can stand in the way* of my being baptized?" (NIV; italics added) The NWT version says, "...what *prevents* me...?" (italics added)

There is nothing said there about "dedication," is there? Philip did not go into a discussion about the need to first get down on his knees and make a solemn dedication to God in prayer. In fact, the word "prayer" does not occur anywhere in this account. It is only said that the Ethiopian was "reading from the scroll of Isaiah" and that Philip "declared to him the good news about Jesus."

Some Witnesses might be inclined to argue that the Ethiopian eunuch was a Jewish proselyte (WTB&TS 1988, p. 767), and so there was no need for him to make a dedication. However, according to the W/W/H's *Comprehensive Concordance* (WTB&TS 1973), the word "proselyte" does not occur at all in connection with the Ethiopian. *Strong's Exhaustive Concordance* (1984) likewise shows an absence of the word "proselyte." Additionally, other accounts to be discussed below definitely do not involve Jewish proselytes.

In the *Authorized King James* version of the Bible, the Ethiopian asked at Acts 8:36, "what doth hinder me to be baptized?" Verse 37 says, "And Philip said, If thou **believest** with all thine heart, **thou mayest.** And he answered and said, I believe that Jesus Christ is the Son of God" (italics and emphasis added).

It is of interest that the large print reference *New World Translation* omits verse 37 but contains a footnote that says, "some manuscripts omit verse 37" and then it adds, "Philip said to him: 'If you **believe** *with all your heart, **it is permissible**'* In reply he said: 'I believe that Jesus Christ is the Son of God." (italics and emphasis added)

The Bible in Living English contains a marginal note for Acts 8:37, which says, *"Var. ads verse 37* And Philip said "If you **believe** *from the bottom of your heart (lit. out of all your heart) **you may.**"* (some italics and emphasis added)

The NIV contains the same footnote.

The fact that the Ethiopian eunuch did listen to what Philip said and did believe "that Jesus Christ is the Son of God" but did not, according to any scripture or Bible translation, make any kind of a dedication indicates that what was necessary to be baptized back then was belief—not dedication. The King James Bible as well as the footnote in the NWT version, in addition to many other translations, indicates that this was the case in the first century.

The next two scriptural accounts about an army officer from Caesarea as well as a jailer in Philippi make it indelibly clear that for Christian baptism to be administered in the first century there was a need for learning and belief (becoming a disciple, a pupil, a learner) *but* not for dedication of any sort.

The first account after the one about the Ethiopian is found in Acts chapter 10; it involves a Roman army officer (a Gentile) by the name of Cornelius. The account says, he and his family were devout, God fearing, and that he gave generously to those in need and prayed to God regularly. That is all we know about him up until Peter called at his house (Acts 10:1–48).

It is noteworthy that the Apostle Peter made an observation at Acts 10:34, 35 that is very relevant to our discussion and which will be elaborated on more in a later chapter of this book. Note what he says: "At this Peter opened his mouth and said: 'For a certainty I perceive that *God is not partial, but in every nation* the man that *fears him* and *works righteousness* is **acceptable** to him'" (NWT; italics added). The NIV says, "I now realize…*God does not show favoritism…does what is right*" (italics and emphasis added).

> ➢ Did you notice that the prayers by Cornelius and the fact that he "fears him and does what is right" or "works righteousness" was observed, answered, and acted upon by God before Cornelius had been taught, received the holy spirit, or was baptized? His baptism symbolized that he had become a disciple (a learner).

- Is it not obvious that Jehovah God can hear and act on the requests of anyone that he observes is "God-fearing and acting righteously," regardless of who or where he or she is? In this case, Cornelius was an active duty army officer, serving with the Roman Empire.

- So much for the W/W/H-sponsored belief that "God will only hear and respond to the prayers of Jehovah's Witnesses" (which has been asserted countless times by the hierarchy). I don't believe it either; the facts prove otherwise. Then the big surprise came: "while Peter was speaking, holy spirit fell upon all those hearing him." (verse 44)

Then Acts 10:47 says, "Surely no one can stand in the way of *their being baptized* with water. They *have received the Holy Spirit* just as we have" (NIV; italics added). The NWT version says, "Can anyone *forbid water*...?" (italics added)

- Notice that here again, there was absolutely nothing said in this account about a need to make a dedication to God before or after water baptism.

- Cornelius was an active duty army officer, yet according to the scriptures, he was anointed with holy spirit even before he was baptized.

- The W/W/H forbids baptism for any person active in military service. The Apostle Peter did not. Do you wonder why?

Let's consider an account from Acts chapter 16; it involves the baptism of a civil servant, a jailer in the city of Philippi. Verses 16–40 give the experiences of Paul and those traveling with him, which led up to their arrest.

Verses 26 and 27 tell us that there was an earthquake that woke up the jailer and led to his question at Acts 16:30–34, which was, "Sirs, what must I do to be saved? They replied, '***Believe** in the Lord Jesus,* and you will be saved—you and your household.' Then they *spoke* the word of the Lord to him…the jailer took them and washed their wounds; then *immediately* he and all his household were *baptized*…set a meal before them; he was filled with joy because he had *come to believe* in God—he and his whole household." (NIV) The NWT version says, "were ***baptized, without delay***… now that ***he had believed God.***" (italics and emphasis added)

In none of these three accounts was there a prolonged study or even one word about making a "dedication" to God first, before baptism. Why not? It was not then and never has been a scriptural prerequisite for baptism in any Bible account. It has just been a bold, dogmatic assertion by the W/W/H.

Do not these accounts make it clear that the hierarchy's position is a deception? In all of these cases, they (the new disciples) listened, learned, and believed.

Recall that is exactly what the word "disciple" means a pupil, one who learns. Additionally, it is not said that the Ethiopian or the jailer, for that matter, had holy spirit poured out on them. They were simply baptized as disciples (learners and pupils) of Jesus Christ.

In view of the documented information presented up to this point, there is no valid basis for the assertion on the part of the W/W/H that dedication to God must precede baptism or that baptism symbolizes dedication to God; it simply is not scripturally true.

Does it chafe your sensibilities to read that the W/W/H has been guilty of deception in such an important matter as what baptism symbolizes? Does it seem impossible that the hierarchy could be wrong, especially deliberately? Before convincing yourself that it could not possibly be wrong, ponder the following points about ancient Israel's history as God's people.

Think about their terrible record, that 85 percent of their kings proved to be corrupt and that for 86 percent of the time between when Moses led the Jews out of Egypt until the first century (about 1,346 years), that nation proved to be corrupt and apostate. It was so bad that its holy temple and the city of Jerusalem were destroyed, first by the Babylonians and then later again by the Romans.

> ➢ An excellent recap of Israel's history, from the time of Abraham until the first century, is recounted by Jesus' disciple, Stephen, at Acts 7:1–60. It will be helpful to you if you read those verses; you will see that religious history has indeed continued to repeat itself.

Stephen had been arrested and falsely accused of speaking blasphemous sayings against Moses and God; worse yet, his accusers could not hold their own against his wisdom and the spirit with which he was speaking, so they panicked and dragged him before the Sanhedrin, the Jewish Supreme Court (Acts 6:8–11). He had been functioning much like a modern-day whistle-blower.

Then things got much worse for members of that religious hierarchy, as Stephen cranked up the heat on them. Here are Stephen's words to that group, from Acts 7:51–53. "You *stiff-necked people!* Your hearts and ears are still uncircumcised. You are just like your ancestors: You always resist the Holy Spirit! Was there ever a prophet your ancestors did not persecute? They even killed those who predicted the coming of the Righteous one. And now *you have betrayed and murdered him*— you who have received the law that was given through angels but have not obeyed it" (NIV; italics added). The NWT version says, *"Obstinate men...resisting the holy spirit; as your forefathers did... Which one of the prophets did your forefathers not persecute?...whose betrayers* and *murders* you have now become, you...have not kept it." (italics added)

Can you sense the hackles up, on the back of the necks of the members of the hierarchy, like angry, trapped animals, their faces red with anger? Is that not how, many times, an exposed religious hierarchy in the past reacted when there was no way to successfully rebut what was being presented against it? (Recall chapter 3, "Whistle-blowers Past and Present...")

Its members' position had reached "critical mass," and they were facing a complete "meltdown." What could they possibly do? What would fanatics do? Acts 7:54–60 tells us, "When the members of the Sanhedrin heard this, they were *furious* and gnashed their teeth at him…they *covered their ears*…began to *stone him* until he fell asleep [in death]" (NIV; italics and brackets added). The NWT version says, "they felt cut to their hearts…put their hands over their ears…began casting stones at him" (italics added).

If one has felt inclined to check the references quoted in this book up till now, he or she will likely agree that there is no way to deny the facts presented. What will such one(s) do; keep on reading and learning, or feel inclined to imitate the actions of the Jewish Sanhedrin? Hopefully keep on reading; there is much more to learn!

Recall again the previously quoted scripture at Ecc. 1:9, where King Solomon points out that there is nothing new under the sun; history will keep repeating itself.

If a person is active as one of Jehovah's Witnesses and refuses to believe that his or her hierarchy could possibly be wrong or corrupt, think again; it is no more infallible than that person is. Remember that the ones who orchestrated Jesus' death were the members of Israel's corrupt, apostate hierarchy—God's own people! They likely did not start out that way, but they became that way, for the same reasons that other religious leaders have become tyrannical, demanding, and abusive in true sect-like or cult-like fashion. Recall Russell's definition of a sect or cult?

The enormous wealth of the W/W/H (the organization is worth billions of dollars in cash and real estate worldwide) makes the Pharisees of Jesus' day look like cheapskates by comparison. (This is one clue as to the agenda of its hierarchy.) All of that wealth, as you will see, has come at the expense (carried on the backs) of unwitting and duped believers and enablers. I was one also. Thank God I'm not any longer!

Let us now take a closer look at the second part of this chapter, "…for Youths: The Dark Side." Do you sense that there may well be the same kind of deception, pressure, manipulation, and tyranny of authority being practiced against the youths of Witness parents? There is!

About this matter of baptizing youths or minor children, recall the quotation earlier in this chapter, from *Reasoning from the Scriptures* (WTB&TS 1989, p. 55), which contains the subtopic and question, "Was infant baptism practiced by first-century Christians?"

Their book says: "Acts 8:12: When they believed Philip...they proceeded to be baptized, both *men and women,*" (notice the words *men and women* are italicized in their book but not in their Bible Translation - NWT)

> ➤ That verse does not say "boys and girls" in addition to "men and women," does it? Why not?

Why do you think the W/W/H writers of their book italicize the words *"men and women?"* It is because they believe that this scripture proves that it is inappropriate for a religious group to baptize infants.

Note the following authoritative definitions of the words "infant," "minor," and "majority" from the *Webster's Revised Unabridged Dictionary (1913 & 1828)*. How do they apply to this discussion at hand?

- infant: "A child in the first period of life... sometimes a child several years of age... (law) A person who is not of full age or who has not attained the age of legal capacity... under the age of twenty-one years; a minor

- minor: "A person of either sex who has not attained the age at which full civil rights are accorded... in England and the United States, one under twenty-one years of age.

- majority: "being of full age, or authorized... to manage one's own affairs."

Reasoning from the Scriptures (WTB&TS 1989, p. 55) notes the following: "Religious historian Augustus Neander wrote, '*Faith and baptism* were always connected with one another; and thus it is *the highest degree probable*...that the practice of *infant baptism* was *unknown* at this period'" (italics added). But this quote taken from Augustus Neander is deceptive; the ellipsis (three dots) indicates that something has been left out of his quote. What do you suppose the writers left out and why?

What is missing? Note the following, from *History of the Planting and Training of the Christian Church by the Apostles* (1864, p. 162): "Neander also acknowledged that 'baptism at first was administered **only to adults,**' because baptism and faith were 'strictly connected'" (430; italics added). You can check this online by using a good web search engine and typing in a phrase like "A History of the Baptism Apostasy." (www.google.com) Retrieved 3/2/2013

As noted above, the meaning of "infant," though applying to a baby, also encompasses all ages up to the age of majority, which is eighteen or twenty-one years old. So then, is baptism of any children, who are not yet full-grown adults, appropriate?

The W/W/H seems to think so, but its beliefs, teachings, and practices fly in the face of the scriptures, historical facts, and definitions of words, as well as common sense, which many times is not common at all. Note this experience mentioned in the *Watchtower* article entitled, "Pursuing a Goal Set at Six Years of Age" (March 1, 1992, pp. 26–28): "In the summer of 1946, I was baptized at the international convention in Cleveland, Ohio. Although I was **only six years of age,** I was *determined* to fulfill my dedication to Jehovah" (italics and emphasis added).

In the experience noted above, do you think that six-year-old Sandra Cowan, whose story is being told there, could have possibly or realistically understood what was involved and hence been, able to be "determined to fulfill my dedication to Jehovah?" Could she have made a "complete, unreserved and unconditional dedication...to do his will when baptized? (Dedication was not **even mentioned** as a requirement for baptismal candidates in 1946 or even in 1950 when I, at the age of nine, was attending a convention, in New York City.

The youngest age I have ever heard of for a child to be baptized as one of Jehovah's Witnesses was only five, which is unrealistic, unreasonable, and unscriptural. Such a baptism also sets such a child up for tragedy. (More specifics will be covered in chapter 10 on the subject of: "Disfellowshipping.")

A further quote from another *Watchtower* article shows just how wrong and unreasonable it would be for parents and the W/W/H to manipulate minors and foist baptism on such youngsters. The article, "Walking With God—The Early Steps," says, "Becoming a dedicated, baptized disciple of Jesus Christ is somewhat *similar to getting married*" (*Watchtower* November 15, 1998, pp. 11–12; italics added).

What would you think if you heard of a six, eight, or ten, year-old child getting married? It would be appalling and illegal in this country. Remember that the "age of majority" is eighteen or twenty-one years of age. Even teenage marriages frequently fail, bringing untold hardship and grief to parents and children. Remember the definitions above, where an "infant" is defined as "a person who is not of full age or attained the age of legal capacity… under the age of twenty-one years" (italics added).

From the evidence presented thus far, it is clear that the procedure of baptizing anyone who is not yet an adult would be unscriptural, unreasonable, and even irresponsible.

There is one more *Watchtower* article I want to call to your attention that clearly shows the deceptive lengths that the W/W/H will go to in an effort to foist baptism on minors as well as their enabling parents. The article is entitled, "Youths Make It Your Choice to Serve Jehovah" (*Watchtower* July 1, 2006, p. 26). But really, it is the choice of the W/W/H, as we will see.

In quoting second-century historian Tertullian, the article says, "Let **[children]** become Christians when they have become able to know

Christ." Interestingly the end of paragraph two says, "But *infant baptism* and *forced baptisms* of adults have no foundation in the Bible." (italics and emphasis added). How about foisting or "forcing" baptism on youths—children?

Did you notice that the word "children" is in brackets? Why is it? It replaces Tertullian's word "them." Although he wanted children eventually to become Christians, what was in fact said by Tertullian was not something that promoted the baptism of infants—children not yet adults. Rather, he took a far more cautious viewpoint.

What I found (www.google.com) with a web search on the question was an article entitled, "Did Tertullian Reject Infant Baptism?" Near the beginning is a section called "Tertullian, treatise on Baptism." To determine what Tertullian actually wrote and recommended, notice the following points that the W/W/H deceptively left out of its *Watchtower* article in an effort to present any possible support, even if twisted a little bit, for child baptism.

Tertullian wrote as follows:

> Let *them* come, then, while they grow up...learn...are taught to whom to come; let them become Christians when they will have been able to know Christ! Why does the innocent age hasten to the remission of sins?...For no less cause should the ***unmarried also be deferred,*** in whom there is an aptness to temptation—in virgins on account of their ripeness as also in the widowed on account of their freedom—***until they are married*** or better strengthened for continence. Anyone who understands the seriousness of Baptism will fear its reception more than its deferral. Sound faith is secure of its salvation! (italics and emphasis added)

Sound, logical reasons for recommending caution include Tertullian's comments and opinions. While not commands, they really are reasonable and well founded. It's better to defer baptism until one is married, because of the "aptness to temptation" and the "ripeness" of virgins or the freedom of those widowed. In other words, we would say in colloquial English, "they're just too horny" (sexually aroused or arousing). They are very apt to stumble morally.

The Apostle Paul used a similar expression and line of reasoning when he was recommending when and why one should get married; he noted in 1 Cor. 7:8, 9, and 36, "Now I say to the unmarried persons and the widows, it is well for them that they remain even as I am. But *if they do not have self-control,* let them marry, for it is better to marry than to be inflamed [with passion]...But if anyone thinks he is *behaving improperly* toward his virginity [or as a footnote says, "virgin"], if that is past the bloom of youth...let them marry" (NWT; italics added). The NIV says, "But *if they cannot control themselves...not be acting honorably* toward the virgin he is engaged to, and if his *passions are too strong*... They should get married" (italics added).

Thayer's *Greek-English Lexicon* (1977, p. 82, # 807) defines the phrase, "not acting honorably" (NIV) or "behaving improperly" (NWT) in verse 36 as, "contextually, to *prepare disgrace for her*" (italics added). The lexicon, in defining the phrase, "passions are too strong" (NIV) and "past the bloom of youth" (NWT), says this, which can help us see the need for caution and for deferring baptism until one becomes an adult: "1. beyond the bloom of life, past prime, 2. Overripe, plump and ripe (and so in greater danger of defilement): of a virgin [R.V. past the flower of her age]" (p. 640, # 5320).

Does not this line of thinking help explain why Tertullian recommended that baptism be "deferred" until one was older (not a young child or infant) and preferably married?

Many hundreds of thousands, if not millions, of Jehovah's Witnesses got baptized as youngsters, having no idea what kinds of problems they would face as teenagers in this regard. Later, as they entered the age of puberty and became "boy crazy" or "girl crazy" (with their hormones running rampant), they found themselves in trouble, facing a judicial committee at their Kingdom Hall.

How do many teens, boys or girls, react to exposure of wrongdoing or criticism when they get into trouble? That's right, they become defensive or even belligerent, which all too often is interpreted by a Witness judicial committee as, "This person is obviously not repentant."

The young person ends up disfellowshipped, thrown out of the congregation, and shunned by friends and family, perhaps for the rest of his or her life, a process that wreaks havoc with untold heartbreak for the young person, his or her parents, and grandparents and others. (See chapter 10, "Disfellowshipping…")

Considering this possibility, which has become the reality for countless numbers of Witness youths, would it not, in their cases, have been far better to "defer" baptism, allowing them time to grow up physically, mentally, and emotionally? What do you think God's will is in this matter? Note what 1 Thess. 4:3–6 says about this: "It is God's will that you should be sanctified…avoid sexual immorality…***learn to control*** your own body…not in passionate lust like the pagans…no one should wrong or take advantage of a brother or sister" (NIV; italics added). The NWT version says, "…***get possession*** of his own vessel in sanctification and honor…that no one…harming and encroaching upon the…" (italics, emphasis added).

Did you notice, in reading the counsel from this scripture, that one must "learn to control" and "get possession" of his "body" (NIV) or "vessel" (NWT)? That takes time. As one who has fathered seven children and faced manifold problems in helping six of them grow from youths to teenagers, through adolescence and finally to adulthood, I know that it takes years, many years, and mistakes are made along the way by both parents and their children. These are all sound reasons not to stampede youths into baptism.

So if the scriptures do not contain even one example or any instruction to baptize young persons who are being raised by a Christian parent or parents, what can be done for them? How can they be saved? Is there any kind of a safety net for such children? Do you think God would just "hang them out to dry" or abandon them? I don't either!

This is the safety net identified by the scriptures for "saving" children and even unbelieving mates. It is an imperative reason for parents not to push their non-adult children into baptism. The details come from the Apostle Paul's counsel for parents not to split up the family for their unbelieving mate's sake as well as for the benefit of their children. In 1 Cor. 7:14, Paul says, "For the *unbelieving* husband *is sanctified* in relation to [his] wife, and the *unbelieving* wife *is sanctified* in relation to the brother; otherwise, *your children* would really be unclean, but *now they are holy.*" (NWT and NIV; italics added)

The *Greek-English Lexicon* (1977, p. 6, # 37) defines this phrase in verse 14 ("has been sanctified" [NIV] or "is sanctified" [NWT]) in this way: "In 1 Cor. 7:14 (Greek word) [*sanctified*] is used in a peculiar sense of those who, **although not Christians** themselves, are yet, *by marriage* with a Christian, *withdrawn from the contamination* of heathen impiety and *brought under* the **saving influence** of the Holy Spirit displaying itself among Christians" (italics and emphasis added). Recall what the end of this scripture clearly says about the children, even if only one parent is a Christian, "they are holy."

Note an additional point about the meaning of the word "children" in the lexicon: "generally of the offspring of men, and in the restricted sense, male issue (one begotten by a father and born of a mother)" (*Greek-English Lexicon* 1977, p. 634, # 5207; italics and emphasis added). And note one more point, so there can be no question regarding the Greek word for "holy." The lexicon provides this meaning: "of sacrifices and offerings; *prepared for God with solemn rite*, **pure, clean:** 1 Cor. 7:14." (*Lexicon* 1977, p. 7, # 40; italics his, and some added emphasis)

In view of the fact that the lexicon, in defining the Greek word used in the Bible for "children," says absolutely nothing about age, we have no right, nor does the W/W/H, to set any kind of age at which this proviso ceases to apply. There is absolutely no age of accountability listed, and no such idea is presented in the verse just considered or anywhere else in the scriptures.

Does not the foregoing clearly negate any supposed rush and/or pressure to get a non-Christian or a non-Witness spouse or a young child, not yet an adult, baptized under the W/W/H's myth that they will "be killed by God's angels at Armageddon, along with all other non-JWs, if they don't get baptized?" You may recall that this stampede mentality was used on me as a child, to get me baptized at the New York City Convention.

One issue that could perhaps cancel the above proviso for the unbeliever might be if the case involves immoral conduct, resulting in the dissolution of the marriage, but that is another subject, not addressed here.

Do you recall the emergency faced by Joseph and Mary, Jesus' parents, when he was twelve? Luke 2:42–48 recounts the fact that Jesus got separated from his family while attending the Passover festival, and he was not found to be missing until they had traveled for a whole day. When they realized what had happened, they rushed back to Jerusalem; it ended up taking until the third day after they had left before they found him in the temple.

Luke 2:47 says, "Everyone who heard him [Jesus] was amazed at his understanding and his answers." (NIV; the NWT version says essentially the same thing). Do you think any parents, whether JWs or others, would have the audacity to assert that their son or daughter who was baptized as a minor was sharper, with more "understanding," or gave better "answers" than Jesus did? I doubt it too. Yet Jesus was not baptized at the tender age of twelve; in fact, he was not baptized until he became an adult. How do we know?

How old was Jesus when he was baptized? Luke 3:23 notes, "about thirty years" (NIV and NWT). And according to 1 Peter 2:21, Christians are urged to "follow in his steps" (NIV and NWT). Does not Jesus' example clearly harmonize with all that we have covered in this chapter about baptism before adulthood? This is especially true in view of the fact that not one single scripture in any Bible translation indicates that anybody other than an adult was baptized, as a Christian, in the first century.

The *Watchtower* (November 15, 2010, p. 8) article, "Young Ones—Resist Peer Pressure," calls a point to our attention that is very relevant to our discussion. Note this statement: *"When you yield to peer pressure from others, you become little more than a puppet"* (italics added).

If that is true of perhaps a fellow student, a neighbor, or even a work mate, would it not be even more true if the pressure was coming from a religious hierarchy such as the W/W/H, one that has become expert at manipulating its believers, having far more resources to foist its dogmatic views on one than just a "peer" would have?

Recall the definitions of a sect or cult? The hierarchy's peer pressure and tyranny of authority have affected far more than just one person; millions of people, especially young ones have been manipulated, becoming little more than puppets, as is clearly demonstrated by history.

That same *Watchtower* article makes a very sobering point with regard to the seriousness of child baptism: "Baptism is a *life-altering step that should not be taken lightly*" (p. 15; italics added). What business would a young person have, taking a "life-altering step" on purpose? Maybe as a result of an accident, his or her parents might be forced to make such a decision—perhaps resulting in an amputation or something equally serious—but not the child.

Being honest, how ready were you, as a young person, to make a decision that would become, "a life-altering step?" Think of some of the youngest ones baptized at five, six, eight, or even ten years of age.

However, the W/W/H has become a master at coercion, deception, and manipulation of Witness parents (as enablers) as well as of their children. First they pressured young ones by warning them that it would be a mistake to postpone baptism, in an effort to avoid accountability. Then deceptive coercion is used, as the publication asserts that "when you have reached **the age of responsibility,** you are answerable to Jehovah…whether you are baptized or not;" then Romans 14:11, 12 is noted; (*Watchtower* July 1, 2006, p. 29; italics and emphasis added).

Do you suppose that the cited scripture supports what the paragraph asserts? *Not a Chance.* Rom. 14:12 actually says, "Each one of us will give an account for ourselves to God" (NIV and NWT). The two verses say absolutely nothing about dedication or baptism involving young children who have not grown to adulthood. Additionally, who is the book of Romans addressed to? Rom. 1:7 points out it is addressed: "To those in Rome and loved by God... his holy people" (NIV and NWT). He does not mention children there.

Even at Pentecost, when holy spirit was first poured out, was the Apostle Paul addressing adults or children? (Acts 2:1–5) It was not children, and no water baptism even occurred at that time.

Under the subtopic of "Facing Up to Your Responsibility" in the above *Watchtower* article, note this dogmatic and pressurizing comment and threat, that the time will come when young people will "no longer be protected," not even if their parents are faithful (1 Cor. 7:14) (*Watchtower* July 1, 2006, p. 28). The scripture *does not say that at all*; the W/W/H just pressures young unbaptized people directly!

Since the scripture does not say anything about young people no longer being protected, as stated earlier, there is no minimum or maximum age or time limit given scripturally for when such protection ceases. Rather, the scripture does say that if at least one parent is a believer, both the unbelieving mate as well as the children are sanctified and considered holy. That stamps the W/W/H and *Watchtower* writers as presumptuous and guilty of deception and fraud, rather than telling the truth. Can you discern these facts?

Is it not perfectly clear that the W/W/H does not mind being deceptive and dogmatic in its efforts to meet its agenda of "getting those kids baptized?" What do you discern that the hierarchy's real reason would be for maintaining and pushing the teaching that young ones must be baptized, especially in view of all of the facts and scriptures we have considered up to this point?

If people can be captured as youths, mentally and emotionally, and can be sold on the idea that the W/W/H is God's *chosen channel for teaching* and must be trusted and obeyed implicitly the organization has another possible lifelong recruiter and worker.

Cognitive dissonance is a cruel and merciless taskmaster, and the W/W/H has become expert at manipulating and abusing millions of its believers from the cradle to the grave. That is a far cry from being Christ-like, don't you think?

At one time, my mother told me that at the age of five or six, I advised her that when I grew up, I wanted to be a "fire engine." I didn't apparently discern the difference between a fire engine and a fireman, at that time. I never became a fire engine or even a fireman.

But a "life-altering" change did come my way when, as an adult, I pursued a flying career with United Airlines. It was truly a life-altering and beneficial decision, though it was opposed by the circuit servant who attempted bullying, intimidating, coercion, and finally threats to try to change it. I shudder to think how different my life would have turned out to be if I had, like a puppet, caved in to his tyranny of authority.

❖ Flight lesson: It was an emergency!

Details of the lesson: When flying a jet airplane, three speeds are calculated before every takeoff: V_1, V_R, and V_2. Note the following with regard to these speeds.

As the plane starts accelerating down the runway, if anything goes wrong (an engine failure; a flock of birds, etc.) before reaching V_1, the captain *must* abort the takeoff. If the speed is past V_1, there is not enough runway ahead of the plane to stop, and the captain *must* continue to V_R. This means rotating (lifting off) and starting to climb as quickly as circumstances allow; additionally, the captain *must* not allow his or her aircraft's speed to drop below V_2 (the minimum speed to maintain flight).

For a veteran airline captain, all of this happens almost automatically; flight crews are trained to react this way.

If all engines have lost thrust, the plane is going down, and the only choice is where—perhaps the Hudson River? There will be no panic on the flight deck, just an understanding and immediate recognition of what must be done to save lives—a decision made by the captain.

Remember Captain Sullenberger's flight from La Guardia Airport in New York (Feb. 5, 2009, US Airways flight # 1549)? He encountered a flock of birds shortly after take-off which destroyed both engines; he did a wonderful job of handling that emergency.

Several options had been considered, evaluated, and then dismissed in the two minutes just after the bird strike and before the Hudson River became the landing option of choice: Could he return to LaGuardia? "We can't do that!" How about Teterboro, New Jersey? "No, it is impossible!" (Thus say the air traffic control tapes.)

With no thrust available from the engines, the aircraft's speed was rapidly dropping, and its nose had to be continually lowered to keep the plane's speed at or above V_2. The best choice, really the only choice that could assure the best chance of survival, was the Hudson River; he no doubt thanked God for that River! This situation called for a trained captain to make that decision—not a child. Even at that, he would have his hands full.

You will see why this information is relevant because of the danger that I *eventually* recognized (as an adult) and my reaction to it. I finally saw the need to call it quits—the W/W/H's pressure to deliberately put children in harm's way, by *pushing* baptism on them, became the turning point for me; let me explain how it came about.

I was already having serious reservations about the propriety of the hierarchy's teaching, nearly demanding child baptism. The study article, "Youths, Make It your Choice to Serve Jehovah" (*Watchtower* July 1, 2006), was becoming more and more troublesome for me as the W/W/H was continuously pressuring Witness parents and their children to *get those kids baptized.* It was not the young people's choice. It was the *hierarchy's choice* and *demand.*

That *Watchtower* was released to the congregations on June 1, 2006. I believed there had to be a hidden agenda, so on June 9, I sent a letter to the Watchtower Branch Office in New York City, explaining the errors that I had found in that *Watchtower* study article regarding child baptism, including what I discovered to be a deceptive quote attributed to Tertullian.

I received a reply back from the Watchtower's Service Desk, dated August 11, 2006, in which they thanked me for my letter. In paragraph three of their letter, they wrote, "As you indicate, it *is not appropriate* for parents or others to put *undue pressure* upon a young one to get baptized. Making a dedication to Jehovah and then getting baptized in symbol of that dedication are steps that the individual must make from the heart and not done because of *what others* might fervently *want for him* or her" (italics added). But next came their double-talk, as their letter to me continued: "Nevertheless, there is a certain **balance** that *must be* **maintained**. Others can *help one who is hesitant* to make a dedication and get baptized, perhaps delaying for the wrong reasons." (italics and emphasis added)

Really, the hierarchy wants "help" from enabling parents or others in an effort to exert pressure on the young ones, because it never loses sight of its agenda: "Get those kids baptized!" But is that the only agenda? Why the stampede mentality?

No doubt they felt compelled to keep their agenda moving forward, so the letter from the society continued as they referred again to the same July 1, 2006, issue of the *Watchtower;* they asserted: "The time will come when a youth will no longer be protected because of the faithfulness of a parent."

Of course there is no scripture, in any Bible translation, that says such a thing. It is just another bold, arrogant, deceptive, and dogmatic statement, a fraudulent assertion that I have already addressed.

That letter from the society' service desk concluded, "Your **concerns**, Brother Staelens, *are valid,* and you can be assured that such are weighed carefully when articles on baptism are prepared. To this end, we appreciate what you have written, and it will be passed along to those who have to do with what is published." (My concerns were valid, but if counsel doesn't fit the hierarchy's agenda, it is discarded and ignored.)

A few months later, we sold our home in Colorado and moved to Illinois to be closer to our youngest son. I was discussing this *Watchtower* and the society's letter with our circuit overseer along with the fact that I understood the reason for continuing to push children into baptism. He interrupted and stopped me cold with the words, "You can *think* what you want, but ***you had better not say it!***"

I quit talking, but I thought to myself, "Why does his comment make me think of Cuba, North Korea, and China?" I was still living in the United States, wasn't I? Is not such suppression of free speech a clear earmark of totalitarian or even a sect-like or cult-like mentality and manipulation?

The beginning of the end of my involvement with the W/W/H was underway. I refused to accept appointment as an elder in the Robinson, Illinois congregation. It wasn't long until I quit going door-to-door and stopped going to the Kingdom Hall. An emergency was occurring; why had I not aborted the takeoff before V_1?

Unfortunately, early on, I did not really appreciate the seriousness of the problem and the danger I was trapped in; I had passed a figurative V_1. Back in 1965, I had stood up to the W/W/H (specifically, brother Patrick) when he insisted that I stop going to college and quit striving for an airline job. However, unfortunately, more time would go by after that incident until I would understand enough to shake cognitive dissonance and get myself out of danger's way.

A whole lifetime had gone by for me, but cognitive dissonance was still creating a war of feelings in my mind and heart. There was fear, embarrassment, and concern over the possibility that our children would shun my wife and me, as had happened to a number of parents that we knew and were aware of and which is the case with some of our children even now.

What was called for, on my part, was a captain's decision: the need for finally "disfellowshipping" and totally abandoning the W/W/H, once and for all. The blinders needed to come off and stay off.

It would have to be *action taken by me—not by the hierarchy!* I had been duped and had been a victim of its manipulation and control. It had started when I was just nine years old; I had reached adulthood, but I was still not completely free of the shackles keeping me tethered to the W/W/H and its organization.

So, as would be the case with an airplane after V_R, the action of identifying the real problem and taking the emergency action that was called for would come, but not until later, after I had been traveling for a while longer, as would be the case in a plane when an emergency occurred on the way up to cruise altitude. Nonetheless, I could no-longer ignore what I had become aware of; although I was retired now, I was still a rated captain—I would respond as such.

There is no substitute for time and experience. Do you remember the fifth bullet on the first page of this chapter? I asked: "If you were a passenger on an airliner, would you want to see a student pilot in the captain's seat?" How about a child?

Did you think much about that question when you first read it? Think about it now. The obvious answer is: definitely not! Especially having considerable experience as a captain, I would not, as a passenger, want to see a student pilot up front, in either seat. There are good reasons for minimum age and experience requirements for captains. And I *definitely would never* want to see a child up front!

When any of us is raising children, we find it is definitely a learning experience for us as well as for our children, and that learning experience brings changes in thinking, plans, goals, and even desires, for all concerned.

In chapter nine, I will discuss my experience of stealing my first push-pedal airplane in Lansing, Michigan, at the tender age of seven. Could I have had any idea, at that time, that I would one day become an airline captain with extensive experience flying nine different jets, including thousands of hours in heavy jets, the ones that have a gross weight exceeding three hundred thousand pounds?

When my wife Dale agreed to marry me, it was definitely a life-altering decision for her. At the very tender age of sixteen, she could not possibly have had even an inkling of how her life was going to change in just six short years. In our fifty-three years together, she has learned to fly several planes and has traveled hundreds of thousands of miles by air, covering over two-thirds of the earth. It is unlikely that any other girls from her small town of three hundred people in Cincinnatus, New York, could have had experiences even remotely similar to hers.

Uncounted numbers of Witness parents have come to despise the pressure that was foisted on them and their children by the W/W/H to "get those kids baptized while young;" later, when their kids slipped into wrongdoing as teenagers, the whole family was pushed by its policies into destruction. That has been my experience too.

Alas, time is only one-directional; it can not to be turned back by humans. Only a clock can be turned back. Both parents and children will go through many life-altering changes as they grow older. To expect any minor child (even a teenager or adolescent) to be responsible for choices that were foisted on him or her by a religious hierarchy that obligates the child to do its bidding and be unconditionally obedient to that hierarchy is nothing short of big time child abuse!

Such abuse can have major negative consequences lasting for a lifetime. Foisting such abuse on any youth is outrageous. It is as bogus as it would be to assert, in a court of law, that a minor is responsible for and must pay a promissory note that he or she was pressured to sign as a youngster. If the child's parents or a religious hierarchy asserted that such a contract was valid, they would be laughed out of court—case dismissed!

If this chapter has been difficult for anyone to read because of his or her present involvement with the W/W/H organization, he or she does have a choice, of course: to believe it or not. Checking all of the references should be done to assure that the person will be able to make a wise choice—at least an informed one!

Some persons are like the proverbial ostrich that supposedly hides its head in the sand (or more correctly, it may, when it perceives danger, lay its head down on the sand), trying to fade into the background in an attempt not to be seen. Of course, with its head on the ground, it can't see either.

There are many of Jehovah's Witnesses who may not wish to see some facts that they consider objectionable. They may even become like the Jewish Sanhedrin at the time of Stephen, who covered their ears with their hands so as not to hear. I was that way for the majority of my life!

They choose not to see (or hear) wrongdoing on the part of the W/W/H, or they may make excuses, trying to justify their hierarchy's wrong actions and failures—if they are even aware of them. Many are not; that is why I have written this book.

Recall Ecc. 1:9 reminds us that history will keep repeating itself. The W/W/H has continued to do wrong, even in the name of God; additionally, the hierarchy has *never* been willing to acknowledge its wrongdoing specifically nor take responsibility for those wrongs and make changes.

Has it become like many in the past who have hungered for financial gain? The lure of huge profits may be too big a hurdle for that organization to get over, regardless of any bold assertions to the contrary. For this hierarchy, there has been a willingness to sacrifice anything and everything for the almighty dollar, including the use and abuse of children.

I hope you have clearly discerned the facts showing the abuse of both adults and youths by the W/W/H, by foisting early baptism on youths under the myth of supposedly saving them while ignoring the safety net" that the scriptures assure us is available to them. (1 Cor. 7:14).

Literally millions of former JWs have already recognized the danger to their own spirituality and that of their families and have made the decision to abandon the unacceptable course that their hierarchy has continued to pursue and foist on unsuspecting believers. That includes me; I am especially distressed that it took me so long to wake up.

What agenda that needs to be fed, in addition to the pressure to "Get those kids baptized," has been at the root of the W/W/H's baptism deception? How have both adults and children been harmed, misled, used, and abused? Why is the mountain of evidence against child baptism ignored? The following section will delve into how and why their deception even rivals the agenda of the first century Pharisees.

Watchtower/Witness Assemblies are
Sponsored with a *Dubious Agenda*

During the 2011/2012 "service year" used by the Watchtower/Witness/Hierarchy, they arranged for a circuit assembly, a special assembly day, and a district convention during the summer.

Each of these assemblies has a highlight—the baptism of new converts. When such a baptism occurs, close to 50 percent of the participants are children, some perhaps as young as five years of age. Each of these candidates for baptism is required to study and answer (before his or her congregation's elders) at least 104 questions before "qualifying" for baptism, in order to be sure that the person has been properly "indoctrinated." Then he or she is approved to be baptized (WTB&TS 2005, pp. 182–218).

At the conclusion of the "baptism talk," two questions are presented to the candidates; they are asked to answer in the affirmative, unanimously and loudly. Here are the questions (italics added):

1. "On the basis of the sacrifice of Jesus Christ, have you *repented* of your sins and *dedicated yourself* to Jehovah to do his will?"

2. "Do you understand that your *dedication* and *baptism* identify you *as one of Jehovah's Witnesses* in association with God's spirit-directed organization?" (WTB&TS 2005, pp. 215, 216)

Remember Matt. 28: 19, 20 contains Jesus' instructions regarding the baptism of his disciples: "Go and make disciples (* or learners) of people, baptizing them in the name of the Father, the Son and holy spirit; teach them to observe everything I [Jesus] have commanded you" (NIV and NWT).

Christian baptism, according to Jesus' instructions, was not a dedication; it was done to identify one as a disciple of Jesus. This raises the questions, "What additional factor may be part of the W/W/H's agenda? Is it simply a matter of baptizing children for their salvation?"

The "service year" used by the W/W/H and its organization in tracking the productivity of all of Jehovah's Witnesses runs from September 1st of one year to August 31st of the following calendar year. The worldwide "publisher report" for all of Jehovah's Witnesses who reported time spent in the ministry, for the 2011 "service year," includes the following information:

- A total of 7,224,930 *individuals* spent time in the ministry carried on by the Watchtower/Witness organization that year (7.2 million people).

- *Collectively,* they spent 1,707,094,710 hours doing so, for that service year (1.7 billion hours).

- The total of *new converts baptized,* including young children, during that "service year" was only 263,131.

Said another way, it took nearly 27.5 Witnesses, working at the Watchtower/Witness ministry for a whole year, to produce *just one new convert* who got baptized.

The W/W/H, to keep its free labor cycle going, has to keep getting new converts. The hierarchy finds it much easier to manipulate young victims rather than adults; hence, foisting baptism on the young becomes a must from that point of view, regardless of all of the evidence that proves the wrongness of such a practice. Can you clearly see that said hierarchy has a multi-faceted and deceptive agenda? Chapters 9, 12 and 13 provide more insight into its agenda.

REVIEW POINTS:

1. Has the W/W/H been truthful and accurate in its teaching about "baptism?" Yes or No?

2. Have you discerned that Christian baptism symbolizes that one has become a disciple, a learner, and a student of what Jesus taught, rather than symbolizing dedication?

3. Do you recognize that the Bible does not teach that "dedication" has anything to do with baptism? It was only the pagan Canaanites who dedicated themselves to their god Baal.

4. Do you recognize that infant (child) baptism was never undergone or authorized by Jesus or practiced by any first century Christians? Remember that the definition of "infant" applies to any person who has not reached the age of majority (eighteen or twenty-one years old).

5. Can you see the enormous wrongs that have descended upon youths who were pushed into baptism by the W/W/H and their enabling parents and who were then held accountable, as if they were mature adults?

Remember the saying by Sir Walter Scott in 1832, "Oh what a tangled web we weave, when first we practice to deceive?" Deception can only result in a greater web of lies and problems and heartaches. History shows that this clearly has been the case.

Such has continued to be the course of action chosen by the W/W/H, and as is unavoidable for all of us, it will continue to reap what it has sown.

Denial will not solve problems for the hierarchy any more than it would work to solve the problems for an alcoholic in denial. Only a changed course and a changed mode of operation can possibly help.

The next chapter, "Doubletalk, Deception, Hypocrisy, and Lying Have Been Rampant," is another eye-opener. It will help you better comprehend that the W/W/H has an agenda and how it has kept it to the fore.

* The list of scriptures that I suggested a person would do well to look up in the Watchtower *Comprehensive Concordance* (WTB&TS, 1973), using the three words "dedicate," "dedicated, and "dedication" are noted here. The Italicized *"d"* represents the key word in each case below.

Dedicate:

- Ho 9:10 *d* themselves to the shameful

Dedicated:

- Matt 15:5 is a gift *d* to God
- Mr 7:11 that is a gift *d* to God
- Lu 21:5 fine stones and *d* things

Dedication:

- Ex 29:6 sign of *d* upon the turban
- Ex 39:30 holy sign of *d,* out of pure
- Le 8:9 the holy sign of *d,* just as
- Le 21:12 sign of *d,* the anointing oil
- Joh 10:22 festival of *d* took place in

CHAPTER 9

DOUBLE-TALK, DECEPTION, HYPOCRISY, AND LYING HAVE BEEN RAMPANT

- The modern-day W/W/H's governing body with its deceptive appearance in 1944 made contradictory changes as recently as October 6, 2012 and July 15, 2013.
- How has it been hypocritical in many other ways, with adverse consequences to countless millions of former believers?
- How and why has it refused to accept responsibility for harm foisted on its believers? What has been its motive?
- ❖ Flying, First Lesson: "You mean you stole it!"

The Watchtower (December 15, 1971, pp. 755–761), in discussing how the W/W/H's governing body appeared, first makes the admission that "there were no apostles of Christ on hand in the nineteenth century." Then referring to its *present-day governing body*, it goes on to say that it [today's governing body] "*is appointed by* the same one who appointed the twelve apostles in the first century, namely, *Jesus Christ*" (italics added).

Was that assertion really true, or was it a deception?

A few paragraphs later, in that same article, under the sub-topic, "How the Governing Body Came to Exist," it is asserted that *C. T. Russell was* a member of the modern-day *governing body*. Then the article states that "he *set himself*, applying his time, energy, ability, *wealth* and *influence*... to spreading the message of God's word" (*Watchtower* December 15, 1971, p. 760; italics added).

> ➤ Obviously he had not been appointed by Jesus in the way that the twelve apostles in the first century were appointed: "he set himself."

Recall what is known about recent cult leaders such as Jim Jones, David Koresh, Warren Jeffs, and others who were proclaimed by others and/or proclaimed themselves to be "the Messiah," "the Son of God," a "Seer, Revelator and Prophet," and so on. Did such assertions make these people's dogmatic statements true? Definitely not! These recognized cult leaders were all proven, in time, to be frauds.

Russell died in the year 1916, so who proclaimed him to be a member of the governing body, in modern times? It was the W/W/H in 1971. That hierarchy did so with the help of the Watchtower Society's writing staff. Why do you think they made that assertion?

It appears that their reason was an attempt to legitimize and solidify their own positions as part of the governing body at that time and to justify their claim to have all the authority that had been previously seized and asserted. Their deception was in order to keep the rank-and-file members of the W/W/H's organization in subjection in true sect-like, even cult-like fashion. Note the following points.

It is noteworthy that the term "governing body" is never used in any scripture, and no man or group of men in the first century were called by that term, name or designation.

That same article, after claiming that Russell *was a part* of the governing body, admits that the members of the governing body back then really **were not** *directly appointed* by Christ (*Watchtower* December 15, 1971, p. 761). How then did the W/W/H's governing body of today really come into existence? That *Watchtower* article backpedals by pointing out that the facts indicate that some of the anointed brothers simply *"accepted"* and *"undertook"* the responsibility of governing Jehovah's people. A far cry from what they originally asserted.

It is important to note that *Webster, (1913)* defines the word "accept" to mean: "to receive with a consenting mind *(something offered)*; to take or *receive what is offered*," Seize means: "To *take* possession of *by force*." Far different than accepting something isn't it! (italics added).

Did God or Jesus offer to the W/W/H the position of becoming part of the governing body? The answer, by the group's own published admission, is no.

That hierarchy had *seized* the position of governing body because no one else, that it could see, was already claiming that position at the time, and it believed that it could get away with doing so. So it simply proclaimed itself to be the "governing body of Jehovah's Witnesses," and got away with it. The hierarchy's claims changed again on October 6, 2012, with more dogmatic assertions on July 15, 2013.

Recall the following: First, this group had *asserted* that the governing body of today *was appointed* by Christ. Second, they admitted that the governing body *was not* directly *appointed* by Jesus. Third, they admitted that these men (members of the modern-day W/W/H's governing body) *"accepted"* and *"undertook"* the responsibility of governing Jehovah's people.

Was this not really double-talk, trying to hide the truth?

- ➢ In other words, by the group's own words in 1971, the governing body since 1944 had not been appointed by anyone with the authority to do so; this hierarchy simply seized the position, proclaiming itself to be the "governing body of Jehovah's Witnesses." This was clearly a dishonest, deceptive, and fraudulent claim, with absolutely no foundation.

- ➢ As you will see, sixty-eight years later, the self-proclaimed governing body would make changes officially transferring any and all authority from thousands (all of the anointed, previously called the Faithful and Discreet Slave) to just a handful of men that now proclaimed themselves to be **both** the governing body as well as the Faithful and Discreet slave.

All persons who have become members of the governing body, after 1944 up to the present, were appointed by whoever claimed and were believed to be the governing body at the time. Sounds like a buddy system, doesn't it?

Any statements by the W/W/H to the contrary are without any validity; they are just dogmatic statements to cover up the facts and keep this group's death grip on what had been seized back in 1944. Have you ever experienced anything like this yourself? I have, so I understand very well what motivated their thinking in this matter.

- ❖ My first flying lesson took place in 1948. The place—Lansing, Michigan. We were visiting my grandparents' home; I was seven years old. I found myself on my own, a couple of blocks from their house, and I noticed an airplane sitting on the sidewalk all by itself, (It was the kind that moved by push-pedals, like a play car but with wings and a propeller).

It was obvious to me that whoever used to own this airplane no longer wanted it, so I climbed aboard and "flew it" (pedaled it) back to my grandparents' home. I was really proud of myself for having found such a gem on my own, so I went into the house to brag to my mom about my new find. "Come outside and see what I just found!" I urged her. She may have thought it was a snake, a frog, or maybe some petrified wood such as I had found in a wooded area near our home. But not so—this was a real treasure!

As soon as she stepped outside and saw what I had "found," it was obvious to her what I had done. "Tell me where you 'found' that airplane!" she demanded.

"Someone just left it on the sidewalk," I replied.

"You mean you stole it!" she countered.

"*No!* It's *mine;* I found it. It doesn't belong to anyone else, I'm sure!" I insisted.

I had, in reality, simply taken it and then *proclaimed myself* its new owner. Sound familiar? A small segment of the W/W/H had done the very same thing in 1944, just four years before my theft of the airplane: its members had assumed the right and proclaimed that their group was the governing body of Jehovah's Witnesses. You will see that history has repeated itself again in 2012 and 2013, with more fraudulent claims and baseless assertions designed to dupe believers.

Although that group had really stolen (seized) the position and proclaimed itself to be the governing body in 1944, its claim has turned out to be just as fraudulent as mine had been. This hierarchy's deception has just lasted longer.

I had stolen my first airplane in 1948, but my claim of ownership was bogus and short-lived. I had been caught red-handed. My mother wouldn't buy my fraudulent claim. "Show me where you found it," she demanded. I reluctantly climbed aboard (she had to walk because she didn't fit) and "flew the plane" (pedaled it) back to where I had found this wonderful, albeit short-lived treasure.

I was forced to go by myself up to the door and ask if anyone there owned the airplane sitting outside. There was a young man about my age sitting at the table, devouring a peanut butter sandwich. He stopped eating, jumped off his chair, and emphatically shouted, "That's *my airplane!* My dad gave it to me for my birthday!"

You can guess the rest; I had to admit to stealing his airplane and apologize to him. I walked away embarrassed and disappointed, but I had learned something from my first flying lesson. It would be another thirteen years till I would again start flying in a real airplane—but this time it would be one that I had not stolen!

It had been a great flight while it lasted, and it did turn out to be a foretaste of things to come. Eventually I would earn the right to fly for myself (owning four different airplanes that I did pay for) and would earn the right to fly for United Airlines—two prop-driven airliners, plus nine different airline jets, over a period of nearly twenty-five years, retiring as a captain at the age of fifty.

The lesson: *taking* or *seizing* something that is not ours and was never given to us, then stating that we found it and decided to take care of it, *so now we owned it* is a lie and a deception. It doesn't matter if we are seven years old or an adult; apparently it doesn't matter to the W/W/H that it has done the same thing over and over again.

In that hierarchy's case, as was true in my case, we had both seized and taken something that neither of us had been given nor were authorized to take. Shame on me! Likewise—shame on them!

I learned my lesson from my wrongful theft, but how about the W/W/H? No! Rather, more deception and presumptuousness and many more dogmatic statements (in sect-like or cult-like fashion) have continually been asserted and have, in fact, become the norm for this hierarchy down to our day, with the most recent examples being the act of solidifying more power to themselves 2012 and 2013.

A *Watchtower* (December 15, 1971, p. 755, points out, that it was not until the year *1944* that the W/W/H *first spoke* about the *governing body,* of the first century or of the ones claiming that position in our day, meaning members of their hierarchy, of course.

That same article *asserts* that the one hundred and twenty disciples [*men and women*] who had met together for Pentecost were granted the appointment to function as the faithful and discreet slave [by whom— Jesus made no such appointment]; this assertion was based on Matt. 24:45–47. However, the new understanding presented on October 6, 2012, explains that those assertions were not true.

Nonetheless, it will be helpful to note what Jesus actually said in the referenced verses, also noting how the W/W/H had applied them in 1971; then make a comparison with what the hierarchy asserts now. Please read the entire account, noted above, in your own copy of the Bible since I'm quoting here only the major points.

Especially note verses 48–51; this will assist your understanding when you consider the upcoming questions, especially in view of the changes that have most recently occurred at the yearly Board of Directors meeting on October 6, 2012 that I alluded to above.

First note Matt. 24:45–47, in the NIV, with a few author notes interspersed: *"Who then is the faithful and wise servant, whom the master has put in charge* [past tense] *of the servants in his household to give them their food at the proper time? It will be good for that servant whose master finds him doing so when he returns...* [Note that the servant is "put in charge" *before* Jesus' return.]

Verses 48-51 continue: *But suppose that servant* [previously considered "faithful and wise" becomes] *is wicked...and...begins to beat his fellow servants...The master of that servant will come...He will cut him to pieces and assign him a place with the hypocrites, where there will be weeping and gnashing of teeth."* NIV - the NWT uses "faithful and discreet" instead of "faithful and wise" and "domestics" instead of "servants." (Italics added to the verses quoted above.)

> ➤ Did you notice that verse 45 is an open question and is never answered? Neither is the slave/servant identified by Jesus.

> ➤ Many individuals and/or groups over the years have *claimed* to be that slave/servant, but *none* have been able to prove their identity scripturally—including the W/W/H, even up to this present time; *their claims*—just bold assertions.

> ➤ Do you discern that this passage also makes it clear that the slave/servant in question (verses 48-51) may turn out to be "wicked" or "evil," by beating its fellow slaves, etc.? Then, as is noted later, "the slave" ("servant") [whose Master is Jesus], rather than deserving commendation as a faithful and wise/discreet servant, would be deserving of condemnation, based on an examination of its own record.

> ➤ Verses 48–51 (above) have usually been ignored by the W/W/H, or else applied to ones they view as apostates (even including the clergy of Christendom).

> In commenting on those verses in the July 15, 2013 *Watchtower,* it now admits that *it,* as the newly identified faithful slave, *could* fall into the category of the wicked slave *if* it were to beat its fellow servants; is that a likely scenario for the W/W/H? They vigorously assert not so—But, indeed it can and as you will see, has already become so.

Recall that the biblical account of God's nation, the Israelites (both the northern and southern kingdoms), was appalling. Eighty-five percent of its kings were corrupt for eighty-six percent of the time, from 1313 BCE to the first century; that nation became corrupt and apostate, over and over again which finally led to its destruction.

Additionally, remember King Solomon's words (Ecc. 1:9) that "there is nothing new under the sun" and "what has been will be again, what has been done will be done again." This book, as an exposé, clearly shows that throughout its history, the W/W/H has been every bit as unfaithful to God as was ancient Israel; the hierarchy has fallen into the same trap for the same reasons—money and power. Truth and honesty have repeatedly been swept aside, while double-talk, deception, hypocrisy, and lying have been allowed to run rampant.

The W/W/H has been presumptuous in that it professes that its members alone are God's faithful people on earth. Yet in agreement with Solomon's words and as shown by repeated history, eventually all such fraudulent claims foisted on hapless religious believers will be exposed. My book's exposé is not the first nor is it likely to be the last!

You will see that not even a self-righteous religious hierarchy can escape the scriptural rule found at Gal. 6:7, which says we must not be misled—we all will reap what we have sown; that principle cannot be escaped by anyone. The W/W/H is even now reaping what it has sown to a large degree, as is evidenced by the decline of its membership with the departure of millions of one-time active Witnesses.

Although the present-day beliefs and assertions changed on October 6, 2012, noting the assertions made about the governing body in 1971 will prove helpful in considering the "new" understanding being foisted on rank-and-file Witnesses. But first, note the following points to ponder:

- Any Jehovah's Witness who claims to be spirit-anointed (going to heaven) *has no proof* to substantiate his or her claim. First century Christians at Pentecost, according to the Bible, did have such evidence demonstrated.

- Likewise the governing body was not given its position; it simply seized it.

- So the entire basis for the W/W/H's claim to authority and power over the lives of Jehovah's Witnesses rests entirely on its assertions, from the time of Russell to the present, that it is spirit-anointed and therefore duly authorized to be the governing body. But its double-talk, deception, hypocrisy and lying, its own actions and record belie its fraudulent claims.

- Complicated specious reasoning, whether from the past or with the new assertions, is presented to "snow" the hierarchy's unwary readers; but this reasoning is not factual. Let us consider why.

It is of special note that from the year 1935 to 1992 (fifty-seven years), the number of Jehovah's Witnesses who claimed that they were spirit-anointed dropped an average of 768 persons per year. The numbers went from 52,465 down to 8,683, for a total of 43,822 people who stopped claiming to be spirit-anointed (WTB&TS 1993, p. 717).

Then the unexpected began to occur. The number of Witnesses claiming to be spirit-anointed (partakers of the bread and wine) started to increase instead of dropping as it had for fifty-seven years. By 2010, the number had climbed back up to 11,000, a number not seen since 1968—forty-four years before (WTB&TS 1993, p.717).

As the number of partakers (of the bread and wine at the yearly JW Memorial celebration) kept growing, articles in the *Watchtower* magazine cautioned Witnesses that many new partakers could not really be spirit-anointed! Why not? Because after all, the number was expected to keep dropping, so that obviously the end of the world could come by the time their number reached zero. All of the anointed, believed to number only 144,000, would then be in heaven.

Can you see the problem this was creating for the W/W/H? If it continued calling into question the legitimacy of the claims of new spirit-anointed ones, then what about the long-standing claims by its own members to be spirit-anointed? Would it not call into question the legitimacy of their claims as well?

The W/W/H's self-asserted claim to all the authority of the governing body as well as its demand for unquestioned obedience from rank-and-file Witnesses was beginning to crumble, just as would occur with any building erected on a faulty foundation. Only disaster awaits such a building.

Do you recall the story, "The Emperor's New Clothes?" It is a short story by Hans Christian Andersen, first published in 1873. It involves two weavers who promised an emperor a new set of clothes that would be invisible to any of his subjects who were unfit for their positions, stupid, or incompetent. "When the Emperor parades before his subjects in his new clothes, a child cries out, 'But he isn't wearing anything at all!'" (*Wikipedia*, "The Emperor's New Clothes" - Retrieved 3/1/2013)

Do you discern the pressure placed on the emperor's subjects? If any of them admitted or stated that he was wearing no clothes at all, that person would be proclaiming himself or herself to be unfit, stupid, or incompetent. Obviously, the only logical choice was to go along with the ruse, even though it was clearly wrong and fraudulent.

The members of the W/W/H, by proclaiming themselves to be God's only favored people, the only ones with the truth, the only ones directed by holy spirit, and so on, and then by demanding complete obedience and absolute unquestioning loyalty, create an environment in which their adherents are embarrassed and afraid to think for themselves or to question anything this august religious hierarchy says. Remember cognitive dissonance?

Do you see the similarity of this situation to that of the subjects in the story about the emperor's new clothes?

Recall C. T. Russell's definition of a "sect," described earlier in this book; the same kind of sect-like, or cult-like pressure which has been applied, and foisted on JWs was also exerted on the believers who followed Jim Jones, David Koresh, or Warren Jeffs.

What about the supposed "new Light" or "revised understanding" of the identity of the governing body and the "faithful and discreet slave" which has been asserted since October 6th of 2012, at the W/W/H's annual board of directors meeting for the WTB&TS of New York?

You may go online to the WTB&TS's official website at www.jw.org to access that report, or you can check the July 15, 2013 *Watchtower* magazine, which contains the same new information, but also adds specious reasoning that it uses in an attempt to *obscure its past history and failures.*

For the section, "When Did Jesus Appoint 'the Faithful and Discreet Slave over His Domestics?" the answer is given that it is logical to believe that "the faithful and discreet slave *must have appeared after Christ's presence began in 1914."* The assertion is also made that even though the apostles and other first century Christians *were* spirit-anointed, that they were *not* the faithful and discreet slave whom Jesus had prophesied about. (*Watchtower*, July 15, 2013, Page 19, ¶ 16)

That contradicts what the W/W/H has taught for many decades and is an obvious attempt *to escape responsibility* for its manifold false prophecies from the 1800s to 1914. You have already seen, in chapter six of this book, the evidence that places the blame for failed prophecies squarely on the backs of the W/W/H - the ones who have made and published those deceptions. But, no one can ever escape from themselves, not even them.

The *Watchtower*, noted above, (Page 19, ¶ 17) asserts that the faithful and discreet slave was appointed by Jesus starting in the year 1919.

> There is of course *no scripture* available *as evidence* in coming up with the date 1919; only specious reasoning.

> The on-line report said, "It is logical," but, again there is no "logic" that can be, or has been, presented.

Let's consider another major reversal of a past teaching, which the W/W/H claims has come about after, "further careful study and prayerful meditation;" it includes the matter of "our understanding of [who] the faithful and discreet slave actually is [and] needs to be clarified," (*Watchtower*, July 15, 2013, p. 20, ¶ 3)

Since I was a youngster in the 1950s the teaching has *always* been that the "faithful and discreet slave (Matt. 24:45-51) had reference to *all* anointed ones on earth at any given time since the first century, when viewed collectively. Now comes a major change: On Page 21, ¶ 9, of the (July 15, 2013 *Watchtower*) the W/W/H stated that the previous view-point was not correct; they declared, "the reality is that *not* all anointed ones have a role in dispensing spiritual food... worldwide." (italics added)

Many times, the "new light" had been as much a surprise or shock to the "anointed ones" in the congregations world-wide, as it was to everyone else. When they opened a *Watchtower*, they found a new foreign idea or teaching that was now being presented as a, for sure new teaching with the usual dogmatism, and tyranny of authority - and of course *without input* from those previously considered to be the faithful and discreet slave (all of the anointed alive).

What? Time and time again over the past many decades, the W/W/H has asserted that *all of its teachings* have come *from that "faithful and discreet slave."* But in reality that has never been true; their teachings, their "new light" has always come from a hand-full of the elite, (i.e. the governing body in New York), who *now have declared themselves* to be that faithful slave.

Does it appear to you that the record that the W/W/H has made for itself over the past 140 years indicates that any of its members have operated as a "faithful and discreet slave?" Or has it operated more like the "evil slave," which is what Jesus said becomes of the faithful slave if and when it abuses its fellow slaves? - Matt. 24:48-51 - Chapters 8, 9, and 10 clearly document how this has become the case.

Is it not obvious that the W/W/H's record of failed prophecies and manifold other wrongs indicates that rather than *commendation*, it is rather in line for *condemnation* because of its "unfaithfulness to the Master," shown by its harming, deceiving, and abusing Jesus' sheep?

Have *money and power* really been at the root of many changes, dogmatism, and demands by the W/W/H over the years? Was that not also the case with the Pharisees of Jesus' day? Was Jesus in the wrong, or was it the scribes and Pharisees who were being exposed?

Do you recall the commendable attitude and conduct of the little old lady highlighted in chapter one? Have you noted even the tiniest hint of a similar attitude by members of the W/W/H? Why do you think such a commendable attitude has been missing?

Actually, the hierarchy has in fact issued orders commanding silence with regard to admitting wrongdoing. Have they really done such a thing? Positively yes! This is how it came about.

During the 1980's, I was appointed to assist a circuit overseer in teaching a Kingdom Ministry School class starting on Thanksgiving day in November and going to the upcoming Sunday, for congregation elders from about sixteen congregations in our area. The fact that other classes were also being taught the same information worldwide makes clear the motive behind the W/W/H's demands for the elders to follow its members' example; what was it? In order to evade accountability, they would simply refuse to accept responsibility, especially for *judicial errors*.

The circuit overseer had received a letter of special instructions from the branch office in New York, containing points that were to be added to the "shepherding books" of all of the elders. That letter explained that "We [actually Witness corporations] have been *sued* having had to pay-out *millions of dollars,* some by court decree, and *other millions* to prevent cases from getting into court..." (In other words, it had become, clearly, a matter of money!)

The circuit overseer read the following: "Therefore there are five phrases that we want you to write in the front of your Kingdom Ministry School textbook, *Pay Attention to Yourselves and to All the Flock,*" (1977, 1979, 1981, 1991).

He continued reading, "You must never use any of these phrases when talking to a person against whom some judicial action has been taken by any of you. Please write these phrases down exactly as I give them to you. You *must never say* any of the following:

1. *We **made** a mistake in handling your case.*

2. *We **might** have made a mistake in handling your case.*

3. *The Society [Watchtower Bible and Tract Society] **gave us some direction** in handling your case.*

4. *Do not ever make reference to the fact that the Society **has its own** legal department.*

5. ***Never refer** to the Society's attorneys."*

Now ask yourself, "Why on earth would any elder or group of elders on a congregation judicial committee feel inclined to tell a person who had been disfellowshipped, "We *made* a mistake in your case" or "We *might* have made a mistake in your case?"

➢ Would not the *only* possible reason be if he or they were certain that such a mistake had been made?

➢ Is it not obvious that the need for such an admission or confession would be plaguing them only if they for a fact *had made* such a mistake?

➢ Would not the person against whom the wrong was committed by the judicial committee have every right in the world to be told the truth rather than having it *deceptively hidden* from him or her by that group of elders, the members of the congregation judicial committee, and forced to suffer the undeserved and unjust consequences?

➢ Recall the little old lady from chapter one? Where have the judicial committee's courage, humility, bravery, and willingness to accept responsibility gone? It does not exist in many cases! The members of the W/W/H, all the way down to local elders, have been hypocritically ordered by their upper echelon to deceive rather than to be truthful—*to live a lie!*

➢ Is it not true that if any corporation had done serious damage to an individual by slandering or harming him or her, that corporation would be found guilty and would be legally liable for such deliberate wrongdoing? Would not a monetary penalty rightly be imposed on it?

Yet the W/W/H has specifically made these demands of congregation elders at the bottom of its hierarchical ladder. These are the very ones whom it has appointed to make judgments for it, disfellowshipping any persons whom it deems deserving of such action.

Is this not clear evidence of the strenuous efforts by the upper echelon of the W/W/H to deny accountability and to refuse to take responsibility for its wrongs or those committed by its appointed elders who follow its demands and example?

> The reason? By that hierarchy's own words—to avoid having to pay millions of dollars to settle very legitimate lawsuits brought about because of its guilt and complicity in wrongdoing.

> There is no way to honestly argue that money, and likely even power, are not major factors in the rationale of the W/W/H.

It refuses to recognize that we now live in a transparent world. Thanks to the Internet, it is impossible, in today's world, for wrongdoers, including those in a religious hierarchy, to continue to hide their bad and worse deeds from eventual detection and exposure. The cat is out of the bag; places to hide are evaporating.

In this book, the exposure comes from published beliefs, policies, and statements made by the W/W/H itself; it has published such in its literature or presented it secretly, via special instructions to congregation elders. This hierarchy has shot itself down by its own words, deeds, and publications. Its own deception, arrogance, dogmatism, and lack of mercy toward those whom it has claimed to have the responsibility to shepherd, as well as its double-talk and unwillingness to accept the responsibility for which it is accountable, have caught up with it.

As previously noted, the departure of countless hundreds of thousands and even millions of formerly active rank-and-file Witnesses—including long-time elders, pioneers, circuit overseers, and former Bethel family members and even some from the governing body and writing department in New York—who at one time trusted and believed in this organization, is proof that its mode of operation is unworkable, unacceptable, and unforgiveable. All these individuals have chosen to abandon a sinking ship.

It is well known, both to active and to former Witnesses that the hierarchy has forbidden any active Witness to read, check out the Internet, or even listen to any information considered to be damaging to it. The fact that you have read these first chapters of my book is commendable. I am hopeful, especially if you are now or were in the past actively associated with that organization, that you have examined and checked many, or preferably all, of this book's numerous quotes from W/W/H publications or from the organization's library or other documents available through a web search.

Perhaps you have experienced feelings running the gamut from doubt to surprise, to disbelief, to disappointment, to anger, or any of a host of other negative feelings. If so, please be assured that you are not alone. Such an enormous range of feelings may well be trying, but they are survivable. Millions of other former JWs have experienced such feelings too (including me); chapter 14 will provide help in the matter of dealing with these feelings. Escaping this oppressive organization and tapping into resources you may not be aware you have going for you will also be dealt with and covered in that same chapter.

Think back to the time of King David, when he had the whistle blown on him by the prophet Nathan. If you had been a loyal Jewish subject in David's kingdom, an admiring acquaintance, or perhaps even a very good and trusted friend, what feelings would likely have overwhelmed you at that time? No doubt many of the same feelings mentioned in the previous paragraph.

Recall that David's actions involved numerous wrongs, including adultery, deception, and even murder. How do you think you would have felt as you became aware of the exposure of his wrongs? How would you have dealt with these new, strange, and even forbidding feelings that you probably never imagined you would experience toward your close friend, King David, the authority figure in your nation?

If such a thing were to happen to a friend of yours, what could you not do about what you had learned? Although you could not change the facts, you might try to ignore them, refuse to believe them, deny them, or even get angry with the whistle-blower who had revealed them, but that wouldn't really change anything, would it? The facts would still be the facts. The embarrassment, the "I wish it hadn't happened to my friend," feelings could not be erased. What to do?

You could recognize that in this case involving your friend, as it was with King David, he or she was in fact just an imperfect person who made one serious mistake, but then by deceptive efforts to hide that wrongdoing, it just led to more deception. Here again we would see the truthfulness of Sir Walter Scott's words, "Oh what a tangled web we weave, when first we practice to deceive."

Of course, if it was deliberate wrongdoing and deception that one must deal with, especially if it had adversely affected you personally, it could be far more devastating and might permanently change your attitude toward your one-time friend. It could, in fact, end a previous long-standing personal friendship. What a price could be exacted because of deliberate deception!

Since King David was repentant, his sin was allowed, by God, to "pass by." But you may recall that the prophet Nathan advised David that he would face many problems, including the death of his newborn illegitimate son. The extreme grief and likely resentment on Bathsheba's part, the embarrassment and tarnished reputation, the shame, guilt, and many additional problems that we may not even be aware of, no doubt flooded in on King David, Bathsheba, and other friends and acquaintances. Even though David's sins had been forgiven by God, what he was reaping for his wrongdoing and deception was going to plague him for the rest of his life.

These became the realities for King David and since we are all subject to the rule stated in Gal. 6:7, we will all reap what we have sown, there is no way of escaping that reality, whether the person is a king, a member of the upper echelon of the W/W/H, or anyone else, for that matter—including ourselves.

Additionally, if it turns out that such a person or group, for whatever reason, refuses to acknowledge accountability or take responsibility for their actions, as has been the case consistently for the W/W/H, the results are likely to become far more devastating for all concerned. Perhaps there will be no way to correct or change the outcome, and disaster and tragedy may well be lurking in the wings.

Below, I will now discuss some additional problems that the Watchtower Bible and Tract Society of N.Y, Inc. (the mother corporation for Jehovah's Witnesses) has had to deal with of late. You will see that the actions that cause these problem areas may well be viewed as deceptive and even hypocritical, especially by any of the W/W/H's rank-and-file members who have personally been touched or harmed by its actions. That would include any who have family or friends who have been victims of its wayward, deceptive policies.

If you have access to a computer and know how to access the Internet, you are already aware of the enormous research tool that you have at your fingertips. It is also true that not everything found on the Internet is factual or truthful. For that reason, I urge you, as I have throughout my book, to please check the information you find for truthfulness and context. Especially look for court documents, IRS records, United Nations records, SEC records, etc. Such records (like published Watchtower literature) well establish the record that the W/W/H has made for itself, and that sort of information is factual.

Since there are two sides to every dispute, I also urge you to check out what the W/W/H has said to try to explain its actions. You will see the same rationale that it has usually displayed; a course of action which includes denial of wrong-doing coupled with specious reasoning in an effort at damage control. Nonetheless, better that you see both sides so that you will have a complete picture.

All of the following points can be explored through a good web search engine (such as Google or Bing); simply type in the phrases that I have noted below in quotation marks, for each of the six main points. The search results will lead to other websites where you will find clear and unassailable documentation of the points being made.

Trust the fact that you have a God-given mind, conscience, and ability to think, reason, and exercise free will to investigate. If you feel uncomfortable about investigating these matters for yourself, perhaps feeling that such action would be disloyal or wrong for any reason, recall what kind of an organization it is that does not allow its followers to investigate questionable conduct, especially in matters that it believes to be detrimental to itself.

Remember the description from C. T. Russell, defining the word, "sect"? Six highlighted points were given to describe both a sect and (although unplanned) a cult:

- The mind must be given up entirely to the sect
- The sect decides what is truth or error, not you
- You must accept the decisions of the sect
- You must ignore individual thought
- You must avoid personal investigation
- Your conscience becomes enslaved to the sect

It may prove to be helpful to go back and re-read the complete quote from Russell's book, *Studies in the Scriptures* (vol. 3, 1911), toward the end of the "Introduction" part of this book.

Recall that Jesus did all of his activities in the open, so everything he said and/or did could be checked out by those who heard him. I earlier quoted the Apostle Paul's words about the Berean Jews; he commended their checking up on his truthfulness (Acts 17:10, 11). Likewise, I cannot overemphasize the request that you check out the following points. Please do not "hide your head in the sand" instead of checking them out, and including their documentation.

Some, or all of these points may at first seem too shocking or unbelievable to be true, but before you dismiss them without checking their documentation, think about the record of deception and hypocrisy that prevailed among those who from 1313 BCE to the first century, had none the less, proudly proclaimed themselves to be God's only chosen people (previously covered). Remember, as King Solomon observed, there is nothing new under the sun.

First:

There has been cover-up of sexual misconduct and abuse of minors due to secrecy policies of the W/W/H. (These findings will include specific court documents awarding millions of dollars charged against it and specifically enumerating its wrongdoing in the Candace Conti case, 2012.)

Use the web search phrase, "Candace Conti." As a youngster, she was repeatedly molested by a man who had previously been a ministerial servant in the Freemont, CA congregation of Jehovah's Witnesses. If you wish to read copies of the actual court transcripts, they can be found and may be checked out at: www.silentlambs.org, www.jwfacts.com, and www.watchtowerdocuments.com. In addition you may find it helpful to examine and retrieve additional points found at the web-site: http://apps.alameda.courts.ca.gov/domainweb/ (Case No. HG11558324).

Second:

The W/W/H has accepted financial gain from the tobacco industry while at the same time disfellowshipping believers who were found to be smoking or even *selling* cigarettes. Even the owner of a store, if he sells cigarettes can be disfellowshipped for not eliminating them from his stock and refusing to sell them. Use the web search phrase, "Watchtower and the tobacco industry," to find ample documentation of these points.

If you search, you will find IRS and SEC documents verifying the truth that the Watchtower organization has received such income on more than one occasion in the past.

Third:

You will find documentation that the organization has pursued get-rich-quick schemes, including how to get into the very risky hedge funds game, by hobnobbing with and imitating some of the country's largest financiers.

www.Wiktionary.org defines a hedge fund as "an unregistered investment fund." They are *considered very risky* and usually involve using other people's money to finance such a venture.

Use the web search phrase, "Watchtower and Hedge Funds," to find links to documentation showing the organization's involvement at special meetings and assemblies with some very heavy hitters from the financial world, learning how to use hedge funds to amass huge amounts of money quickly. One needs millions of dollars to get started in this risky game, so it is not for the average guy or gal.. Where do you think the organization would "find" that kind of cash? Large financial and religious institutions use money from others—like from whom, I wonder?

Fourth:

Political involvement (including lobbying) on the part of the W/W/H includes UN documents proving its NGO (nongovernmental organization) membership for years.

If you do a web search on the phrase, "Watchtower and UN," you will find links to considerable documentation verifying this fact. You will also note what the W/W/H has said and published about the UN that makes it seem inconceivable that it would ever consider joining the United Nations for any reason.

The W/W/H's claim that it "joined to get a library card" (that is, to have access to the UN's library) is fraudulent; anyone can get a library card. If the hierarchy really believes that God has condemned the UN, why would it risk God's wrath by joining that organization?

Fifth:

There has been considerable and consistent involvement by the W/W/H as a major stockholder in a company that had been involved in research and development of an engine being designed for use by the United States military.

When you do a web search using the phrase, "Watchtower and rand cam engine," you will find that the Watchtower Society held 50 percent of the stock in that company. Many sites and youtube.com videos "tell all" and can be found in your web search.

You will also be able to access SEC filing records; if you follow the links, they make denial by the W/W/H organization fraudulent and futile.

Sixth:

The W/W/H practices a double standard in the matter of disfellowshipping members for joining the military or for taking blood transfusions in most countries. It has made major compromises in Bulgaria on these issues. Do you wonder why?

Since the W/W/H has consistently made sure that it takes care of number one (itself) *first*, it always gets priority; so in order for it to obtain legal recognition as a religion, compromise became acceptable and desirable in Bulgaria.

When you do a web search on the phrase, "Watchtower and blood transfusions," you can learn of these compromises in both areas, joining the military and blood transfusions, compromises that *would never be tolerated* in other parts of the world for Jehovah's Witnesses. Note the previous dogmatic policy stance: "For this important Bible reason they tell officials of the government that *they conscientiously object* to serving in any *military* establishment *or any civilian arrangement that substitutes for military service*." (*Watchtower* February 1, 1951, p. 26; italics added)

However after many decades, the W/W/H changed this policy, but not before thousands of young Witnesses, including personal friends of mine, spent years in prison. They carry the scars of a criminal record and years lost from their lives, "not for righteousness sake," but for the sake of the W/W/H's policies, (which always revolve around money). It has gone way beyond the things that are written in the Bible. What an outrage was foisted on these many duped followers!

Do you smell something "rotten in Denmark" (or New York)? How do you feel about these facts? Do you care?

Have you noticed that this chapter has involved a number of practices by the W/W/H that certainly seem to have been hypocritical? Note the meaning of that word from *Webster (1913)*: "Dissembling; *concealing one's real character or motives*... Proceeding from hypocrisy, or marking hypocrisy... as a hypocritical face or look." (ital. added)

The Hebrew and Greek words for hypocrisy, as found in the Bible, have the same meaning. How serious do you consider the practice of hypocrisy to be? If you were asked to name the groups that were given the most scathing denunciation by Jesus, in the first century, which groups would come to mind and why?

Would it not be those among the Jewish hierarchy known as the scribes and Pharisees? They were the very ones who orchestrated the execution of both Jesus and Stephen; many were members of the Sanhedrin (Jewish Supreme Court).

What were they guilty of that earned them such a denunciation? The answer is given at Matt. 23:2, 3, where it says, "The scribes and the Pharisees have seated themselves in the seat of Moses...but do not do according to their deeds, for they say but do not perform" (NWT). The NIV uses "teachers" instead of "scribes" and "do not practice what they preach" instead of "do not perform."

The twenty-third chapter of Matthew uses the phrase, "scribes and Pharisees, hypocrites," at least five times. Other phrases used in this chapter are "blind guides," "fools and blind ones," and "serpents, offspring of vipers." And note, in the same chapter, how reprehensible Jesus viewed their conduct to be, when he says "how are you to flee from the *judgment of Gehenna?*" (Matt. 23:23, 33) NWT - The NIV says, "escape *being condemned to hell?*"

Strong's Greek dictionary defines the word used here as, "gheenna, ghehennah; valley of (the son of) Hinnom; a valley of Jerus., used (fig) as a name for the place (or state) of everlasting punishment: hell" (*Greek Dictionary of the New Testament*, p. 20, # 1067).

Thayer's Lexicon adds the following: "Gehenna, the name of a valley on the S. and E. of Jerusalem...which was so called from the cries of the little children who were thrown into the fiery arms of Moloch...The Jews so abhorred the place after these horrible sacrifices had been abolished by King Josiah (2 Ki. xxiii, 10), that they cast into it not only all manner of refuse, but even the dead bodies of animals and of unburied criminals who had been executed." (*Greek-English Lexicon* 1977, p. 111, # 1067)

Jesus ate with tax collectors such as Zacchaeus (Luke 19:2–8) and allowed a sinful woman to wet his feet with her tears and wipe them off with her hair, kissing his feet and greasing them with perfumed oil. (Luke 7:36–40) Jesus did not condemn either of these sinners; yet he roundly condemned the Jewish religious leaders (members of the hierarchy) for their practice of hypocrisy. Why so?

Which people do you discern to be more reprehensible, the known sinners such as the tax collector and the sinful woman, or the religious leaders who proclaimed themselves to be holy and righteous? As Jesus said over and over again in Matthew 23:2, 3, 13, 15, 23, 25, 27, 29, and 33 "Woe to you, scribes and Pharisees, hypocrites!"

Where do you think the W/W/H stands (all things considered) in the matter of hypocrisy? In view of the record the scribes and Pharisees of the first century made for themselves and the condemnation they received from Jesus, what kind of a judgment do you think the hypocritical W/W/H is in line for?

Looking at scriptural history as a barometer of things to come, that hierarchy will not be found "faithful and discreet;" rather, it will be found deceptive, dishonest, and hypocritical. I would not want to be found standing in its shoes (or sandals) when it comes time for judgment by God or Christ. Would you?

Remember, history keeps repeating itself, and this really is noticeable in the religious venue that we have been considering in this book. How would you answer the following questions?

REVIEW POINTS:

1. Do you discern deception in the claims made by the W/W/H in reference to its governing body and how it came into existence?

2. In what way were its actions involving the governing body similar to my acquisition of my "first airplane" while visiting my grandparents?

3. Do you think God's view of its claims would be any different than my mother's view was of my fraudulent claims of ownership of a push-pedal airplane in 1948?

4. How would you view a (non-religious) business that refused to take responsibility for its wrongs and demanded that all managers do likewise?

The next chapter gets into a procedure that has been the practice and norm for the W/W/H since 1952. It has resulted in considerable harm to millions of Jehovah's Witnesses, all of whom have or had been charged with violating what this hierarchy classifies as serious sins.

Millions more than just the alleged wrongdoers have been harmed and pressured by the W/W/H, with the result that countless families have been torn apart and destroyed.

Jesus said that a tree could be identified by its fruitage (Matt. 7:15–20). What are the realities of a procedure that has been foisted by the W/W/H on its followers? What kind of fruitage has it produced?

Let us delve into this archaic and draconian procedure which will be covered in great detail in the next chapter.

Chapter 10

DISFELLOWSHIPPING:
THE DARK SIDE LEADING TO
THE DESTRUCTION OF FAMILIES

- Are people born deceptive, wicked, or cruel?
- How does wickedness come about and why?
- How does the W/W/H define its "disfellowshipping
- and shunning" procedures?
- Why does it disfellowship, expel, or shun anybody?
- When was disfellowshipping implemented?
- How are wickedness and weakness different?
- What about "not saying one word" to people?
- ❖ Flying - trying to avert a tragedy.

What do the names Bernie Madoff, Adolph Hitler, Jim Jones, David Koresh, and Warren Jeffs bring to your mind, and why? They were all deceptive either in the financial, political, or religious arenas. They were all frauds.

Did they start out life that way? Of course not; but, whether they accidentally became that way or slipped into their positions through conspiring as they grew older, nonetheless they brought great harm, financial loss, heartache, and even death to others—sometimes even to millions.

What went wrong? A clue comes from a "dirge" (or "lament" in the NIV) concerning the king of Tyre (Ezekiel chapter 28). The verses coming up seem to parallel the account found at Genesis 3:1–5, where verse one (NWT) carries a marginal reference to Rev.12:9, "the original serpent...called Devil and Satan." What went wrong in the case of the king of Tyre, or Satan?

If neither of these two started out wicked or lawless when they were born (or created), then what went wrong? What contributed to their downfall? Read the whole account in Ezek. 28:11–19 to get the context, and you will note that verse 15 says, "You were [past tense] *blameless* in your ways from the day you were *created* [born] till wickedness was found in you" (NIV; italics and brackets added). The NWT version says the same, except that it uses the word "faultless" instead of "blameless."

Does that account not indicate the truth of the idea that persons, or spirit creatures, for that matter, do not start out bad but become that way over time? That is true of hijackers, terrorists, drug pushers, pedophiles, or really, any wrongdoers. They are not born that way or in those positions, but they become such as they grow older and as wickedness gradually creeps into their lives as they gain more experience. Other factors likewise exert an influence.

Notice some of the things that preceded their downfall: wisdom and beauty (verse 12), position of responsibility as a cherub; (verse 14), and being viewed as faultless (verse 15); then success in business "widespread trade and violence," (verse 16) and excessive pride led to downfall (verse 17).

Then followed the outcome (verse 18): "By your *many sins* and *dishonest trade* you have desecrated your sanctuaries. So I made a fire come out from you, and it consumed you, and reduced you to ashes on the ground" (NIV; italics added). The NWT version uses "errors" and "injustice of your sales goods" instead of "sins" and "dishonest trade."

The saying, pride comes before a crash is true and is based on a scriptural proverb (Prov. 16:18); pride can even consume one who in his or her younger years started out humble and unassuming. Many things can contribute to a person's humility evaporating, leaving room for undesirable traits to flourish and become dominant.

For example, consider this. In 1933, Adolph Hitler became Chancellor in Germany. The Great Depression of 1929 had devastated Germany as well as the United States. Hitler embarked on trying to improve the German economy and met with a good bit of success. He improved the Autobahn system and accomplished many other public works; by

1938, unemployment was nearly unheard of in Germany. Who at that time would have imagined or ever dreamed of the horrific abuses that were about to come? Good works, yes…and the German people were pleased with the turnaround in their economy. But disaster was waiting in the wings; for many "unsuitable ones" from his viewpoint—the good turned to bad, and then to the outrageous!

Many others could be mentioned; remember Jerry Sandusky, discussed in an earlier chapter? Did his accomplishment of some good deeds—excuse the extreme bad or abusive sexual misconduct that resulted after he gained status as a benefactor for disadvantaged boys?

The W/W/H is no exception. In the matter of disfellowshipping; there may well be a need for some form of discipline in a congregation, but, what should dictate the proper degree to prevent a miscarriage of justice and heartless abuses from occurring?

Do you remember my own grave mistakes and wrongdoing involving my son Jimmy and the thirty-nine strokes? I had done some good things too, but that did not excuse my abusive wrongdoing. I felt absolutely compelled to take responsibility for my wrongs, admit them to the ones I had harmed (my own children, especially Jimmy), and try the best I could to correct them and try to prevent them from happening again.

You are likely aware of the fact that many persons never admit faults or wrongs and flatly refuse to take responsibility for them or make corrections. Do you recall an exception related in this book? Think about the commendable conduct of the little old lady, related in chapter one; can you remember her story?

This also brings to mind a relevant scripture involving God and his discipline, administered to the ancient Israelites, mentioned in the Bible at Jer. 30:11, where it says, "I will discipline you but only in due measure; I will *not* let you go entirely *unpunished*" (NIV). The NWT version says, *"to the proper degree"* instead of "due measure" (italics added).

This scriptural statement, attributed to God by the prophet Jeremiah, I believe serves as a benchmark, as to God's view of a proper as well as an improper degree of discipline. If this benchmark was applied to the W/W/H and its disfellowshipping and shunning procedures, it would call for dramatic changes on its part, as you will see.

This hierarchy has waffled in its demands to congregation elders about how severe to be in the administration of discipline. The approach has sometimes been balanced, but much more often, it has seemed to be more of a shotgun or even a draconian (harsh or severe) approach to discipline (since its implementation in 1952 by Nathan Knorr, President of the Watchtower Society at the time).

For example, even when a wrongdoer has stopped his or her wrong conduct, the person may continue to be dealt with unkindly, even cruelly, unless he or she is willing to grovel before the elders while begging for reinstatement. This reinstatement is often denied—sometimes for years on end—or perhaps it never occurs, and at times, without just cause. Why? Sometimes it's because of bias or prejudice on the part of the elders. Such abuse happens all too often; it is uncalled for and is unscriptural, as well as unreasonable.

Consider the following illustration. If one of your kids had to be punished for stealing five bucks from you, would you ostracize him for years on end, making him grovel before you; never letting him forget for a minute what he had done? Should not reasonableness play a part in the discipline you would choose? Should the child's punishment be as severe as would likely be the case if he or she had stolen a gun and then shot and seriously injured a schoolmate? Of course not!

Remember my son Jimmy? A punishment of thirty-nine strokes with a belt was outrageous, even criminal!

A very relevant scripture in this matter is (Phil. 4:5): "Let your ***reasonableness*** become known to all men. The Lord is near" (NWT). The NIV version says, *"gentleness"* in place of *"reasonableness"* (italics added). Other related word choices can be found in Thayer's *Greek-English Lexicon* (1977, p. 238, #1933): "seemly, suitable... equitable, fair, mild, and gentle."

Yet many times the W/W/H has, by its own policies, proven to be senseless, irrational, and unreasonable, bordering on the fanatical. Its conduct reminds me of a scripture involving an asinine zebra, mentioned in the Bible book of Job, specifically Job 11:12, which says, "Even a *hollow-minded man* himself will get good motive As soon as *an asinine zebra* be *born a man*" (NWT). The NIV uses "witless" and "donkey's colt" instead of "hollow-minded" and "asinine zebra" (italics added). *Webster (1913)* defines "asinine" as: "Of or belonging to, or having the qualities of... stupidity and obstinacy... asinine nature."

I have seen enough "asinine behavior" on the part of the W/W/H to last a lifetime. I will relate two accounts involving two of my seven children who were dealt with in that manner. See if you agree.

The first account involves my fifth child and fourth son, Joseph. He was born on May 25, 1975, the year our little son, Ronald, died as the result of a tragic bicycle accident. You may recall that this was just four months before the last *for sure date* that the W/W/H had prophesied for the end of the world; not a good year!

By 1994, Joseph had become a young adult (nineteen years old) and was living on his own in New Albany, Indiana. He had attended a trade school in Superior, Wisconsin, to learn the trade of welding, but he really wanted to become a deep-sea diver.

Training for that job costs a great deal more than training to be a welder; so on one occasion, he, along with a friend (another young Witness man), after drinking more than was prudent, got a bright idea. Let's join the navy and let them pay for the training; good idea! At least it seemed so to them at the time and in the condition they were in. So they signed up to join on a future date—they were going to become divers!

What would you call their decision? Was their idea likely wickedness or perhaps just weakness? Does it matter?

When the due date arrived to pay the piper, Joseph decided not to go through with it; however, it was too late—the navy's MPs would never agree. They picked him up and shipped him off to Great Lakes Naval Training Station. At this point, he found himself suffering from a severely guilty conscience (because JWs are not allowed to join the military). So he refused to continue with the enlistment, which in turn landed him, not on an aircraft carrier, (as a Navy Seal), but in prison. He was threatened: "You can choose a four-year enlistment or ten years in prison. What will it be?" They were tightening the screws on him, but he was, after all, a Staelens. He flatly refused to continue; I can't imagine where he acquired such a stubborn streak! His friend went ahead and did join; Joseph did not.

We had no idea anything was going wrong in his life; the first hint of trouble came with a shocking call from his apartment manager after his rent was past due. Joseph had simply disappeared from the earth without a trace. His personal belongings had been confiscated. The months crept by with no Joseph, no explanation, and no facts available. How could someone just disappear?

Can you even begin to imagine how we felt? Where was he? What had happened to our son? No one could say; there were only guesses and no facts. The pieces of this puzzle would eventually be found, but ever so slowly.

In the meantime, the elders in the New Albany, Indiana congregation got wind of what *they thought* had occurred—mostly guessing—but they took judicial action and announced it to the congregation. If any of them knew where he was, they kept their lips sealed. Although they had our names and address, no one called us!

We eventually learned (from his friend's mother) that the congregation had announced that "he disassociated himself," rather than using the word "disfellowshipped" (to avoid getting into trouble with the government for punishing Witness youths who joined the military). But *he had not joined!* The end result is the same: the "wrongdoer" is shunned. These days, in such cases, they will just announce that the person is "no longer one of Jehovah's Witnesses" but still shun them, unless they grovel at the feet of the elders begging to be reinstated in the congregation, which most refuse to do.

Cornelius was mentioned in the chapter on baptism; he received holy spirit and was baptized while still an *active-duty army officer* for the Roman Empire (Acts 10:1–35). The scriptures never say he left the military, yet the Apostle Peter stated that "he was acceptable to God." But the W/W/H's *actions* show it disagrees with the way God dealt with Cornelius. Do they have a right to question God Almighty's acceptance of someone in the military back then? How about now? What presumptuousness!

In Joseph's case, we eventually learned that there had never been a judicial hearing or conversation of any sort with him by the elders in New Albany, Indiana. Their judicial decision was based solely on "hearsay," with no two witness testimony and no opportunity for any kind of explanation from Joseph. No facts; what a travesty!

Eventually we found out that he was in prison at the Great Lakes Naval Training Station, just northeast of O'Hare Field in Chicago. I had flown over him countless times on my approach to Runway 22 Right at O'Hare, with no idea that he was only four thousand feet away—below me.

I called the training station's commanding officer and learned that Joseph's actions had been recorded by the navy as an "aborted enlistment." But *wait a minute!* To an airline captain, an "aborted take-off" means that the plane did not continue down the runway. It never got airborne but had stayed on the ground. The *take-off never happened!*

Something was "rotten in Denmark" (or New York), so I called the Watchtower Society's Service Desk (the ones responsible for confirming disfellowshipping action) in New York. The brother I talked to there did not care that Joseph had never gotten a hearing and that there had been no witnesses or that a decision had been based on hearsay only or that the navy had aborted his enlistment. No! Come hell or high water, the judicial committee's decision would stand. Common sense was non-existent.

In discussing this with one member of the hierarchy, I used myself as an airline captain in an example: What if, while on a layover at the other end of the world, I invited a flight attendant up to my hotel room, stripped down and hopped in bed with her? (No I have never done this, ever! It's just an illustration.)

At any rate, that would be dumb, stupid, reckless, and all sorts of other bad things. But! What if I came to my senses in time, got my butt out of that bed, and never touched her—would I have been guilty of committing adultery? What do you think: adultery or not? Yes or No?

Should I, in such a case, be disfellowshipped for adultery?

No! I was crazy and irresponsible, but I never touched her; it was like aborting a take-off. The take-off never happened.

But the upper echelon would not hear of it. Its members had made up their minds. In Joseph's case, facts, reason, and common sense would not rule. They stuck to the congregation's fraudulent decision, as they have done so many, many times before. After all, they can never be wrong, and even if they are—they will never admit it.

Eventually, Joseph ended up back in Superior, Wisconsin, and he was trying to get reinstated. It was the dead of winter, and he was walking a couple of miles, one way, to meetings at the Kingdom Hall. He had no transportation.

The temperature was forty degrees *below zero*. Some in the congregation asked for permission to stop and give him a ride, but only one person ever did stop, just once. The elders' orders were, "No, absolutely not; he made this mess for himself. So if it is tough on him, that's his problem, not yours." Was inappropriate pressure applied? You bet! Was any kind of reasonableness shown? *No!* The shunning procedure stays in place—keep the pressure on!

Were those elders in the Superior, Wisconsin Congregation of Jehovah's Witness guilty of stealing the faculty of individual conscience from their members? Absolutely yes; there can be no question about their travesty! The hierarchy decides—not the individual Witnesses. But those are sect-like traits, right? *Right!*

"The mess" that had been foisted on Joseph was due to a bogus, fraudulent decision having been made *without due process*. Neither the elders from the New Albany, Indiana Congregation or Superior, Wisconsin Congregation made any efforts to meet with him to address his situation or provide any kind of help. He was simply thrown-out, discarded, shunned and ignored. Why does that make me think of Jesus' or Stephen's fraudulent kangaroo court trials?

Joseph continued making that walk several times, but he finally gave up, feeling that it was useless and impossible; no help, not even some encouragement would be allowed. What would you have done?

His decision, although aborted, alienated him from the Witness organization and from most of his immediate family. But he has continued to mature and has become an excellent father, husband, and son. He has also provided considerable help and support for Dale and me, struggling with the problems of aging while some of our staunch Witness children have decided we are not worthy of their help. Joseph has turned out to be a very special son to us.

Two-thirds of the persons who are disfellowshipped by Jehovah's Witnesses never return. Is it any wonder why?

Second account: Literally a near tragedy

My wife and I had just landed in Alamosa, Colorado, in our own plane, on a trip back home from Florida, where we had been visiting some of our family. It was December twenty-first.

As we walked through the door at home (about 10:00 p.m.), we heard the phone ringing; the person calling us was a friend of our son John. We learned that he had just interrupted an attempted suicide by John—"could we possibly come up? He drastically needs your help!" Of course we would! I would make sure, if humanly possible, to be landing at the Bozeman airport in Montana before noon the next day.

Both Dale and I needed sleep badly, but we were in for a short night—back in the air at first light. Bozeman was over eight hundred miles away, and we would have to fly the Front Range over Denver because of heavy weather over the mountains (which would have been the preferred, direct route from Alamosa). That adjustment would require more time than desirable.

We had just completed a flight from south Florida, over thirteen hundred miles away; with direct GPS navigation capability, we could cover a great deal of ground in short order, but there are limits…

As I lay there in bed trying to sleep, I thought back to how John (our sixth child, fifth son) had come into this world at 1:00 a.m. on December 29, 1978. I had been in Denver (with my family), attending DC-10 school at United's flight training center. To make a long story short, we delivered John ourselves in our hotel room. That has made a special bond between us and him, understandably so.

Though I had been in on two previous deliveries by my wife (at the hospital), with a doctor assisting the delivery, this time, it was just Dale, me (and John, of course). It turned out to be the easiest delivery she had ever experienced with any of our seven children (that is her assessment). Never let it be said, in this case, that I didn't finish what I started! Time marched on.

By now, John had become a young adult living on his own in Montana. He had gotten into trouble with the congregation in Bozeman and had been disfellowshipped. That and other issues had led him to believe that life was not worth living anymore, which had led to the cry for help from his friend to us; thank God he called us!

I knew that Dale and I would likely be condemned by some of our staunch Witness relatives for even thinking of providing assistance to him, let alone actually doing it. That was just not allowed for "loyal, obedient JWs." They believed, we should just have covered our eyes and ears to his plight. He would have to come back to the organization and grovel first, before they would ever consider helping or trying to understand his problem; that's the W/W/H way.

I was very accustomed to making captains decisions—what is right is right, and to hell with what my relatives might be thinking or what the hierarchy demanded; John was our beloved son—another human *needing our understanding, love, and help* - not a shove off the edge of a cliff. Jesus would never have acted the way the W/W/H, pressures both elders and the rank-and-file members to act.

This helps explain, in part, why I have such very strong personal feelings against the W/W/H's long-standing tyranny of authority. That is especially true of their demanded disfellowshipping and shunning procedures.

We did get professional help for John, and tragedy was averted. And we were condemned, as expected. But as time marched forward, more disdainful treatment was heaped upon him, even as he tried to live by W/W/H policies in a judicial matter.

When John was ordered to attend his last judicial hearing, he asked that an elder known as "the hanging elder" not be involved in the hearing. The elder's secret book that was used at the time, *Pay Attention to Yourselves and to All The Flock* (WTB&TS 1991), contained specific instructions to the affect that if a brother facing judicial action, does not want an elder to be present, that *brother **must not be used under any circumstances***. As the book pointed out, brothers for a judicial committee can be borrowed from a neighboring congregation if needed; the alleged wrongdoer has the right to never have any elder he feels would be unjust in dealing with him, *present at the hearing*. No exceptions!

However the Bozeman, Montana judicial committee refused to honor John's request, the meeting occurred, and John was disfellowshipped. When I learned of this injustice and clear violation on the part of the judicial committee, I called their circuit overseer. I was still at that time serving as an elder, back in Colorado, and I had assisted over the years in helping to teach no fewer than three different "Kingdom Ministry Schools." I knew that book, backward and forward, including the proviso mentioned above.

This circuit overseer was brand new to the congregation and was in fact only a week from his first visit to them. I called his attention to the specific instructions and procedures that had been violated. There was no disagreement on his part; he knew I had their judicial committee "dead to rights."

But *he refused to intervene* or in any way bring this travesty up to the committee. Why? There was absolutely no question about its failure. As we continued talking, he simply said, "I am brand new to the congregation, so I am not willing to bring up this kind of a distasteful problem on my first visit." *Period.* He would discuss the matter no further.

The obvious translation: "On my first visit I get to find out who is most favorable to the circuit overseer, who's the most affluent and most generous to the traveling brothers in any given congregation. I want to keep relationships with them cordial; it will benefit me for the next three years. I *want the goodies!* So I'll just keep quiet, thank you very much." Justice and honesty became nonexistent, yet again.

It turned our stomachs too, worse than if, in our plane, we had hit severe air turbulence at altitude, leading to a near crash.

Some of John's Witness family members continue shunning him to this day, although it has been many years since he was disfellowshipped. He has refused to grovel before the congregation elders; instead, he has made a new life for himself. He has turned out to be a wonderful man; just ask his new family. We, of course, feel the same way about him.

He too has turned out to be of great help to Dale and me as we have aged and have to deal with the limitations that are typical of this time of life. Both he and Joseph have shown us unconditional love because we gave them life and cared for them as youths. They have no hidden agenda for us to be acceptable to them and deserving of such care.

Does it help you to see where I am coming from? I have seen, on the part of the W/W/H, a continuing sick, asinine mentality. Common sense, good judgment, and reason have been ignored by elders, circuit overseers, and the brothers on the Service Desk at their New York City Bethel headquarters, over and over again. I quit tolerating it years ago, and I will *never tolerate* it again!

Happily, some of our Witness relatives have cautiously extended some help to us and deal with us to a limited degree, though we have not been active as JWs for many years. They have not totally succumbed to the hierarchy's cult-like policies that dictate their every move involving family matters. However, most of them still refuse to close the gap that separates them from Joseph and John; action that they have been forbidden by the W/W/H to take and may later regret.

The reality is that as was the case in my relationship with my father in 1950, the W/W/H is still in the business of destroying families by means of its draconian policies. How many more millions will abandon the organization instead of their families? Only time will tell.

Some years ago, I personally, and unilaterally, disfellowshipped their upper-echelon hierarchy from my life and abandoned it, as millions ahead of me have already felt compelled to do. I never have and never will shun individual family members who are still staunch Witnesses, unless I am being reviled abusively; then I'll just get out of the way. I refuse to imitate what I consider to be a Pharisaical mentality of abridging anyone's right to free speech, including my own. I believe it is a constitutional and scriptural right, regardless of what others think.

Getting back to Phil 4:5, that counsel, to "be reasonable," would surely have been appropriate rather than the judgmental attitude displayed by many JWs toward my sons, don't you think?

Let's continue to see this verse's application in this case involving the merciless disfellowshipping and shunning procedures, practiced by the W/W/H; its procedures have produced some very rotten fruitage, which have needlessly harmed and alienated millions of past as well as present believers. (Note Matt. 7:18–21 for "fruitage.")

The Bible is filled with God's counsel and discipline administered to the nation of ancient Israel, and so it is to be expected that such a need for discipline would be found among all Christians today, including Jehovah's Witnesses. The problem is not that of whether there is ever a need for discipline. Of course there is in any kind of society; but what about the matter of the degree of severity? What kind of discipline is needed; what would reasonableness dictate to be "to the proper degree" (Jer. 30:11)?

Abuses and extremes can easily occur; the Bible clearly shows this could be and has been the case in the past. Such abuses have continued into the present, by the W/W/H, toward any members it judges to be wrong-doers, and anyone sympathetic toward them.

So let's check it out. What is discipline "to the proper degree?" Let's not relegate common sense to the closet either; what does it teach us? Let's use some discernment. The Watchtower/Witness book, *Reasoning from the Scriptures* (WTB&TS 1989), does not contain the words "disfellowship," "disfellowshipping," "shun," "shunning," or "congregational judgment" (That book refers only to "resurrection of judgment," one time; p. 338.)

The NWT, the hierarchy's preferred Bible translation, contains the word "shun," but only three times (WTB&TS 1973, p. 1,032). In Prov. 4:15, the word is used in "Shun it; do not pass along by it." In 2 Tim. 2:16, the phrase containing the word is, "But shun empty speeches that…" And at Titus 3:9, it says, "shun foolish questionings and…"

Noting the applications of the word will teach us much about what is wrong with the W/W/H's procedures of disfellowshipping and shunning. What do these scriptures actually say? *What* should be *shunned?*

First usage: Prov. 4:15 "*Avoid it,* do not travel on *it;* turn from *it* and go on your way" (NIV). The NWT version uses "Shun" in place of "Avoid." The "it" is identified as the "path" or "way" (verse 14) in both translations. So it was *not a person* that was to be avoided or shunned; it was a "path" or "way."

Second usage: 2 Tim. 2:16 "But *shun* empty speeches that violate what is holy; for they will advance to more and more ungodliness" (NWT). The NIV says, "Avoid godless chatter" (italics added).

Last usage: Tit. 3:9 "But *shun* foolish questionings and genealogies and strife and fights over the Law, for they are unprofitable and futile" (NWT). The NIV says, "foolish controversies and genealogies and arguments and quarrels." (italics added)

Not one of these scriptures is talking about *shunning a person,* one who had been a fellow believer but is now to be shunned by the congregation. Is that not true?

Five words (or expressions) similar to "disfellowshipping" are used in some Bible translations: "put out," "expel," "expelled," "excommunicated," or "banned." Only one of these words or phrases is used, in two different places, for disciplinary action in the W/W/H's NWT. The word "expelled," found at John 9:22 and John 12:42, will be quoted shortly; attention will also be given to the matter of not speaking in any way or about anything to disfellowshipped persons.

In spite of the fact that the word "disfellowshipping" is *never used* in the NWT, published by the WTB&TS of New York, the hierarchy practices disfellowshipping and shunning of previous fellow believers for many various infractions. There is no scripture that gives this as a directive (that is, a formal congregation action) to be leveled against one accused of wrongdoing.

Their book, *Organized To Do Jehovah's Will* (WTB&TS 2005, pp. 153–156), discusses the disfellowshipping and disassociation procedures and policies that its judicial committees in the congregations are ordered, by the W/W/H, to follow. Under the subtopic, "If the Decision is to Disfellowship" (p. 153), the book says, "In some cases the wrongdoer may be hardened in his course of sinful conduct and thus fail to respond to efforts to help him. Fruitage, or works befitting repentance may not be in evidence, nor may genuine repentance be apparent at the time of the judicial hearing. What then? In such cases, *it is necessary to expel* the unrepentant wrongdoer from the congregation." (italics added)

Who says "it is necessary to expel the unrepentant wrongdoer?" It is not a Biblical directive; no, it is the W/W/H, following the example of the Pharisees of the first century, as you will see.

It is of interest to note that the *Comprehensive Concordance* (WTB&TS 1973) of the NWT does list two scriptures in their translation that use the word "expelled, with a reference to persons being expelled, but neither of these verses is referenced in the *Organization* book on pages 153–156. Do you wonder why? How could the hierarchy have neglected referring to those two gems? Wonder no more…

Note that the next two verses reference disciplinary action taken by the Pharisees against Jesus' disciples. John 9:22 says, "anyone who acknowledged that Jesus was the Messiah would be *put out of the synagogue*" (NIV). The NWT version says, "confessed him as Christ" and "*expelled* from the synagogue" (italics added).

Next, John 12:42 reads, "All the same, many even of the rulers actually put faith in him, but because of the Pharisees they would not confess [him] [Jesus], in order not to be *expelled* from the synagogue" (NWT; first brackets theirs, italics and second brackets added). The NIV says "for fear they would be *put out.*"

Of the thirty-five scriptures listed in the NWT *Concordance* (p. 314) for "expel," "expelled," "expelling," or "expels," thirty-two refer to actions against demons, one refers to "the error of Jacob," and the two just quoted refer to the Pharisees expelling anyone confessing Jesus.

But, not a single verse refers to a person being removed (expelled) for wrongdoing, as a formal procedure, from the Christian congregation. Is there an exception? It may look that way, so therefore, I will shortly give special attention to 1 Cor. 5:13; you will see a reason for caution.

Meanwhile, biblically, only the Pharisees had the audacity to take such abusive action. No wonder the *Watchtower* writers chose to leave the two scriptures regarding the Pharisees out of their supposed proper reasons to disfellowship or expel one from the congregation. No such formal action was ever taken by any congregation of Christians in the first century. You will soon see why.

For now, let's look carefully at the verses that the W/W/H does use in trying to justify its position favoring disfellowshipping of those who are felt to be unacceptable from the W/W/H's viewpoint, regardless of what the scriptures, common sense, or good judgment dictate should be done.

The scriptures that are referred to in the *Organized* book (WTB&TS 2005, p. 153) are the following:

First: Deut. 21:20, 21. I will cover verses 18–21.

If a stubborn and rebellious son *doesn't obey* his father and mother and *won't listen* to them when disciplined, his parents should bring him before the elders of his town, at the gate, with the complaint that, our son is *stubborn and rebellious,* he won't even obey us, in fact he is a glutton and a drunkard. As a result, "all the men of his town should *stone him to death*, so they could purge the evil out of their town" (NIV). The NWT says substantially the same, except in verse 18, where it uses the words, "they've corrected him" instead of "they've disciplined him."

Notice that this was not to occur in the back room of a synagogue or a Kingdom Hall, in a cloak-and-dagger fashion.

Second: Deut. 22:23, 24 (read also verses 25–27). This account deals with a situation where a man had sex with a virgin engaged to a different man; the man and woman are *both stoned to death*. In this case, the girl was stoned to death (if this violation occurred in a city) because she did not scream. If it was in the country that this crime was committed, no death for her; it was assumed that she had screamed but that there was no one to rescue her.

What if the two had just committed fornication, but neither one was engaged? Neither of them was stoned to death. Instead, a penalty of fifty silver shekels (about $110.00 in today's currency) was imposed on the man, the couple had to marry, and the man was not allowed to divorce her for all his days (Deut. 22:28, 29). The penalty could turn out to be far greater. How? They both would do well to think twice before engaging in sex, because he would be forced into marriage to a gal who might turn out to be a real wench, with no way out, and the wife's "prize" might turn out to be a "surprise," a real loser!

Among Jehovah's Witnesses, if a couple did the same as just covered in the preceding paragraph, they both could be disfellowshipped, and especially if they had sex more than once; this would mean they were unrepentant. But it is not the whole congregation that makes the decision (though C. T. Russell believed it should be). Instead, the judicial committee makes the decision, in a back room, with no observers and no advocate for the accused—in a cloak-and-dagger fashion—allowing plenty of room for abuses. We've already observed how this became the situation in the judicial actions imposed on two of my sons.

Third: 1 Cor. 5:5, 11–13. This case involves incest—a man had sex with his stepmother, his father's wife. It was considered more shocking than things done "even among the nations." Please read the whole account (verses 1–13). The man is handed over to Satan (verse 5). Verses 11–13 state, "you *must not associate* with anyone who claims to be a brother or sister but is *sexually immoral* or greedy, an idolater or slanderer, a drunkard or swindler. Do not even eat with such people… *Expel* the *wicked person* from among you" (NIV).

The NWT version puts it, "quit mixing in company...Remove the wicked [man] from among yourselves." *Thayer's Greek-English Lexicon* (1977 p. 601, # 4874), "not associate—company." It goes onto say, "*to keep company with, be intimate with,* one: 1 Cor. 5:9, 11; 2 Thess. 3:14" (italics Thayer's,). Did you notice that the biblical Greek includes, "be intimate with?" Note also that both 1 Cor. v. 9, 11; 2 Thess. iii. 14 carry this same meaning, which will become very important later. For now, please note this fact.

Paul says, at 1 Cor. 5:3, "even though I am *not* physically *present*... I have already *passed judgment*" (NIV). The NWT says, "judged already..." (italics added). He had not been present, had not been part of any judicial committee, and had not gotten firsthand information, but he had an opinion, had made up his mind on hearsay, and had then passed judgment. Does that not sound a lot like the way the congregation in Indiana, as well as the Service Desk (in New York) dealt with my son, Joseph? It did not matter what the facts were; their judgment, made and passed already, would stand.

Concerning the words "judged" and "judgment," Thayer's *Lexicon* (1977 p. 360, # 2919) gives this definition: "1. *to separate, put asunder, to pick out, select, choose...3. to be of opinion, deem, think. 4. to determine, resolve, decree. 5 a. to pronounce an opinion concerning right and wrong.*"

Please give attention to this point from the Apostle Paul, in recommending that others stay single and not get married. Note his words at 1 Cor. 7:25, 26, 40: "I give *my opinion*...I think this to be well in view of the necessity...continue as she is [unmarried]" (NWT; italics added). The NIV uses the words, "I give a *judgment*," "I *think*," and "*in my judgment.*"

Is it not clear that Paul was expressing an opinion, his thought in the matter? Do you think that if one who was single wanted to get married, the person should be disfellowshipped and shunned, based on Paul's opinion that singleness was better? Of course not; how ridiculous!

- Additionally, note that this was not a ruling from the "apostles and older men:" it was Paul's opinion, the same meaning as contained at 1 Co. 5:3.

- Acts 15 is the only place where a written directive came from "The apostles and elders, your brothers" (NIV). The NWT version says, "apostles and older men:" (the very ones who were asserted, in the past, by the W/W/H, to be the "governing body" of the first century).

- Even the words of the apostles and older men, mentioned in Acts 15, were not directed to every congregation but just to, "the Gentile believers in Antioch, Syria and Cilicia" (Acts 15:23, NIV). The NWT version puts it, "to those brothers in Antioch and Syria and Cilicia who are from the nations."

Note their comments, in Acts 15:29, "You are to abstain from food sacrificed to idols, from blood, from the meat of strangled animals and from sexual immorality. You will *do well* to avoid these things" (NIV; italics added). The NWT version is similar, but it concludes with the words, "If you carefully keep yourselves from these things, you will *prosper. Good health to you!*" (italics added)

The meaning of the words, "you will do well" and "good health to you," are according to Thayer's *Lexicon* (1977 p. 256, # 2095): "*well… to do well* i.e. *act rightly…to be well off, fare well, prosper.*"

- The apostles and older men did not say, "If you don't do what we say you will be disfellowshipped, expelled, or shunned for the rest of your life."

- The teaching of disfellowshipping, expelling, and shunning of wrongdoers is a fabrication by the W/W/H, to keep excessive control over its members—manipulation by fear tactics.

Of further note is this point by Paul, found at 2 Cor. 1:24, "*Not that we lord it over your faith*, but we work with you for your joy, because it is by faith you stand firm" (NIV). The NWT version says, "not… masters over your faith" (italics added).

However the W/W/H's actions show that it does indeed "lord it over" duped and manipulated believers.

Some scriptures come to mind when it comes to judgment, which should engender due caution by those who judge others. For example, Rom. 3:23, states, "for *all have sinned* and *fall short* of the glory of God" (NIV and NWT; italics added).

Or note 1 John 2:1, 2: "My dear children, I write this to you so you will not sin. But if anybody does sin, we have an advocate with the Father—Jesus Christ, the Righteous one…the atoning sacrifice for our sins, and not only for ours [Christians'] but also *for the sins of the whole world*" (NIV) The NWT version uses the words, "a propitiatory sacrifice" rather than "atoning" (italics added).

> ➤ Notice that Jesus' ransom sacrifice was "for the sins of the whole world," and not just for current JWs; it would include all sincere persons in need of ransoming would it not?

I earlier discussed the fact that the W/W/H frequently follows a shotgun or draconian approach to discipline. For example, what is the difference, scripturally, between one who is "weak" and one who is "wicked?" If you were being judged and you were weak, how would you feel if those sitting in judgment viewed you as wicked instead?

Note 1 Cor. 8:9, which says, "Be careful, however, that the exercise of your rights does not become a *stumbling block to the weak*" (NIV and NWT; italics added). Those words would apply equally as much to a judicial committee of Jehovah's Witnesses—(the higher-ups) as they would to rank-and-file Witnesses as well as others. If it is good for the goose, it's good for the gander, wouldn't you agree?

If one were to cause stumbling for a person who is weak, that one will have to answer to God and Christ, in due time, for such action. The rule surely applies equally to all groups of people, the leaders and the rank-and-file; any groups of persons.

Thayer's *Lexicon* (1977 p. 80, # 770) notes the following, concerning the Greek word translated "weak" in this verse: "1 Cor. viii. 9 who is weak (in his feelings and conviction about things lawful), and I am not filled with a *compassionate sense* of the same weakness?" (italics added) Additionally, Paul notes at Rom. 15:1, "We who are strong ought to *bear with the failings* of the *weak* and not to please ourselves" (NIV). The NWT says, *"weaknesses"* rather than *"failings"* (italics added). Thayer's Greek-English *Lexicon* (1977 p. 12, # 102) says about this word for "failings" (NIV) or "weakness" (NWT): "1. *without strength, impotent*...fig. of Christians whose faith is not yet quite firm, Rom xv. 1." (italics his)

Should the weak be cut a little slack? Yes, of course!

Keeping in mind that *all have sinned* and fallen short of God's glory, what comes to your mind when you read the word "wicked?" Both Matt. 5:39 and 1 Cor. 5:13 use the same Greek word for "wicked." Matt. 5:39 says, "But I tell you, do not resist an *evil* [wicked] person...turn the other cheek" (NIV and NWT; italics added). 1 Cor. 5:13 says, *"Expel* the *wicked* person" (NIV). The NWT version has it, *"Remove* the *wicked* [man]" (italics and brackets added).

Thayer's *Lexicon* (1977 p. 530, # 4190) defines the word "wicked" in both of these verses in this way: "2. *bad, of a bad nature* or *condition*; b. in an ethical sense, *evil, wicked, bad,* etc...the evil-doer spoken of, 1 Cor. v. 13; *the evil* man, who injures you, Mt. v. 39.... is used pre-eminently of *the devil, the evil one.*"

Do you recognize that there is a very wide range of conduct, common among humankind that is called wicked? Since all have sinned and fall short of God's glory (Rom. 3:23), would you not expect that every human would be considered wicked or evil in at least some sense of the word, or to some degree?

Notice this point from Jesus' Sermon on the Mount found at Matt. 7:11, "if you, then, *although being wicked,* know how to give good gifts to your children, how much more so will your Father who is in the heavens give good things to those asking him?" (NWT) The NIV uses, *"though you are evil"* (italics added to both).

It is noteworthy that the words "wicked" or "evil," used above, are also used by Paul at 1 Cor. 5:13, where he says that such a man should be expelled or removed "from among you." These words could apply to any of us. Should all of us be removed? Would that make sense or be reasonable?

Matt. 7:11 is part of the Sermon on the Mount, so let's take a closer look to see who Jesus was talking to and what this really teaches us. Notice that Jesus' sermon starts out as he was talking to "the crowds" and his "disciples" (Matt. 5:1). Then, a little later, Jesus gives the command, at Matt. 7:1, 2, *"Do not judge,* or you too will be judged. For in the same way you *judge others, you will be judged,* and with the measure you use, it will be measured to you" (NIV and NWT; italics added).

Keeping in mind what Jesus said at Matthew 7:11, to the effect that even the wicked know how to give good gifts to their kids, he was obviously indicating that even his disciples and that crowd were to at least some degree considered to be wicked. This fact must always be considered in judging others or injustice will prevail.

What kind of people did Jesus come to the earth to save, anyway? Matt. 9 tells us that Jesus called as his disciples (and even ate and had association with) "tax collectors and sinners" (verses 9, 10). This, of course, upset the Pharisees, who complained to his disciples about his eating with such people (verse 11). But Jesus heard their complaints and said at Matt. 9: 12, 13, "It is not the healthy who need a doctor, but the sick. But go and learn what this means: 'I desire mercy, not sacrifice.' For I have not come to call the righteous, but sinners" (NIV) the NWT version is similar.

Do you recall Jesus' illustration concerning the Pharisee and the tax collector (Luke 18:9–14)? Please read all six verses to get the full flavor of what Jesus was teaching, by using these men as examples.

Both men went up to the temple to pray. The Pharisee's attitude was, "Thank God I am not like other men, extortioners, unrighteous, adulterers, or even as bad as this tax collector." He bragged about his fasting and giving of the tithe. (Look how good I am he thought) He really looked good...*to himself!*

The poor tax collector didn't even raise his eyes heavenward; he just kept beating his chest, saying, "God, have mercy on me, a sinner" (Luke 18:13, NIV and NWT).

The next verse of that illustration (Luke 18:14) shows Jesus' judgment in the matter: "I tell you that this man [the tax collector], rather than the other, went home *justified* before God. For all those who exalt themselves will be humbled and those who humble themselves will be exalted" (NIV). The NWT version uses the term "more righteous" instead of "justified."

The word "justified/righteous" according to *Strong's Greek Dictionary*, (1984, p. 150, # 1344) means: "*to render* (i.e. *show or regard* as) *just or innocent:* free, justify (-ier), be righteous."

If we consider the basic meanings of the words associated with sin, it assists our understanding. Thayer's *Lexicon* (1977, p. 30, # 266, 265 and 264) gives these definitions:

- sin: A failing to hit the mark, a bad action, evil deed

- sins: a sin, evil deed

- sinned: *to miss the mark, then to err, be mistaken,* lastly *to miss or wander from the path of uprightness and honor, to do or go wrong*

If we think of it like target practice with a bow and arrow, it will help our understanding. If we hit the bull's-eye, we would have hit the exact center of the target—perfect! If we hit within the third circle out from the center, that's not bad. But if we don't even hit the target, we would need a lot more practice.

If we turn our back to the target and shoot in the opposite direction, we would have *deliberately missed* it. So it is with sin. We can miss the mark by a little or miss by a mile, or we can, not even try to do what is right, having an "I don't care" attitude. Sinning is a matter of degrees. What kind of sin is one talking about, and how much sin is to be forgiven? Further, what kinds of sin are forgiven, and what kind cannot be forgiven?

Let's examine the Apostle Peter's question to Jesus about how many times he had to forgive a brother who sinned against him? Jesus' reply was "seventy-seven times" (Matt. 18:21, 22 - NWT). In discussing the need for mercy, Jesus gave an illustration (Matt. 18:23–35) about the unforgiving slave. He was shown mercy (by his master) when he begged for it, but then denied mercy to a fellow slave who likewise begged for it. That attitude landed him in prison for being unforgiving. The conclusion of the story says, at Matt. 18:35, "*In like manner* my heavenly Father will also deal with you *if you do not forgive* each one his bother from your hearts" (NWT; italics added) The NIV makes the same point. Does that not cover all sins others may commit against us?

Perhaps you recall the "Lord's Prayer" (also referred to as the "Our Father" prayer), where we ask God to forgive us "*as we also* have *forgiven our debtors*" (Matt. 6:12, NIV and NWT; italics added). Notice that, when any person or group refuses to be forgiving, they are begging for the same type of treatment from God when they need and ask for his forgiveness.

But is there anything that God will not forgive? The answer is found in the Bible at Matt.12:31, 32, which says, "Anyone speaking a word against the Son of Man will be forgiven, but *anyone who speaks a word against the Holy Spirit will not be forgiven*, either in this age or in the age to come"

(NIV; italics added). The NWT version uses the word "blasphemy," and "holy spirit" is not capitalized.

Think of what that scripture is saying: *one will be forgiven for speaking against Jesus*, but not for speaking against the Holy Spirit (NIV) or holy spirit (NWT). However the W/W/H will not forgive anyone for even questioning it, let alone speaking against it or its failed prophecies or other errors. Isn't something wrong with this picture? How unreasonable, unrealistic, unthinking, and hypocritical they have become!

No one was ever disfellowshipped, expelled, or shunned for speaking against even an apostle in the first century. Recall Acts 17:10 and 11 where the Beroeans were commended for checking the scriptures each day to check up on Paul's truthfulness. What is the hierarchy afraid of?

Remember, Jesus died for the forgiveness of the sins of all mankind. Rom. 5:12, tells us, "death spread to all men because they *had all sinned.*" - NIV and NWT (italics added)

According to the Bible, the only human exempted from that statement was Jesus himself.

Another relevant scripture is Rom. 6:7, "because *anyone who dies* is *set free from sin*" (NIV; italics added). The NWT version uses the term "acquitted" instead of "set free." The words, "set free from sin" and "acquitted from sin" are defined by Thayer's *Lexicon* (1977, p. 150, # 1344) in this way: *"to make, to render righteous or such as he ought to be; to show, exhibit, evince, one to be righteous, such as he is and wishes himself to be considered."*

In other words, we are all imperfect and sin (miss the mark), with no exceptions, yet we are "freed, acquitted, considered righteous from sin" at death.

Look up the word "judge" in any concordance, and you will find that although some men did judging, God is definitely spoken of as the final judge of all humankind. After Jesus' arrival in the first century, a change in procedure, one more beneficial for humanity than judgment by imperfect men came into being; what was that?

Jesus' words show that "all judging was committed ('entrusted,' NIV) to him" (John 5:22). So any and all judging done by men, whether it be on the part of the Pharisees, the members of the W/W/H, or others regardless of who they are, their judgments represent *their opinions*. At times those judgments have been proven to have been flawed; sometimes they have been deliberately wrong—and so they can by no means represent one's final judgment.

Aren't we happy to leave the final judgment of all persons in the hands of God through Jesus Christ? Thus they will receive a judgment based on true justice and mercy!

Since all wrongdoing and sins are "a matter of degrees," and all people are totally deficient in the matter of reading hearts, unable consistently to render accurate judgments regarding a person's motives and feelings about God and what his will is, the wise course is to leave judging up to God and his son rather than to make a major issue over what any individual man or religious hierarchy demands to be their right in the matter of judging fellow humans.

Don't Even Say Hello!—What?

The W/W/H insists that loyal, obedient JWs not speak even one word to anyone who is disfellowshipped, one who is deemed should be shunned; it doesn't matter to it what the reason was or how serious the alleged offense was deemed to have been. The Watchtower (September 15, 1981, pp. 24–26) says, "And we all know from our experience over the years that a simple 'Hello' to someone can be the first step that develops into a conversation and maybe even a friendship. Would we want to take that first step with a disfellowshipped person?"

Obviously, the writers of that Watchtower (actually the W/W/H) want you to think, "No, of course not. I would be scared to death to do such a thing." That kind of question is manipulative and indicates excessive control; both are sect-like and cult-like traits are they not?

So what does the Bible really say about not "speaking a single word" to a so-called disfellowshipped person? (The relevant scripture is 2 John 7–11 please read all thirteen verses.)

In verses 7–9, note that there are many deceivers, who do not acknowledge Jesus Christ as having come in the flesh; such ones are called "deceivers" and "the antichrist." Then we are cautioned to watch out because if anyone does not continue in the teaching of Christ, he does not have God either. Then 2 John 10 tells us, "If anyone comes to you and does not bring this teaching, [Which teaching?] Verse 7, "not confessing Jesus Christ as coming in the flesh," never receive him into your homes or 'say a greeting'* to him" (NWT; brackets added).

The footnote * on the word "greeting" says, "Lit., to be rejoicing." Strong's Greek Dictionary (p. 77, # 5463) says of this word, "to be "cheerful, calmly happy or well-off...be well...be glad, God speed, greeting hail, joy (fully), rejoice" (some italics added).

Does 2 John 10 seem to prohibit saying anything, even one word, to this wrongdoer, the antichrist? Or is the writer suggesting prohibiting, friendly, cordial, joyful, rejoicing, or glad greetings? Does the verse prohibit asking a wrongdoer, perhaps a family member, if he or she is OK or if the person needs help?

The elder's book, *Shepherding the Flock of God* (WTB&TS 2010), lists no fewer than thirty-four major categories of wrongdoing that one can be disfellowshipped for, with an additional thirty-plus additional sub-points which list specific actions that can bring judicial action and disfellowshipping (for a total of sixty-four wrongs). From this book, compare two of these. Should they carry the same sanction? Which would God consider to be worse—murder (p. 59) or heavy petting? (pp. 61–65) Both are disfellowshipping offences, and the W/W/H applies the identical penalty—*shunning!*

Listed under the heading, "Greed, gambling, extortion" (WTB&TS 2010, pp. 70), we find the offence of one "who is greedy and unrepentantly extorts *a high bride price*." Yes, that is a disfellowshipping offence. How about gluttony? (p. 67); those are both disfellowshipping offences with the same sanction.

Do you think all of the above highlighted "wrongs" should carry the same penalty—disfellowshipping and shunning—with the additional penalty that any active JW who is caught talking to or eating with such a disfellowshipped person could likewise be disfellowshipped? Do you think that would be discipline "to the proper degree" (Jer. 30:11), from God's viewpoint? I don't either.

Recall the statement made earlier, that the W/W/H follows a shotgun, draconian approach to its disciplining procedures and practices toward any who are disfellowshipped. One size fits all! One is not "sort of" disfellowshipped. It's like being pregnant; you either are, or you are not. Does this approach make sense? *The same sanction?*

If it does not make sense to you, what do you think of the W/W/H that has ordered such a practice from its appointed elders? Recall my example of one who stole five bucks, compared to the one who stole a gun and shot a fellow classmate. Are not the W/W/H's disfellowshipping and shunning procedures cult-like, void of all logic or reason and not in harmony with the scriptures Such a shotgun approach, with the same penalty for every offense, is dead wrong.

The "one size fits all" mentality in the matter of discipline would not be acceptable in any other venue (for example if a judge handed out exactly the same penalty to a sex offender as to one who simply ran a red light). How can it possibly be considered proper? It does not make sense in either secular justice or so-called religious justice.

Getting back to what the apostle John wrote, who is the book of 2 John addressed to? Verse one provides an answer: "The older man to the chosen lady and to her children whom I truly love" (NWT). The NIV says, "The elder" to the "chosen lady."

- ➤ Second John is not from the apostles and older men, nor from some so-called "governing body."

- ➤ It is not addressed to even one congregation, let alone to the whole body of Christians back then.

- ➤ It is not discussing expelling wrongdoers. The only ones who expelled others at that time were the Pharisees.

- ➤ It does not say that all wrongdoers are the antichrist, just as not all wrongdoers making a court appearance in our day are guilty of murder.

- ➤ The only wrongdoer who is discussed in these verses is the "antichrist."

Strong's Greek Dictionary (p. 13, # 500) defines the antichrist as "*An opponent* of the Messiah—antichrist." Who does John himself identify as the "antichrist?" Please note what is said at 1 John 2:22, "Who is the liar if it is not the one that denies that Jesus is the Christ? This is the antichrist, the one that denies the Father and the Son" (NWT; the NIV says the same).

Do these facts not prove that the W/W/H has indeed gone way beyond the things that are actually written in the Bible, in its efforts to foist a draconian style of discipline on some of its members? Such an idea is not even taught in the Bible, This type of discipline was not practiced in the first century, by Christians, or in fact even by this hierarchy until 1952.

The elaborate and specious reasoning presented in the September 15, 1981 *Watchtower* (pp. 24-26 - previously considered) is based on one verse only (2 John 10) in the hierarchy's attempt to justify its precious, controlling doctrine of "disfellowshipping and shunning" of those whom it has judged to be wicked.

It has used its shotgun, draconian mentality to foist the doctrine of disfellowshipping and shunning on millions of former and present believers, by using or inventing words not to be found in any Bible translation (including its own). It has applied verses completely out of context that are contrary, not only to reason, but also to the meaning of the biblical Greek words they are taken from, while it proclaims itself to be the guardian of truth.

This hierarchy has also failed to instruct elders of the need to exercise mercy and compassion in the manner in which they judge their rank-and-file members, who are considered wrongdoers. Otherwise they will bring an unwanted adverse judgment back on themselves. Indeed, the hierarchy's merciless doctrine has produced rotten fruitage that can be smelled all around the world, resulting in millions of God-fearing persons abandoning the organization in disgust; no doubt such actions will result in many more following suit for the very same reasons. They refuse to tolerate further deceptive and hypocritical abuses to be heaped upon them and their families.

We all will reap what we sow; what kind of judgment are the elders likely to get if they follow their hierarchy's oppressive procedures? The members of the W/W/H have become exactly like the Pharisees, of whom Jesus said their traditions had made God's word invalid (Matt. 15:6).

About Apostasy:

I now want to draw your attention to the word "apostasy." It is the first or second most common reason given by a judicial committee for disfellowshipping one who is even questioning why the W/W/H has been guilty of proclaiming over thirty false prophecies about the end of the world or events related to that end.

So how does the hierarchy define that word, and has it been deceptive in this teaching also, as it has been in so many others?

Reasoning from the Scriptures (WTB&TS 1989, p. 34) gives this definition of the word: "Apostasy is abandoning or deserting the worship and service of God, actually a rebellion against Jehovah God. Some apostates profess to know and serve God but reject teachings or requirements set out in his Word. Others claim to believe the Bible but reject Jehovah's organization."

The following facts about the word "apostasy" or related words found in the Bible are relevant to our discussion:

1. *Strong's Exhaustive Concordance of the Bible* (1884, © 1994) does not contain the word "apostasy" even once.

2. The *Comprehensive Concordance* (WTB&TS 1973), lists a total of nineteen different scriptures found in their own NWT which uses that word "apostasy" or a related word.

3. In comparing those same verses in eleven of my personal, collection of different translations, the vast majority use other words such as "villainy," "profaneness," "corrupt," "lies," "futile hopes," "iniquity," "ungodliness," "impious," "hate," "wickedness," "wickedly," "hypocrite," "hypocritical," "hypocrites," and "worthless"—words that do not even imply a falling away or apostasy.

4. In not one single instance, not even in the NWT version of the Bible, does the verse in any way imply that any person was formally expelled, removed, or disfellowshipped from a Christian congregation because of being labeled an apostate.

However there is a term, "blasphemous words," that some were killed for by enemies of Christianity asserting false accusations against them. The Jewish hierarchy and members of the Sanhedrin were quick to search for people who were willing to testify falsely against such ones.

For example, the charges, by the false witnesses against Stephen were that he spoke "blasphemous words against Moses and God" (Acts 6:11

NIV) based on such false testimony, he was executed. The exposé he gave as recorded at Acts 7:1–60, about Israelite history was truthful and stung those religious leaders roundly.

In the case of Jesus' execution (Mark 14:55–65), false testimony with a charge of "blasphemy" was involved. As was the latter case with Stephen, it was the Jewish Sanhedrin who again orchestrated the whole "kangaroo court" proceedings against him as well.

So what is blasphemy? Thayer's *Greek-English Lexicon* (1977, p. 102, # 988) defines that word to mean "railing, reviling, slander, detraction, speech injurious to another's good name."

There is no record at all in the New Testament of first century Christians disfellowshipping, excommunicating, or expelling anybody for "blasphemy," just as there is no record of anyone being "disfellowshipped" for "apostasy." So what could be the rationale for such action to be taken on the part of the W/W/H against its members?

First, consider this warning given by the Apostle Paul, which is very relevant. 1 Cor. 4:6 says, "learn from us the meaning of the saying, *'Do not go beyond what is written.'* Then you will not be puffed up in being a follower of one of us over against the other" (NIV). The NWT version has, *"learn the [rule]"* (italics added; brackets theirs).

The *Watchtower* (April 1, 1986, pp. 30, 31) asks, "Why have Jehovah's Witnesses disfellowshipped or (excommunicated) for apostasy some who still profess belief in God, the Bible, and Jesus Christ?" Before I note their answer, please recall that the word "disfellowship" and related words do not occur at all in the Bible. The word "expelled" is used only twice in connection with actions taken against a human, and it only involves actions by the Pharisees in the first century against persons who expressed faith in Jesus.

As you consider the W/W/H's answer, given in the abovementioned Watchtower, please ask yourself this question: "Has the hierarchy gone beyond the things that are written?" And if so, what could possibly be its motive?

In the specious answer given by the hierarchy in the above referenced *Watchtower* (April 1, 1986, p. 30), it asserts that many religious organizations which claim to be Christian don't have a problem with allowing opposing views. The W/W/H feels justified in its opposite position because its members say that those who permit contradictory views cannot feel certain about what Bible truth is or what it is not.

Then they assert that, unlike the Pharisees who couldn't speak with authority, they can. How can they say that honestly? They have failed more "end-of-the-world prophecies" than any other group since the first century! Please recall what you learned in chapter 6, that the W/W/H has proclaimed over thirty such false prophecies—not one of them came true. What basis could there possibly be for that hierarchy's members to claim to speak with truthful "authority?" - They have a 100 percent failure rate for *their prophecies!*

Next, the article refers to 1 Cor. 1:10 as a basis for not tolerating divisions in the congregation. Is that what the Apostle Paul really said, or are the writers starting to go "beyond the things that are written" again? These are Paul's words: "I appeal to you, brothers and sisters, in the name of our Lord Jesus Christ that all of you agree with one another in what you say and that there be no divisions among you, but that you be perfectly united in mind and thought" (NIV). The NWT version says the same. Is there any example of what was going on? Oh, yes, verses 12 and 13 continue: "What I mean is this that each one of you says: "I belong to Paul," "But I to Apollos," "But I to Ce'phas," "But I to Christ." The Christ exists divided" (NWT). The NIV makes the same point, but uses the words "I follow," rather than "I belong."

Is it not clear that what Paul is cautioning against is the congregation following different Christian elders back then [their hierarchy], rather than Christ Jesus?

The W/W/H, by going "beyond the things that are written," has over and over again had to change its teachings because of its failures. That would not be a problem if it had just stuck to what the Bible does say rather than presenting prophecy or other matters for which there is no scriptural proof only specious speculation (such as the identity of the "governing body" or the "faithful and discreet slave").

That *Watchtower* article (April 1, 1986, pp. 30, 31) also refers to Gal.1:8, 9 as further proof that there should be no divisions; but the first part of the book of Galatians is dealing with the issue of circumcision and how Gentiles should be viewed. Gal 2:11–14 points out that it was the elders Peter, James, and John in the congregation who were causing the problem in putting on a pretense and that even Barnabas was tripped up by their actions. It was their hierarchy that was causing the divisions!

The *Watchtower* article contains specious reasoning, but such reasoning is false. Then the writers cap the article off by referring to Hymenaeus and Philetus. Pay special attention to what these two men were actually being accused of. What was their fault that was so wrong? As 2 Tim. 2:17, 18 explains, "their word will spread like gangrene. Hymenaeus and Philetus…have deviated from the truth, saying that the *resurrection has already occurred,* and they are subverting the faith of some" (NWT).

Next that same *Watchtower* article makes the point that "Nothing indicates that these two men didn't believe in God, or the Bible or even Jesus sacrifice. Yet *on this one point [alone] they were 'branded apostate.'*" (Such a branding was *not* by any scriptures, but rather, by the W/W/H.)

There are two points here to recognize. Paul said, in verse 16, to "shun empty speeches," not to shun Hymenaeus and Philetus. Nor are either of these men called "apostates" in the scriptures; nor is there any comment about congregational action being taken against them. They were never disfellowshipped or excommunicated from the congregation. That is simply a dogmatic statement by the W/W/H.

Additionally, there is a major point one may not have thought about. If we check back to chapter 6, and refresh our memory, guess what we will find? There were numerous prophecies given by the W/W/H that involved the "resurrection." What specific dates were prophesied by that hierarchy for when the resurrection *would occur?*

Of the list of over thirty failed prophecies, pay attention specifically to these:

- # 12. 1914: the Rapture
- # 21. 1925: the Rapture again
- # 23. 1925: the resurrection to life on earth of the faithful men of old
- # 32. 1975: the Rapture (for the third time) and the start of the Millennium.

Is it possible, that the W/W/H's failures "subverted the faith" of many rank-and-file JWs? Absolutely yes! And on that same one point.

Do you wonder why three different dates were given? Each one in turn failed to be a true prophecy; and again, all four of those prophecies involved the "resurrection."

Lest we miss the fact: It was on this "one basic point," of the resurrection, that the *Watchtower* article claims that Hymenaeus and Philetus were "branded apostates." So then, how do you think the W/W/H should be branded? Would not is fallacious prophecies regarding the resurrection, brand it as apostates as well? Yes, absolutely! The hierarchy stands condemned *by its own* words and actions!

Can you discern these facts? Or might you feel you should cover your ears and eyes? Has not the W/W/H clearly been like the "pot" that called the "kettle" black in this matter? What gross hypocrisy! What can help one decide?

Recall that there are only two scriptures (1 Tim. 1:20 and 2 Tim. 2:17), listed in the W/W/H's *Concordance*, that even mention either of these men. Neither account says one word that indicates that any formal congregational action occurred, such as shunning, disfellowshipping, excommunicating, or expelling them.

In 2 Tim. 2:16, quoted earlier, the writer says to "*shun* the empty *speeches* that violate what is holy." It does not say to shun the two men whom the W/W/H insists on branding as "apostates" (even though the scriptures never say that was the case). Has it not clearly gone "beyond the things that are written–again?

Why do you think this is so? Why does this hierarchy seem to be hell-bent on preventing anyone from in any way questioning its errors or the honesty of its procedures? Do you recall the six earmarks of a religious sect or cult listed by Witness founder, C. T. Russell, as quoted in the Introduction of this book? They are as follows:

- The mind must be given up entirely to the sect
- The sect decides what is truth or error, not you
- You must accept the decisions of the sect
- You must ignore individual thought
- You must avoid personal investigation
- Your conscience becomes enslaved to the sect

Has not such extreme control been clearly in evidence in the disfellowshipping and shunning procedures, especially against anyone who questions the legitimacy of those procedures or teachings (ones they label as "apostates")?

Do you recall Jesus' words recorded at John 8:32? "The truth will set you free!" NWT

Is there anything to be feared if one is teaching or believing what is the truth? Can you imagine Jesus, God's perfect son, resenting or condemning anyone for investigating what he was teaching? What would be the only reason for fearing such an investigation or fearing a probe into one's actions? Would it not be only if one was trying to hide the truth?

It is in many ways like trying to remember what you said about a matter. If you always tell the truth, it is easy to remember what you said. It only gets difficult if you have not told the truth and have been deceptive. Remember the words of Sir Walter Scott: "Oh, what a tangled web we weave when first we practice to deceive." The W/W/H has been spinning such complex webs for so long that not even that hierarchy can remember what it has previously said.

Thank God for the printed page. If a person is shown what he or she has already written, and it is factual, it becomes impossible to deny. Of course, that is what Stephen did in recounting Israelite history to the members of the Jewish Sanhedrin. Because there was no way to rebut or deny the truth of what he said (it had been recorded in the biblical scrolls), they panicked. They put their hands over their ears to stop hearing, and they killed him. Clear earmarks (no pun intended) of those who hated and could not tolerate the truth; their conduct labeled them as panicky fanatics.

Recall that I mentioned, earlier, that the W/W/H has waffled many times in its demands to elders regarding how to handle the disfellowshipping and shunning procedures. The following are some examples of going from the strict and draconian to the more reserved and merciful and then back again to a strict mode of operation.

Starting in 1952, when the disfellowshipping procedure was implemented, an ever increasingly harsh approach to discipline became the norm. In the *Watchtower* (November 15, 1952, p. 703), the writers noted regarding apostates, "Being limited by the laws of the worldly nation in which we live…we can take action against apostates only to a certain extent…The law of the land and God's law…forbid us to kill apostates." (Sounds like, "Oh what a shame we can't kill them," doesn't it?)

Then this hierarchy, through the *Watchtower* (July 15, 1961, p. 420), tightened up the screws a little more, even trying to negate what Jesus said. That *Watchtower* says, "Jesus encouraged his followers to *love their enemies*, but God's word also says to 'hate what is bad.' When a person persists in…badness after knowing what is right…, then in order to hate what is bad *a Christian must hate the person* with whom the badness is inseparably linked." [That is not what Jesus said! Do not their words contradict his directive?] (italics added)

Here they negated scriptural counsel and replaced it with their own ideas and agenda. Is that not clearly going beyond the things that are written? No one gave them permission to rewrite Jesus' counsel, did they?

Next came the *Watchtower* in 1974 (August 1, pp. 460–473) with a less harsh, more balanced viewpoint. For example, after referring to the lax position, taken by the congregation in Corinth, in the first century, they said, "There is a parallel danger…going too far in the other direction…to rigidity and hardness." The article goes on to give examples of a "balanced viewpoint", saying not to be "needlessly unkind and inhumane…So, not '*mixing in company*' with a person, or treating such one as '*a man of the nations*,' does not prevent us from being decent, courteous, considerate and humane." (italics added)

Later, the W/W/H *went back to a more draconian mode of action* and so tightened up the screws again; the *Watchtower* (January 15, 2007, p. 20) saying: "While caring for *necessary family matters* may require *some contact* with the disfellowshipped person, a Christian parent should strive to *avoid needless association.*" (italics added)

Most recently the January 15, 2013 *Watchtower* arrived and on (p. 15), the W/W/H tightened up the screws again: "Jehovah knows your pain, but it would be unwise to take a course of action toward a disfellowshipped family member that might displease Jehovah." Then the article recommends that the JW try to cope, but they should never blame themselves for the way they are treating their family member who was disfellowshipped. Indeed, each one must carry his own load, *but,* what they really mean is for rank-and-file JWs to conform to the load the W/W/H has imposed upon them; an unscriptural harsh load.

Although the article admits that Jehovah has given all of us the freedom to think for ourselves it adds a *Watchtower* twist by applying more pressure to force adherents to conform to their spin by allowing the W/W/H's directives to become the controlling factors in any decisions they make on disfellowshipping issues. In other words one has free will, but, *don't use it*; just do as the hierarchy dictates.

> Do you recall the earmarks of a sect or cult?

An area I haven't yet discussed is how some circuit overseers will go to extremes to get local elders to do their bidding for them, even if it means perverting justice. I have served on many, many appeal judicial committees. One in particular comes to mind. It was a Sunday afternoon, and I got a call from the circuit overseer asking me to serve as the chairman of an appeal committee for a congregation in northern Minnesota at 8:00 p.m. that evening.

I advised the brother, "I have to leave on a flight at 4:00 a.m. That would not work for me; I need some sleep first."

"No problem," he insisted. "It is an open-and-shut case. There are two eye witnesses; it will take no time at all." Guess how it went?

The young man, sporting several tattoos, had been accused of smoking (not allowed for JWs), and there were two "eye witnesses." But what we found out was that the two witnesses were two (literal) sisters, aged nine and seven.

When we questioned them, we learned that the nine-year-old thought she might have seen the young man smoking, but she really *was not sure*. She told her seven-year-old sister what she thought she had seen. And those two were what were called the "eye witnesses."

Needless to say, the members of the appeal committee reversed the decision by their judicial committee to disfellowship the young man; he had continually denied that he had been smoking. There were no legitimate witnesses who could testify that he had been smoking. To have upheld the original decision would have been fraudulent.

That does not guarantee that he was telling the truth. But it was a fact that there *were not two eye witnesses*. When I told the circuit overseer of our decision, he was noticeably disappointed and definitely irritated. He did not apologize for the pressure tactic he had pushed on me either.

Two of the elders on that congregation's judicial committee had an obvious disdain for any brother with tattoos, such as this young man had. Some months later, both of these two brothers ended up removed as elders over another matter.

I could name at least three appeal committee cases where this same type of problem occurred, where the elders had been prejudiced and deliberately rendered fraudulent verdicts. I have never personally recommended (as part of a judicial committee, regular or appeal) that a person be disfellowshipped unless I felt absolutely sure he or she was guilty, with an admission or with two valid witnesses. If I was going to make a mistake, I wanted it to be on the side of mercy. Even at that, I am aware of the possibility that I could have been wrong in my assessment of any case. If I have made any mistakes in this area, I certainly apologize for my wrong at this time; I am truly sorry.

As a final point that clearly brands the W/W/H's procedures involved in "disfellowshipping" to be totally without any scriptural basis, please note the following from *Insight On The Scriptures* (WTB&TS vol. 2, 1988, pp. 233–235), under the heading, "Legal Case," and the subtopic, "Procedure." (Please read all three pages dealing with the Israelites.) "If a case could not be cleared up by the parties involved; then the legal cases were heard, publicly at the city's gates. The procedure was available to Israelites, including women, slaves, as well as alien residents."

The entire proceeding was open to the public. Witnesses faced each other and heard one another's testimony. It was not private, hidden, or conducted in cloak-and-dagger fashion, as is *always* the case with W/W/H judicial committee meetings. It is a fact that the legal proceedings conducted by its judicial committees are never allowed to be recorded. No legal representation is ever allowed. The entire case is heard behind closed doors, and witnesses are not allowed to hear each other's testimony. Can you imagine a legal court hearing in the United States without the whole case being recorded?

In the first century, such a case, involving Jesus, was conducted by the Jewish Supreme Court. The W/W/H style of justice is similar in many ways, as you have seen from this chapter: conducted behind closed doors, lacking real justice. Its judicial procedures are often conducted in "kangaroo court" style. Even *Insight on the Scriptures* (WTB&TS 1988, Vol. 2, p. 235), mentioned above, under the heading, "Jesus' Trial," calls those proceedings to be: "The greatest travesty of justice ever committed."

And yet that is the way the hierarchy has directed legal cases in its congregations to be handled for disfellowshipping procedures. (This has especially been the case if the ones dragged into the judicial meeting are accused of exposing any of the W/W/H's wrongs). Such have been their normal procedures since 1952, when the disfellowshipping, shunning procedures came into existence.

What would I call it? Not the "greatest travesty of justice ever committed," but "a great travesty in *imitation* of the greatest travesty ever committed," mentioned above.

Shame on the W/W/H! The results of its judicial proceedings, as the title of this chapter suggests, have proven to be "Disfellowshipping: The Dark Side leading to the Destruction of Families."

Rather than the W/W/H displaying a truthful and Christ-like mode of operation, its lack of mercy and its deception are obvious, given the facts just presented; this is also attested to by millions, of at one time loyal members having abandoned not Jehovah God but this apostate organization. It has followed the Pharisees' example and has proven to be every bit as corrupt leading toward its eventual demise, just as became the fate of ancient Israel in the first century.

REVIEW POINTS:

1. People are not born deceptive; they become that way.

2. The W/W/H's disfellowshipping procedure *does not* imitate any procedure of a Christian congregation in the first century.

3. The actions of disfellowshipping, excommunication, and expulsion were not Christian procedures. The closest thing to any such action was practiced by the Pharisees against those who believed in Jesus. Disfellowshipping is fraudulent.

4. While the Bible does approve "of shunning false words or empty speeches," no such formal procedure was ever practiced by congregations in the first century against any person.

5. God definitely recognizes that there are "degrees of wrongdoing." This fact is clearly shown by the way he disciplined the ancient nation of Israel "to the proper degree." You may be thinking, "I agree; there is something radically wrong with the W/W/H's teachings and procedures of disfellowshipping, expelling, or shunning wrongdoers. OK, but if its procedures are wrong, what scriptural procedure is there for disciplining a wrongdoer and doing it to the proper degree?" How would it work?

The next chapter, entitled, "If Not Disfellowshipping: What Could Work, and Has Worked—and How?" will explain.

CHAPTER 11

IF NOT DISFELLOWSHIPPING: WHAT COULD WORK, AND HAS WORKED–AND HOW?

- Do you discern a difference between laws and principles? Can one "trump" the other?
- Can either one provide an advantage for the person trying to follow a Christian course of conduct?
- What do the scriptures say about man-made laws that negate God's words?
- What kind of fruit do you expect from a rotten tree?

A Quick Review:

As you noted from chapter 10, especially if you checked all of the references, the teaching by the W/W/H on the matter of both disfellowshipping and shunning (since the policy's inception in 1952) has produced rotten fruitage; it is unscriptural and unreasonable, and you will see in this chapter that it violates a manifold number of basic Bible principles.

- The word "disfellowshipping" is never used in the Bible; the closest thing to it (being expelled from the synagogue) was a procedure the Pharisees foisted on any Jews who confessed Jesus.

- The word, "shun," is mentioned in the Bible, but is never applied to a person, only to things such as empty speeches, gossip, and foolish questioning.

- The only thing that disfellowshipping and shunning conform to, as noted by Jesus, is that "a *rotten tree* [teaching] produces *rotten fruit*" (Matt. 7:18–20).

- Also, millions of past and present believers would characterize the disfellowshipping teaching to be rotten to the core; it has produced nothing but rotten fruitage—fruitage suitable only to the W/W/H.

- But is there a scriptural procedure that can protect both the individual and the congregation from lawless people? Of course. But first, some preliminary information will help lay the groundwork for it.

Webster's Dictionary, (1913) defines a "law" as "a general rule established by authority." The word "principle" is defined as "A fundamental truth; a comprehensive law or doctrine, from which others are derived… a general truth, an elementary proposition."

Some of the positive advantages of a principle as opposed to a law are that a principle is basic and broader in scope, and it allows an individual to think and make decisions by being able to apply the principle in his or her own life. The person, and not a self-righteous religious hierarchy, chooses to take responsibility for his or her own decisions and actions (Rom. 14:12).

Let's consider some basic principles (ignored by the W/W/H) that will help us to see why the disfellowshipping procedure produces rotten fruitage.

First of all, recall the "Golden Rule" (Matt. 7:12). "All things, therefore, that you want men to do to *you*, you also must likewise do to *them*; this, in fact, is what the Law and the Prophets mean" (NWT; italics added). The NIV says "this sums up…" instead of "this, in fact, is what…"

- Does that principle tell us exactly what to do?

- Or does it require us to think and make application?

- That principle "trumps" a lesser, man-made rule.

IF NOT DISFELLOWSHIPPING: WHAT COULD WORK, AND HAS WORKED—AND HOW?

The scriptural procedure that trumps the disfellowshipping and shunning procedure is called, in the NWT, being marked [or marking]. A majority of other translations use words such as "note," "take note," "take special note," or "noting," depending on which translation you choose to check.

So before we go further, what does the W/W/H say about its teaching on "marked" or "marking?" It's book, *Organized to Do Jehovah's Will* (WTB&TS 2005), explains their policies; under the subtopic, "Marking Disorderly Ones" (pp. 150–151), the book makes the following statements and assertions based on 2 Thess. 3:6–15. It will help you to read all of the verses in that passage. Page 150 asserts that this applies to "certain ones who were walking disorderly...could exert an unhealthy influence." You will find that the W/W/H includes some practices for noting or marking which are not given in the scriptures. These are noted in the list below with bold type.

- Such people display a "**flagrant disregard for theocratic order.**"

- These people engage in "**scheming to take material advantage of others.**"

- They engage in "**indulging in entertainment that is clearly improper.**" (Whose viewpoint rules?)

- "**After giving repeated admonition**...[if] **he persists**...*talk should be given* **to the congregation.**"

- The *Organized* book (WTB&TS 2005, p. 150) says that it is the **elders that make the decision *about marking first***, and then the members of the congregation jump onboard and comply. The scripture **does not say that either.**

- The W/W/H says to give admonition first; then, if there is no response, a talk is given. But notice that at the conclusion of the account in 2 Thess. 3:15, it says, "**continue admonishing him**

as a brother," not to admonish him and then give a talk. The W/W/H puts the cart before the horse, doesn't it?

- Notice that six out of these six assertions made by the W/W/H *do not harmonize* with what the scriptures say. Do you realize that represents 100 percent of the time that the hierarchy has it wrong?

- Is it not, as usual, going "beyond the things that are written?" The W/W/H's words negate God's words. Why wouldn't that surprise many?

It applies its own twist; it wants to "do the marking" (as if putting a literal mark on the wrongdoer).

In this way, it gets to be in the driver's seat and keep a stranglehold on its followers. This prevents rank-and-file JWs from using their own heads in the marking matter.

Clearly, the W/W/H's actions are all about keeping control of the minds and consciences of its members, in true sect-like and cult-like fashion as has been its mode of operation for the majority of its modern history.

You no doubt recall that the six ear-marks by C. T. Russell have continued to come back to haunt the upper echelon of the W/W/H, because of its decisions that it insists must be accepted without question.

With the W/W/H, it is not just a problem of how scriptures should be understood, interpreted, or applied. There are numerous Bible principles that this hierarchy flagrantly violates in addition to the Golden Rule, in order to make room for its pet disfellowshipping and shunning procedures of "extreme control" (a cult-like trait). These will be considered shortly.

Strong's *Greek Dictionary of the New Testament* (p. 65, #4593) gives the following definition of the word "note:" "to distinguish, i.e. mark (for avoidance) note." Thayer's *Greek-English Lexicon,* (1977, p. 574, # 4593) adds the words, *"to mark or note for one's self"* (italics his). This is significant. Why so?

This involves all in the congregation since the book of Second Thessalonians is addressed to the whole congregation. It *does not say* in 2 Thess. 1:1, "This is a *secret letter* just *for* the *elders.*" (Only the W/W/H feels that way.)

If we examine a couple of scriptures, we will be helped to catch on to how, and to whom, we should apply principles such as the Golden Rule. Consider the word "neighbor," to get a better appreciation of what Jesus commanded and how his words would apply to us. After discussing the greatest commandment, to "love God first of all," Jesus noted at Matt 22:39 and 40 that "The second [principle] like it is this, 'you must love your neighbor as yourself.' On these two commandments the whole Law hangs, and the Prophets" (NWT and NIV). What a profound statement!

The "Law" refers to the Pentateuch, the first five books of the Bible—Genesis through Deuteronomy. The "Prophets" refers to all the rest of the Old Testament books of the Bible.

Can you think of two commands that the whole Constitution of the United States of America hangs on? I can't either. What a dynamic way to impress the importance of this principle on our minds.

A scripture that will help us understand who Jesus meant by the word, "neighbor," is the account known as the parable of the Good Samaritan. Luke 10:25–37 tells us that a man called "an expert in the law" asked Jesus what was needed to inherit eternal life. Jesus called his attention to the two great commandments. But that wasn't good enough for him; "wanting to *prove himself righteous*" (verse 29), he asked specifically, "Who is my neighbor?"

No doubt you recall the account Jesus gave of a Good Samaritan who helped a Jew who had been robbed and beaten. But wait—Jews didn't have dealings with Samaritans, did they? (John 4:9) First a priest and then a Levite saw the injured man, but they crossed to the other side of the road, hypocritically *pretending* they did not see him.

Then along came a Samaritan (heaven forbid, a man from a race hated by many Jews), but unlike the priest and Levite, who should have felt compelled to render aid to a fellow Jew, but refused, the Samaritan compassionately rendered considerable aid, even paying out two denarii to the innkeeper (two denarii was two days wages), to help the injured man get back on his feet.

Think of that; the last man on earth any Jew would expect to provide such help to him, a man who was from a nation hated by most Jews! What a sterling example and illustration is provided by Jesus of how a principle can trump any law, especially a man-made law, whether from the Pharisees of old or from the modern W/W/H.

Jesus summed up the account by asking the "expert in the law" a question to drive home the point of his parable; it can help our understanding too. As recorded at Luke 10:36 and 37, Jesus asked, "Which of these three do you think was a *neighbor* to the man who fell into the hands of robbers? The expert in the law replied, 'The one who *had mercy on him.*' Jesus told him, 'Go and do likewise'" (NIV; italics added). The NWT version is similar.

That must have stung a lot. Remember, "the Jews did not have dealings with Samaritans," and yet Jesus commanded him to do the same himself as the Samaritan had done. That clearly drives home the application of the principle taught by the Golden Rule, doesn't it?

Do you recall the experience that my son Joseph had, after he was "disassociated" (same as disfellowshipped) and therefore shunned by local Witnesses? While living in Superior, Wisconsin, he was attending the Kingdom Hall, hoping to be reinstated in the congregation. Because he had no transportation, he had to walk, and it was two miles one way; the temperature was forty degrees *below zero*.

Other Witnesses who wanted to give him a lift were told, *"No!"* Do you think anyone in that congregation would have liked to have been treated as they were forced (by the demands of their congregation elders) to treat Joseph? Nor do I!

Why was the Golden Rule not applied? Because the rules of the W/W/H demand that Jesus' instructions, as stated in the parable of the Good Samaritan, *must be ignored.* Who do you think the W/W/H was imitating? Was it the Good Samaritan or the hypocritical priest and Levite who pretended not to see the Jew, or even the Pharisees, who invalidated God's words by their traditions?

Do you think those instructions should apply to us also? Would it be excusable for us to ignore the Golden Rule as well as Jesus' parable of the Good Samaritan and what it teaches us about "our neighbor," just so we would not violate the rules and demands of the W/W/H? Do you really think it would be excusable, from God's viewpoint, for that hierarchy's man-made rules to cancel God's law?

Notice this telling comment that will help us decide.

Thayer, in his *Lexicon* (1977, p. 518, 519, # 4139), in defining the word "neighbor" as used in the scriptures, says, *"friend...any other person...*acc. to the teaching of Christ, any other man *irrespective of race or religion* with whom we live or who we chance to meet" (some italics his, some added).

Keeping these scriptures in mind, please recall Jesus' words to the Pharisees as recorded at Mark 7:1–8, but especially verses 6–8: "He [Jesus] said to them, "Isaiah aptly prophesied about you hypocrites, as it is written...'It is in vain; that they keep worshiping me...they teach as doctrines commands of men'... *Letting go the commands of God, you hold fast the traditions of men*" (NWT and NIV; italics added).

Now let's carefully return to 2 Thess. 3:6, 14 and 15, where we began before the discussion about the Golden Rule and the Good Samaritan.

Recall that Thayer, quoted earlier, as well as most translations, use a word like "note" (i.e., note for one's self) in these verses; it may well be more meaningful, as you will see, to refer to this as a "noting procedure" rather than as a "marking procedure." Why is this so? Because, no literal mark is to be put on a person.

In other words, what kind of a threat was being noticed about people in the congregation who were problems? They were called "disorderly;" what did that mean? Being "lazy," and/or "meddling with what did not concern them" would be examples in this case, but "disorderly" means more than just these two things.

Thayer's *Lexicon* (1977, p. 83, # 812, 814) defines the Greek word for "disorderly" to mean "*to be neglectful of duty, to be lawless...to lead a disorderly life*" (italics his). So different people might note different actions of others, and as a result their own reactions likely would vary, depending on what they individually noted.

Consider this example of noting something. If, while driving your car, you *noted* a chipmunk on the road in front of you, would your reaction be the same as if you had *noted* a moose? I experienced that, once, in northern Minnesota. If we had not stopped driving and given the moose the right-of-way, who do you think would have been the bigger loser? He weighed close to eighteen hundred pounds, and his belly was above the hood of my car. Bigger problems require more notice; perhaps a faster reaction or solution. In this case, "Note—Don't mess with Mr. Moose!"

Let's look specifically at what the scripture says one should note and what he or she should do about it, in 2 Thess. 3:6–15, where it says, "*withdraw from every brother walking disorderly...keep this one marked** ["note that man" in other translations], *stop associating* with him...yet *do not* be considering him *as an enemy*, but *continue admonishing him* as a brother" (NWT; italics added). (* Lit., "be you putting sign on")

> ➤ Did you notice that the scripture in 2 Thess. 3:14 says, "stop associating with"? This is the identical Greek word used for

the phrase, "quit mixing in company," found at 1 Cor. 5:9, 11 (*Greek-English Lexicon* 1977, p. 601, # 4874).

The W/W/H *does not apply shunning* in 2 Thess.3:14, yet it does in 1 Cor. 5:9, 11, involving the incestuous man in Corinth.

- ➤ Do you see a double standard in its application of shunning in those two scriptures? Even though the same Greek meaning applies in both cases, the W/W/H twists its application to suit its agenda. Of course, shunning, as we have seen, is not scriptural in either case if applied to a person.

- ➤ Recall what Thayer's *Lexicon* said of the word "note" (i.e., note for one's self). The *individual*, and not the congregation, takes note and determines the proper action to take.

- ➤ Notice that 2 Thess. 3:6 uses the word "withdraw" to describe how to treat this type of person; the word is defined in Strong's *Greek Dictionary* (p. 66, # 4724) in this way: "abstain from associating with…avoid, withdraw self."

- ➤ This scripture continues, "And yet *do not be considering him as an enemy*, but *continue admonishing him as a brother*." That could facilitate readjustment on his part, and that would definitely benefit both him and the congregation, don't you agree?

- ➤ Nowhere does that scripture say that the members of the W/W/H should be the ones to make the decision to "mark" or "note" a person first, followed by the rest of the congregation jumping onboard to complete the process.

Rather, if one was to note a wrongdoer, individually, and then apply the noting counsel correctly, there would be no violation of the Golden Rule or any other principle, would there?

How about this principle from Matt. 7:1–5: Stop judging or you will get the same treatment; don't try to take the straw out of your brother's eye, when you have a rafter in your own eye; hypocrite, get the rafter out of your own eye first! - (This account is part of Jesus' Sermon on the Mount).

Recall the tax collector described, at Luke 18:13, and mentioned in chapter 10, who asked God to have mercy on him, "a sinner;" he was viewed by God as more righteous than the self-righteous Pharisee, who mistakenly believed that he was doing everything right and therefore was better than the tax collector. As Luke 18:14 subsequently says, "I tell you that this man [the tax collector] rather than the other, went home justified before God. For all those who exalt themselves will be humbled, and all those who humble themselves will be exalted" (NIV).

As Gal. 6:1 advises, if a person takes a false step (footnote* says: "Lit., should be overtaken"), those with spiritual qualifications should try to restore him in a spirit of mildness, but you had better keep an eye on yourself, because you also could be tempted and end up going bad.

Note what Jas. 2:13 admonishes: "For the one that does not practice mercy will have [his] judgment without mercy. Mercy exults triumphantly over* judgment." (*footnote says: Or, "as superior to.") (NWT) This scripture is actually saying that mercy trumps judgment. Don't you agree?

The point of all of this is quite simple. Each of us is expected by God to shoulder his or her own responsibility in how to apply any principles, even in the matter of noting (or marking) someone. We are not told that the W/W/H should shoulder our responsibility for us. That hierarchy doesn't even take responsibility for its own errors.

The hierarchy claims it has been given authority from God and Christ and therefore has the right to tell others what they must do in all areas of life (total control). But it may help us to take a closer look at what was given to first century Christians in this matter of authority.

Jesus said that he had been given all authority in heaven and on earth from his Father (God) (Matt. 28:16–20); he *did not say* to his apostles,

"I am giving you all of the authority that I have…so now you are the bosses," did he? Nor did he say, "In the future it would be given to the W/W/H so they can treat people in a cruel way."

So, in this matter, it is *"noting"* the wrongdoer ("marking," NWT), *rather than* disfellowshipping and shunning, that is the scriptural procedure given to all in the congregation. It does work for the disciplining of nearly all wrongdoers. (An exception and how to handle it will be discussed below.) And it falls within the parameters of the authority and responsibility allowed and permitted by Jesus.

What makes it possible for a wrongdoer to benefit from the marking (noting) procedure? It includes admonition, with a view to restoring him or her without stripping away such one's dignity and/or violating other basic Bible principles we've just examined. That makes sense, doesn't it?

Will adequate protection be afforded to the congregation as well as to individuals? Yes; but how so? Not everyone in the congregation has the same worries or concerns; some have children and some do not, some are elderly and some are young, and so on. Those directly affected in some way can "take note" and *react in a way appropriate* to their circumstances.

Consider a Serious Scenario:

What would be the difference in the feelings or needed protection of an elderly couple compared to a couple with a seven-year-old child, if a pedophile (one whom the elders come to know is or has been a child molester) moves into the congregation?

Think about the chipmunk and the moose. Which family would have the greater need for knowledge of the presence of the pedophile, so safeguards could be applied by the parents? In addition, needless to say, multiple safeguards must be put in place and monitored by elders and others. Common sense should rule in such cases. Obviously, the parents of the seven-year-old would be outraged if such a sex offender moved into their congregation, but the elders who were aware of the problem decided to keep their lips sealed, and then later their daughter was molested by this person. How would you feel if you were in that family?

Would the elders be accountable? Absolutely! Following the procedure of keeping silence—as in the case involving Candace Conti, considered earlier—cost the Watchtower Society a twenty-eight-million-dollar judgment for such negligence and for its secrecy policy, which resulted in her being violated repeatedly over a period of years.

Did that judgment and others like it, some of which resulted in award costs of additional millions of dollars, cause the W/W/H to change its secrecy policy? No! There were other similar situations that cost the Watchtower Society millions more to prevent such cases from getting into court in the first place. (Where do you think all of that money comes from?)

Up to this point in time, the W/W/H has made some very serious and costly mistakes in these areas; its members are not policemen; nor are they professionals prepared to deal with physical, mental and emotional issues. That is in no way their job.

Like it or not, the W/W/H will be forced, one way or another, to conform to the laws of the land. The policies it has been following for years have not been working (as shown by the Candace Conti case). What to do? What is really the problem, and how can it be fixed without making things worse or violating Bible principles?

Recall that Rom 13:1–7 discusses the superior authorities (governing authorities) in some Bible translations. No matter which government in the world one is talking about, democratic, dictatorial, or otherwise, those verses say that "the *existing authorities* stand placed in their relative positions by God...it [the existing authority] is *God's minister*... it *bears the sword*...it *is*...an avenger *to express wrath* upon the one *practicing what is bad*" NWT. (italics added)

It is not for the W/W/H to take over the role of the government. The members of that hierarchy do not bear the sword; the government does, and such an authority is only a phone call away.

Congregation Elders, (not the New York honchoes), must call local authorities *immediately* when such a situation arises; *this is not optional.* If these elders wait, greater damage will be done. Make a captain's decision and do what common sense, good judgment, and the law of the land require. After all, that is why God has, "placed [them] in their relative positions." (They "bear the sword!")

Recall: "Don't mess with Mr. Moose!" Some problems are outside the realm of the elders to handle, and attempting to handle them anyway would be like trying to borrow my airplane and take it for a spin when you don't know how to fly. Only disaster awaits such irresponsible action!

It must be admitted that the vast majority of wrongdoers that the W/W/H disfellowships are not a threat to life and limb (or to children). Additionally, many, many wrongdoers are not wicked; they are weak (the same as the elders who are sitting in judgment of them). They do not need to be pushed off the edge of the cliff by elders applying and using W/W/H's disfellowshipping and shunning procedures. Such action by them will not rehabilitate a wrongdoer or restore him or her; in fact, many times it causes irreparable damage.

Do you think the W/W/H would not have the problem of two-thirds of those disfellowshipped refusing to grovel before the elders in an effort to get reinstated, if it eliminated its manipulative and draconian procedures in the first place? If these were replaced by noting or (marking), how many more weak people could be helped in line with Bible principles, counsel, and admonition?

The W/W/H has become its own worst enemy because of its draconian procedures that violate so many basic Bible principles. The hierarchy is playing with nitroglycerin if it doesn't recognize the need to change its attitude and then apply the changes called for.

But let's suppose, for a moment, that the wrongdoer whom the elders are concerned about and dealing with really is wicked, as in the case of a present or past child sexual abuser. What should be done? (Information on this specific kind of case is available through a *web search*. Enter the phrase, *"Child Welfare Information Gateway"*, and the search results will provide definitions of such abuse as well as state laws for mandatory reporting of such abuses.)

The *web search* reveals: "It is noteworthy that the tide is changing as far as clergy responsibility to report cases of child sexual abuse.

The same date Jerry Sandusky was convicted for his sexual abuse of minor boys, in 2012, Philadelphia's *Monsignor William Lynn* was convicted of felony child endangerment, which brought a prison sentence of three to six years." (October 10, 2012)

Lynn's conviction was the first time a senior church official in the United States was convicted of covering up sexual abuse by the priests he supervised. Lawsuits filed against the Catholic Church, with settlements of upwards of two billion dollars, underscore big reasons for all religious hierarchies to take seriously any and all reporting laws involving sexual abuse of children.

At Monsignor Lynn's trial, prosecutors pushed for a seven-year (maximum) sentence, saying that it was because of "[h]is active, even eager execution of archdiocese policies, carried out in the face of victims' [innocent minor children] vivid suffering, and employing constant deceit, required a more amoral [against moral standards] character, a striving to please his bosses no matter how sinister the business" (brackets added).

Is there a lesson here for elders of the W/W/H? Indeed there is: violate laws of the land that are there to protect innocent minor children, and you may well land, not at an airport but, in prison. Would obeying the W/W/H's secret policies be suffering for "righteousness' sake?" No! Absolutely not; it would be done to satisfy the whims of the bosses, in this case the upper echelon of the W/W/H.

IF NOT DISFELLOWSHIPPING: WHAT COULD WORK, AND HAS WORKED—AND HOW?

This hierarchy has never provided such warning, and to this day, it requires that elders *notify them* of alleged child sexual abuse problems *first*, before the state authorities are advised. This organization is playing with nitroglycerine—again.

JW elders take note: what does the Bible indicate is the answer to such a situation? What would common sense as well as good judgment dictate? Wouldn't it be much better to listen to your own conscience and the law of the land rather than to the demands of the upper echelon of the W/W/H? Recall that Rom. 13:1–7 makes it clear that the "superior authorities" (governing authorities) wield the sword by God's permission. Would it not make perfect sense for the W/W/H to use the tools that it already has available rather than risk the alternative and be accused of negligence in how it handles sexual child abuse cases?

What is done at a Watchtower sponsored convention if a troublemaker appears? A phone call is made to 911, and he or she is handled by the police. If the same type of problem were to occur on an aircraft, the captain would land SAP (steps are usually not taken at altitude, for obvious reasons), and the troublemaker would (forcibly if necessary) be removed from the plane by the FBI or local authorities. The point is to let the governmental authorities do what they have been elected, appointed, and God-ordained to do. Neither the elders in a congregation nor airline captains, for that matter, have that responsibility.

There is an exception, of course, in the case of terrorism on an aircraft. Efforts may have to be made to expel the terrorists by any means possible in such a life-threatening emergency; the exception based on altitude may have to be ignored. Would not the same be true at a convention, in a movie theater, at Wal-Mart or anywhere, for that matter, if there was no time for a phone call and only immediate action would do? Isn't that what the exercise of good judgment (not necessarily a rule) is all about?

However, the problems in the congregation that can be cared for without resorting to violence or the breaking of Bible principles can usually be cared for by each member applying what has been referred to, in this chapter, as the noting procedure (called "marking" by the W/W/H).

Returning therefore to the matter of noting or marking, a term that the Bible does use and describes, is protection afforded to the congregation as well as to individuals within the congregation? Yes, definitely, as our investigations have shown us thus far.

Now let's look specifically at what is correct as well as what is incorrect with the W/W/H's procedure, teaching, and action involved in marking (noting) wrongdoers in the congregation.

The elders' secret book, *Shepherding the Flock of God* (WTB&TS 2010), which contains rules on disfellowshipping and shunning, lists about sixty different disfellowshipping offences which the scriptures actually show to be "marking" or "noting" offences as listed below:

> - Page 70 of that book lists as a disfellowshipping offense, "Adamant *refusal to provide materially* for one's own family." But recall that 2 Thess. 3:11 mentions marking (or noting) for the "disorderly among you, not working at all."
>
> - The disfellowshipping offense of extorting a high bride-price" (WTB&TS 2010, pp. 69, 70) is also listed. Can you think of any scripture that defines an exorbitantly high bride price? I can't either, and of course it is not even applicable in the United States
>
> - Another offense listed for disfellowshipping is "insulting speech" or "reviling" (p. 68), also termed "loose conduct" (especially if critical of any policy of the W/W/H).

Regarding the last offense listed, Matt.12:32, says: "… whoever speaks a word against the Son of man, *it will be forgiven him*" (NWT) But apparently the W/W/H feels it is more important even than Jesus by applying no forgiveness for such action against it.

The organization calls this offense "apostasy," and it disfellowships any rank-and-file Witness who says anything against it or questions its failures and wrongdoing. The W/W/H is still going "beyond the things written." What is the point? It has set its structure of rules to give itself the right to do as it pleases, without regard for Bible laws or principles, to handle the situations just mentioned.

Do you recall an earlier quoted scripture that states that it is "through use" that perceptive powers are trained? (Heb. 5:14) The scripture does not say that the W/W/H is to impose its perceptions on you. It is our use of our own perceptive powers that trains them.

Another scripture that I quoted earlier in this book makes a point that is relevant to our personal obligation of learning. That scripture directs, "make your mind over and prove to *yourselves* the good, acceptable and perfect will of God" (Rom. 12:2). So on with your thinking cap, as you consider and perceive the following relevant points.

The "noting procedure," called the "marking procedure" by the W/W/H, has enormous advantages as a disciplinary standard, which *can be exercised* to the "proper degree" (Jer. 30:11), without the abuses that are part of its tyranny of authority.

There are additional points you might want to consider. When a wrongdoer is put in prison in our day, the goal is to rehabilitate him or her. If the person is locked up in solitary confinement, tantamount to shunning, how much rehabilitation do you think will take place? If a parent locked up a child in his or her room indefinitely and kept that child isolated from the rest of the family, what kind of a youngster (or adult for that matter) do you think he or she would become? Is not extreme treatment in today's world (whether in the family, at the workplace, or in school) often a prelude to extreme tragic conduct in retaliation against the tyranny of authority?

What kind of treatment do you think the W/W/H is asking for as a repayment for its harsh, draconian and bullying treatment (which it tries to disguise as discipline) done to members of its congregations? Considering this question helps one to understand the extraordinary efforts put forth by its hierarchy to secure anonymity for its members because of its craven activities; you will perceive and appreciate this even more as you get into the next chapter.

What usually happens to those who practice tyranny of authority when the tables are turned? Do you recall the lessons learned from events in history, such as the French Revolution (1789–1799)? Heads rolled!

Think about God's dealings with the ancient nation of Israel in the matter of discipline; it was always done to the "proper degree" and was not a "more or less situation" (Jer. 30:11). But, was it not repeated failure on the part of the higher-ups in ancient Israel to conform to God's requirements that eventually led to the downfall of their nation? Eventually they lost it all. The reasons why are specifically addressed at Jer. 5:27-31, where it says the following:

"…their houses are full of deception…they have grown fat…overflowed with bad things.* [*Or "words; matters"] No legal case have they pleaded, even the legal case of the father-less boy, that they may gain success; and the judgment of the poor ones they have not taken up. Should I [God] not hold an accounting with [them]…a horrible thing, has been brought to be in the land: The *prophets* themselves *actually prophesy in false-hood*…the priests, they go subduing according to their powers. And my own people have loved [it] that way; and what will you men do in the finale of it? (NWT)

Can the W/W/H see itself in this lesson from the past, this "mirror?" What will it "do in the finale of it?" Just how much more abuse will God tolerate from this hierarchy? Please recall that Solomon said: There is nothing new under the sun, history will keep repeating itself. (Ecc.1:9)

Is it not clear that the W/W/H has continually and dogmatically thrown reason out the window, as if there would never be an accounting demanded of it? What does that scripture found at Gal.6:7 indicate? Oh yes, we will all reap what we have sown—if we think not, we are misleading ourselves! There are no exceptions to that principle, not even for this hierarchy.

In summary, note the following:

- First of all, no scriptural procedure exists or is recorded in the Bible in which the Christian congregation disfellowshipped or shunned anybody. Only the Pharisees demonstrated such audacity.

- There is the procedure to take note or mark one who is not doing as he or she should; association with this person is curtailed, to some degree, but each one in the congregation shoulders his or her own responsibility in determining how to apply this; that is not the responsibility of the W/W/H.

- The wrongdoer is not to be viewed or treated as an enemy, but is to be admonished as a brother or sister.

- His or her dignity is not to be stripped away by shunning—which could lead to suicide. Recall my son, John?

- The procedure of taking note or marking of a wrongdoer does not violate or negate basic scriptural principles. The wrongdoer gets help for rehabilitation, by "continuing admonition for him."

- The "noting procedure" allows mercy to triumph over (or trump) judgment.

- *If* the W/WH would properly apply the "noting procedure" it would not find itself facing probable adverse judgment, because it has continued to insist on going "beyond the things that are written," it would be well advised, for them, to take note of the ominous hand-writing on the wall. There will be an accounting; we will all, *eventually*, reap what we sow!

- The congregation members *would* end up treating wrongdoers the way they would *want to be treated*, if they were in the same shoes. (Golden Rule)

➤ What do Bible principles, common sense, reason, and good judgment indicate to be the proper course of action, for the Christian congregation, in the matter of discipline? Would it be, "disfellowshipping and shunning" or would the "noting procedure" be a far better way to go?

➤ If the wrongdoer is really wicked—a real threat—it is out of the elders' hands and should be handled by the ones who have that responsibility as well as the authority to act—governmental authorities.

REVIEW POINTS:

1. Is not the disfellowshipping, shotgun approach to discipline practiced by the W/W/H, where one size fits all, unreasonable, unfair, and even unscriptural? It is not discipline "to the proper degree," as God decreed for the nation of Israel.

2. Is it not clear that the disfellowshipping and shunning procedures practiced by the W/W/H since 1952, with growing severity, is really in harmony with the sect-like and cult-like traits that the W/W/H has exhibited over and over again?

3. Does the harsh, draconian procedure demonstrate the hierarchy's growing need to keep a death grip on its adherents, for fear members will be "lost to the sect"—as C. T. Russell indicated would be an earmark of sect-like and cult-like organizations?

4. What kind of fruitage (results) has the W/W/H seen from its disfellowshipping and shunning procedures?

5. Can you perceive that scriptural principles, common sense, and good judgment all dictate that a change is long overdue for the W/W/H?

6. Will the hierarchy have the courage to admit failure and make such changes? What does its record indicate?

How has the W/W/H sought to hide accountability and evade responsibility, and what bad affects have come from its cowardly procedures? Chapter 12 will cover these points in detail.

Chapter 12

HOW AND WHY THE W/W/H HIDES ACCOUNTABILITY AND EVADES RESPONSIBILITY

- Accentuate the positive!
- Hide, or better yet, eliminate the negative.
- Burn those bridges…
- Say it frequently enough, and people will believe it.
- What does the "olfactory system" have to do with understanding?
- A stench cannot be ignored. Why not?
- ❖ Flying: If you are on an approach to land, and you find yourself going down because of wind shear, you must never…

In 1945, a song by Johnny Mercer climbed to the peak billboard position of number one song. It was entitled, "Accentuate the Positive," and two lines from that song go like this:

You've got to accentuate the positive
Eliminate the negative

What do those two lines have to do with the Watchtower/ Witness/ Hierarchy? (W/W/H) Although it has accomplished some good things, as enumerated in chapter 4, all too often, when those good things have morphed into something bad, the inclination of the W/W/H and mankind in general, has been an attempt to accentuate the positive and try to hide or better yet, eliminate the negative.

As an example, people who have just agreed to a Bible study with one of Jehovah's Witnesses are assured of many things that they really love to hear. This practice is similar to promising one, "You are going to win the lottery—we can guarantee it—but first, it will be necessary for you to 'buy' this ticket…" What is that saying? "If it seems too good to be true…"

The W/W/H has become a master of deception by accentuating the positive while hiding or masking the negative. Sometimes they will even attempt "eliminating" it, by denying, or even trying to change their own published history—that is really a lesson in futility.

But, think of how good these promises would sound to a new, unwary potential JW recruit, one who has just agreed to a home Bible study; such ones are commonly referred to by their JW teacher as: "*My* Bible study."

- Here are some examples of the big promises made to such people:

- You can be positive that Armageddon is very near.

- You will live to see the end of all wickedness.

- The "new world" will bring everything you have ever wanted or could imagine!

- Jehovah has *chosen you*; that is why you are studying with us. How special and blessed you are!

A thinking new "Bible study" participant might begin to smell that something is "rotten in Denmark," however, as these next dubious points are foisted on him or her with friendly persuasion:

- Don't be afraid to burn your bridges behind you; if your family or past friends refuse to join you in your new found faith—ditch them. You are getting a huge, brand new family of *loyal* brothers and sisters to replace them. What a wonderful blessing!

- The great thing about us is that *everything is free;* we never pass a collection plate or charge anything.

- Your faithful brothers (the W/W/H) in New York are the head ones of Jehovah's Organization; they can *always be trusted,* and we must never doubt them. Even if you don't understand the reason for some new truth (some new light that has just been revealed by them), no problem. Jehovah will make it all clear to you, in his own due time.

- Remember; there is no such thing as a "free lunch." There is always a catch!

The last four bullet points, with the promise of a free lunch, eliminate any past support group you might have had and leave JWs to be your only friends and support group. Does this sound dangerous? It is, much like insidious wind shear on a short final approach to an airport for an airline crew, (to be discussed later)

Then there are things that the Witness teacher will try to *prevent* his Bible student from hearing before he or she gets baptized and joins:

- ➢ If you ever disagree with the W/W/H, you can think what you want, but you had better not say it! Do so, and you will likely face disfellowshipping. (Recall my experience with the circuit overseer, when I brought up the matter of child baptism?)

- ➢ The congregation stays faithful to Jehovah and will disfellowship any baptized brother or sister who has the audacity to cause divisions in the congregation by questioning or complaining about past or present organizational errors and/ or disagreeing with statements from the Faithful and Discreet Slave.

- ➢ The W/W/H has prophesied the end of the world (or events associated with it) over thirty times—more than any other group over the past two thousand years—and although these prophecies all failed, *keep your lips sealed.* Never talk about that, because "we must have 'unity.'" (No investigation is allowed.)

Why do you suppose they don't tell new "Bible studies" these things? You've got it—there would be no new recruits!

JIM STAELENS

The *United States Office of Strategic Services* issued a report during World War II, describing the *psychological profile of Hitler*. Who else might this profile fit? The following is a paragraph from this report, quoted in the *Wikipedia* article, "*The Big Lie:*" (Retrieved 3/15/2013)

> "His [Hitler's] primary rules were: never to allow the public to cool off [i.e. keep them busy]; never admit a fault or wrong; never concede that there may be some good in your enemy; never leave room for alternatives; never accept blame; concentrate on one enemy at a time and blame him for everything that goes wrong; people will believe a big lie sooner than a little one; and if you repeat it frequently enough people will sooner or later believe it."

Does this information sound familiar in the way the W/W/H handles its failures and wrongs? Do you recall, from chapter six, what was said (about the failed prophesy for 1975?) Who got the blame? *The Watchtower*, (July 15, 1976, p. 441) said: "If anyone has been disappointed... he should now concentrate on adjusting *his* viewpoint... *his* own understanding was based on wrong premises."

The governing body has never admitted wrongs or fault; regardless of what the facts show. It just ignores these as if they had never occurred. Instead, for example, comments like this are printed in the *Watchtower* article, "Trust Your Proved, Faithful Brothers," (May 1, 1957, p. 284), which says: "Showing respect for Jehovah's organization really revolves itself down to our attitude toward God's visible channel and the *trust that we place in our proved, faithful* brothers. If we have become thoroughly convinced that this is Jehovah's organization... we shall not be unsettled by anything that happens... we will wait." (italics added) Of course some have waited for a whole lifetime.

These are dogmatic assertions that have been made by the W/W/H countless times, but there is no basis for such trust and confidence. Quite the opposite; its continual stream of failed prophecies belies such fraudulent claims.

So what can be done if a potential new believer begins to discern that there are problems with the teachings of the W/W/H; teachings that paint such a rosy picture? The teachings not only conflict with reality but are dubious promises at best and lies and deception at the worse. They need investigation! What can one do who finds himself or herself in such a situation?

We know that growing up takes time and requires acknowledging mistakes and learning how to cope with and correct (not hide and deny) them—or better yet, trying (if possible) to prevent them from occurring in the first place. It is not an easy task, is it? Good luck in your efforts. However, an illustration may help in learning how to recognize potential areas of concern that could prevent one from making serious mistakes in the first place.

Think back to your childhood school days, in health class. Do you remember learning about our olfactory system, our sense of smell? It works for us, even if we cannot see with our eyes the exact cause of the smell—whether it's a nice smell or especially if it is a repugnant, unpleasant odor.

An expression I have used more than once in this book is, "There is something 'rotten in Denmark' (or New York)." The "rotten in Denmark" phrase is from Shakespeare's Hamlet, and it basically means that there is something very wrong. In an airline context it means, *you must do something—now!* You may not know the full story of what is going down, but you realize that something is definitely wrong. As an example, if you have ever returned home from vacation and been greeted by a pungent odor as you walked into your house, you know the sensation I am talking about. "Yuck! What is that awful smell?"

We cannot ignore the smell—it is overpowering—we are compelled to do something about it—so we have to open the windows and investigate. Maybe it is coming from the cupboard. Is it a leftover meal on the kitchen counter? Oh look, a dead mouse in the corner who greedily dined on some cheese in a trap! No matter the source or cause, it must be found and eliminated. Could the problem be far more serious than we first imagined? Is someone dead in the bathtub? Let's hope not!

Might we, in handling the problem, do something stupid, making things worse? For example, if the unpleasant odor is coming from a broken gas line to your furnace; would you light a match so you could see into a dark corner and check it out? *No! Stop!* If you don't stop, you may well find yourself heaven-bound sooner than you planned, and that, without an airplane. Not a good idea!

How about just putting a clothespin on your nose to block the smell? That's an idea, but not a good one either. It would only help in giving you a sore nose, but it wouldn't solve the problem; it could in fact make things worse. You would become like the proverbial "ostrich."

So what about problems we may face religiously in our lives? If we sense that something is wrong, what will we do? In the religious venue, what if it involves things we may have been taught from the time we were youngsters, things that may have been foisted on us as by a religious hierarchy displaying sect-like or cult-like traits? Such longstanding, entrenched problems (or teachings) can be difficult to discern in the first place and can be far more difficult to overcome.

The religious teachings may have been rammed down our throats plunger-style, by force, or more gently, using friendly persuasion, shoehorn style. Whatever the case, the problem can become like a bad odor that starts out barely discernible but which then gradually gets worse and worse, eventually becoming so pungent that it can no longer be tolerated. We may finally reach the conclusion that something is dead wrong with what we have been taught. It must be discerned first; then there is a need for corrective action.

How could one handle this kind of problem, if he or she was faced with it? Would one even discern it in the first place? If the person did, but then ignored it, would the problem go away? Not likely; think of the leaking gas line.

So how much effort do you think one should expend in trying to care for a matter when the person's senses tell him or her that something is "rotten in Denmark" and is definitely wrong? Could it be life-threatening? What kind of price might be exacted from the person if he or she chooses to ignore it, when the person's senses are saying, "Do not ignore it"? Could the person stay focused in trying to correct the problem? How might one decide? Does it matter?

When flying, why is wind shear so difficult to notice in the first place? In what way is it like a bad odor, barely discernible at first, but likely to bring tragic consequences later if it is ignored (as would be the case with a leaking gas line)?

> ❖ *A Flying Lesson* will help us to evaluate those questions sensibly, so buckle up your seat belt again, and come along with me to Denver for one of my biannual proficiency checks on the Boeing 767 (the plane shown on the back cover of this book).

First, some preliminary information about wind shear is necessary. It can be vertical or horizontal. A microburst, which creates wind shear at low altitudes, has the following characteristics:

- It is a localized column of descending air, producing both damaging divergent and straight-line winds; it is associated with thunderstorm activity.

- When a microburst is close to the earth's surface and an aircraft on approach to land will have to fly through it, it becomes especially dangerous; a number of fatal aircraft crashes have been caused because of this phenomenon.

- Many times, nothing is seen. There may be no turbulence, and that powerful column of descending air may last for just a few seconds; but when it continues for over thirty seconds, it can seem like an eternity, and it quickly becomes deadly.

Here's the point. A problem of faulty religious teachings can be like wind shear or a microburst. How? What can possibly identify and solve the problem? Where do we start? The following true account will aid comprehension in that it discusses the way a catastrophic problem involving wind shear as well as microburst recognition was addressed and dealt with by the airlines in order to be able to save lives. You will see the relevance shortly, but for now let me fill you in on my real life story. Obviously it must have had a successful ending, though it could have been a tragic one instead.

I had encountered only one really serious problem with a microburst prior to our wind shear training. I was flying a segment from Chicago, Illinois to Dallas, Texas; I was at the controls, flying a stretch Boeing 727. By modern standards, that 727 was an underpowered airplane. We expected to land to the south, on runway 18-R.

Dallas-Fort Worth had experienced some thunderstorm activity a short time before our arrival, but it had all moved off to the east, and we were well in the clear. We were cleared for the approach about seventeen miles out, north of the airport, inbound to runway 18-Right. So I began a gradual descent to that runway.

I was on speed, on profile, and on glide slope (angle of descent for a visual approach). All was well, but very slowly, things started to change. My airspeed started to decay, so I added power. I started descending below glide slope, so I raised the nose of the aircraft. But my speed was still decaying, so I added more power; it got worse, and I added still more power. "*This is not good,*" I said to myself.

In short order, I found myself with takeoff power on the engines, and we were still below our proper glide slope and still descending. Remember my discussion, in chapter 2: the mandate is always to keep the aircraft approach stabilized. (I said to myself, "Don't start your descent too soon—you know better than that—you're not a new kid.")

But I was already at takeoff power. If I added any more power, I would be over-boosting the engines past the red line power limit; I was a gnat's eyebrow from doing exactly that! Thankfully, the plane started responding, and we were flying out of the microburst. Our speed started increasing as we approached a "fix" (16 miles) from the runway 18-R threshold, and I did not have to over-boost the engines.

"Welcome to the world of wind shear, Jim," a voice inside me said. Believe me, it was an extremely uncomfortable feeling, and I was very glad the problem had started when we were just above five thousand feet instead of down at one thousand feet.

But I was still about thirty feet below what should have been a normal glide-slope, so the approach controller called and asked, "United triple seven, are you OK up there?" He was on the ball and had noticed on radar that something didn't look right. Our speed had been decreasing, and we were below the glide slope. Airline pilots never do that on purpose—never!

I keyed my mike and replied, "Yeah, we're OK, but you've got a hell of a wind shear up here, no turbulence, but a very intense downdraft. I'd call it moderate, bordering severe; we're flying out of it now." Our report was acknowledged, and we continued the approach.

The rest of the trip was uneventful, thank God! But I kept going over things in my mind. What had gone wrong? With most aircraft problems, such as an engine fire, rapid decompression, or a hydraulic failure, there would be an obtrusive audible sound such as a bell, a siren, or a horn, and there would also be a visual signal such as a "Master Caution" red light on the glare shield.

This time, there had been no advance notice. Why? The problem that I had failed to recognize in advance was that wind shear, and especially microbursts, can sneak up on a crew stealthily, with no warning—not even turbulence. We would really benefit from the wind shear training to come, but it was still a few years away.

All of us had missed an earmark of wind shear and especially of microbursts. They can especially become a threat just after thunderstorms have passed through an area. Our wind shear training (when we got it) would correct that lack of recognition and a great deal more.

But since it is impossible for airline cockpit crews to be trained for every conceivable problem they might face, including wind shear, what can they be taught in order to give survival the best possible chance? How can it be taught? What does the crew need to know and do? What will be the *best way to teach* what must be learned? Let me explain what was eventually done about wind shear training.

I was relatively new at flying the Boeing 767. The year was 1985, and I was in Denver for one of my biannual proficiency checks (PCs). We had just finished our normal PC, and our instructor advised us that United had recently implemented wind shear training into all PCs for all flight crews. The reason, he noted, was because of the recent string of airline crashes caused by wind shear and experienced by a number of different crews with several different airlines. He said, "The FAA has mandated that thorough, vigorous wind shear training be commenced immediately, so that's what's coming next."

By this time in my career, all of United's PC training was given in cockpit simulators. The DC-10 had been the first high-tech simulator with realistic motion that United had installed at its training center. Our plane, the Boeing 767, had a glass cockpit (described in chapter one); it was newer and more sophisticated than the DC-10; so it was the one United decided to be the best choice for wind shear training.

That simulator is so realistic that all of my initial training for the 767 was done in it. In fact, the first time I flew a real 767 was with a load of passengers on a regular flight. (No, I didn't tell them it was my first time flying the actual plane. I didn't want to make them nervous, you know.) The 767 simulator is so close to the real thing that if you were blindfolded and brought onboard, and then you sat down and took off your blindfold with the cockpit door closed, you would swear you were on an actual Boeing 767. Truly amazing!

The visual presentation for this PC was a nighttime scenario. When we took off from the Denver airport, there to the west on the mountain was the huge lighted cross, and to the north was the big dipper; everything was right where it belonged as would be seen for a real night flight. If you have ever flown out of Denver at night, you know exactly what I'm talking about.

The flight data recorder details from several actual crashes caused by wind shear had been programed into the 767 simulator. (There had been *many* fatalities.) Each scenario gave us the identical problems that other crews had already experienced and which had led to crashes: the same stresses, same "G" forces, same wind speeds, *exactly the same problems*. How would we handle those situations? That was what this was all about—could we survive?

We had already received the specifics of the procedure that United and the FAA had determined to be the best way to get out of the problem and to make severe wind shear survivable. But why were so many professional flight crews making the same mistakes that led to crashes? Something had to be missing to have caught so many professionals unaware and which had led to such fatalities. What was missing?

Remember chapter 2 and the discussion about our initial Crew Resource Management training. The instructors had made a major point: "CRM teaches that when there is a discrepancy between what is happening and what should be happening, an error is likely already occurring."

That was the missing link. There was a problem with perception and discernment by flight crews; by the time they caught on to what was wrong, it was too late. They were in too deep, and it was no longer possible to avert disaster, especially without the training we were about to receive.

Obviously, the first and best choice is to know where wind shear is occurring and to divert to a different airport until it has passed. That way, it will never be a problem in the first place. But that is not always possible; the clues that disaster may be only moments away can sneak up insidiously on the crew. So the crew members must be taught what to look for, to *sharpen* their discernment and help them be alert to even the possibility of wind shear, especially if there are, or have recently been, thunderstorms in the area.

This was training for when there was no advance notice of any problem, and wind shear had insidiously found us. We were experiencing an actual wind shear emergency, and a crash was inevitable unless we immediately and vigorously implemented the wind shear profile procedure.

Both of us actually did very well. By applying the training, we were able to avoid crashing for every one of the previous scenarios that had killed a number of passengers. Our instructor asked me how I felt about the training so far. I replied, "Good!" We had done what several other crews before us, from different airlines and without this training, had proven unable to do.

"You won't feel so good about the next one," the instructor noted.

"Why not?" I asked.

Very soberly, he replied, *"Because it is not survivable."* And so it turned out to be.

The Boeing 767 was a wonderful plane to fly, from a pilot's point of view. It has incredible power, over forty thousand pounds of thrust from each engine, and a "super critical wing." It is the only plane I have ever flown to forty-two thousand feet—about eight miles above the earth. But even it was no match for what we were about to experience. The exercise was downright embarrassing; it seemed like a giant flyswatter had hit us, and down we went. We tried our best and did everything right, as far as the training was concerned, but to no avail. There was in fact no way out of this one, and in a few seconds, it was all over. You can crash in a simulator without getting hurt, and I was really glad about that.

I kept thinking about that last scenario as we finished up and exited the simulator. Our instructor showed us printed graphs that had tracked us for all of the profiles that we had flown—including the last one, which was not pretty. We had done well on all but that last one. True, for a couple of them we came within about twenty feet of the tree tops, and in real life, it would have been scary, even for a seasoned airline captain. But we survived.

I had to ask, "My God, if it's not survivable, then why on earth put us through it? It's disheartening."

He looked me straight in the eye and replied, with the sternest face I have ever seen on a flight instructor, "Jim, there is no one on earth that can tell you in real life which wind shear is survivable and which one is not. We want our crews to be able to discern a potential wind shear problem and avoid it. If it is too late, and you find yourself involved with this problem, we want you to never stop trying to pull out of it. *Never give up—as long as you are alive!*"

Enough said. It was truly a matter of life or death training, and I never forgot it. That training attitude—never to give up and to keep trying as long as you're alive—has saved my life from disaster, more than once.

- Do you understand? Have you gotten the point? CRM training (discussed in chapter 2) usually involves problems that one has time to work on, like the crash at Salt Lake City or the one at Portland. Application of CRM concepts has helped solve those kinds of problems.

- But wind shear problems can come upon crews sneakily and with tragic consequences. They are easy to miss unless you have been trained and are looking for them.

So it is with religious deception and abuse, especially if you have experienced them since you were a youngster. As I have personally found out, it can take nearly a whole lifetime to recognize and then eventually to be successful in overcoming them. Like trying to break any bad habit, it takes time, and there will likely be setbacks along the way.

What can possibly help a person in such a situation to catch on? The following are specific earmarks of deception used by the W/W/H, to try to keep a person in the dark:

Hide Accountability:

Example one: This example is especially for present JWs.

> ➢ Letters to congregations or elders from the W/W/H never carry a signature; they are just stamped with a designation such as "Christian Congregation" or "Watchtower Bible and Tract Society."

What do you think the reaction would be from a brother at the Watchtower's Branch Office, if a judicial committee sent a "disfellowshipping report" just stamped with the designation, "Centerville congregation," but bearing no personal signatures?

Would that brother not fire back a letter immediately, demanding the signatures of all the men on that committee? Yes he would, but why? The hierarchy wants to know who to hold responsible in the event that there are problems or possibly legal concerns that could lead to a lawsuit. But wait—why won't the W/W/H, then, allow its own letters to be signed with personal signatures? Obviously because the members of the hierarchy have always refused, as you have seen countless times in this book, to take responsibility for what they say or do.

Do you discern how and why they hide accountability? Is it not true that even the woman from the phone company who promises to give you a credit on your next bill, due to the company's error, will gladly give her name and not hide it from you? She is accountable for what she promised, and she will take responsibility, even to the point of giving her name, so that you know specifically who to call if the credit doesn't show up.

Example two: How the W/W/H Evades Responsibility

As came to light over and over again in chapter six, in discussing the thirty-plus failed prophecies, the W/W/H has never admitted fault or blame. However, if you ask the next Witness who calls at your door whether it has ever admitted fault, the person will reply, "Of course." But let's review the facts. When you look at anything even vaguely resembling accepting fault, making an apology for wrongdoing, or taking responsibility for a mistake or a failed prophecy, here is a reminder of what you will find.

From chapter six, discussing failed prophecy number 12, we saw that the W/W/H admitted that failed expectations and failed millennial promises led to a dramatic drop in meeting attendance (WTB&TS 1993, p. 633). But neither the W/W/H's governing body nor any members of its hierarchy admitted any fault on its own part, did it?

Notice how they handled their false prophecy number 21 (1925) from chapter six: "The year 1925 is here...Christians [JWs] have...*expected that all members of the body of Christ will be changed to heavenly glory*...Christians *should not be so deeply concerned* about what *may* transpire this year [i.e., what the W/W/H had promised] that they fail to joyfully do what the Lord would have them do" (*Watchtower* January 1, 1925, p. 3; italics added). Did you see an admission of fault? Neither did I.

Here's what the W/W/H said about false prophecy number 25 (also for 1925): "Some anticipated that the work would end in 1925, but the Lord did not state so. The difficulty was that *the friends inflated their imaginations* beyond reason; and that when their imaginations burst asunder, they were inclined to throw away everything." (*Watchtower* 1926, p. 232; italics added) Was it "the friends fault"—or was it clearly the fault of the W/W/H.? Would you like to be blamed for something that was clearly the fault of somebody else?

With a record of twenty-five false prophecies since the 1800's (over a 131 year period of time), might you have been, in 1925, inclined to *throw away* everything, meaning the hierarchy's dogmatic and fraudulent promises and prophecies?

I have admitted that I too had succumbed to their sect-like and cult-like manipulation; I found myself being subjected to their manifold errors since 1950 and it did take me over fifty years to catch-on and abandon the W/W/H organization.

I am ashamed that it took me so long to really comprehend the enormous wrongs that had been foisted on me, since the tender age of nine. Needless to say the W/W/H works diligently to keep the facts, of their wrong-doing, hidden from new recruits as they come along.

It doesn't really make me feel better to realize that there were millions of others, besides my wife and me, who have been duped in the same way. What a monstrous deception has been perpetrated by the W/W/H, on deceived believers, for two lifetimes!

Do you recall that there are still more points that relate to false prophecy number 25? "There was a measure of disappointment on the part of Jehovah's faithful ones on earth concerning the years 1917, 1918, and 1925, which disappointment lasted for a time... and they also learned to quit fixing dates." (WTB&TS 1931, p. 338)

That publication had asserted that "Jehovah's faithful ones" *had learned not to fix dates*. But, was that true of the W/W/H, who had been responsible for all of those failed prophecies? No they actually set at least an additional seven specific dates for the end of the world and/or events connected with that end, after the *Vindication* book had been published! Does that sound like the W/W/H took responsibility for the false prophesying? Not to me either.

Notice this example of the "pot calling the kettle black," for false prophecy number 30: "True, there have been those in times past who 'predicted an end to the world', even announcing a specific date. Yet nothing happened...They were **guilty of false prophesying**. Why? What was missing...? Missing from such people were God's truths and *evidence that he was **using and guiding them**."* (*Awake!* October 8, 1968, p. 23; italics and emphasis added).

What kind of arrogance does it take for the W/W/H to make a statement like that? It is the world record holder for false prophecies about the end of the world or for events connected with it. You may recall that over 200 false prophecies have been given in total since the first century; of that number the W/W/H is responsible for 16 % of them.

The *Proclaimers book* (WTB&TS 1993, p. 632), regarding false prophecy number 32, for 1975 asserted that millennial events and the heavenly resurrection would start that year. The question is asked, "Did the beliefs of Jehovah's Witnesses on these matters prove to be correct?"

Notice that the W/W/H refers to "the beliefs of Jehovah's Witnesses" about these matters, but nobody from the governing body on down ever admitted fault or took the blame. Is it not perfectly clear that it was the beliefs foisted on them by the hierarchy which proved to be incorrect? It never was or has been the fault of rank-and-file Witnesses. It has always been the fault of their hierarchy.

By the way, if any of this sounds familiar, you might want to look back not just on chapter six but also in the early pages of this chapter, where I have quoted the paragraph from the profile of Hitler. There I asked the question, who else might fit this profile?

- Do you recall the earmarks of "the big lie" mentioned in that profile?
- Keep them (the public) [or Witnesses] busy.
- Never admit fault or wrongdoing.
- Never concede any good in your enemy.
- Never accept blame.

➤ Always blame your enemy for anything wrong.

➤ Repeat *even a big lie* often enough and the public will believe it to be true.

I want to remind you of the demand that was made of all elders in the 1980s by the upper echelon of the W/W/H through its branch office instructions: No one in their hierarchy was ever to admit even the possibility of having made a mistake or to admit that the organization had a legal department and a huge crew of university-trained attorneys. Why was that?

It was because the real issue was (and still is) *all about money*. The Watchtower Bible and Tract Society (their mother corporation) has been sued for many millions of dollars. Trusting members of the W/W/H organization have been severely harmed and damaged, mentally, emotionally, and even financially, due to its failed prophecies and secret policies, and have said, "Enough is enough! Is it past time to force them to accept responsibility for their bad deeds—will any of those who have been so injured decide to hit them in their wallets?"

REVIEW POINTS:

1. How has the W/W/H accentuated the positive and eliminated the negative in the matter of its teachings and course of conduct?

2. Why does it want "Bible studies" to burn their bridges behind them? Who becomes their support group then?

3. Thinking of the quote from The United States Office of Strategic Services and that office's profile of Hitler, do you discern the very same profile evidenced on the part of the W/W/H?

4. If your powers of perception are telling you that there is something "rotten in Denmark" (i.e., New York, in connection with the W/W/H organization), will you continue to investigate further?

5. How is the W/W/H's manner of teaching new "Bible studies" similar to wind shear facing an airline crew?

6. Why does the W/W/H deny and vigorously quash, or try to forbid and stop anything from being spoken about or published that exposes its wrongs to others?

7. Many Witnesses, even after proofs are given of the W/W/H's, failures, still assert that, "Being one of Jehovah's Witnesses is still the best possible way of life to live on this planet." Perhaps you feel that way too; I used to, but *not any longer.*

You do have a choice here; let's try a good old-fashioned "multiple choice" set of questions. From what you have read in this book up to this point and have examined in the references concerning the WWH's record, is it imitating:

➢ The Pharisees of the first century?

➢ Sect and cult leaders in modern times?

> Hitler's psychological profile?

> Or is it…all of the above!

I already took this test and passed with flying colors (pun intended). How did you do?

Is deception necessary for a Christian to be ready for the future?

The W/W/H has often said, for example when the circuit overseer has his talk with the local elders, that it is necessary to "keep pressure on the brothers, so they won't slow down; they must keep believing that the end is imminent, immediately ahead of us—or they may not work as hard as is needed." Why would that matter? You guessed it. More work = more money—for the W/W/H, of course!

In the airline venue, if a captain and his crew stayed "spring-loaded" for a probable disaster, how do you think they could deal with it? If such reported to dispatch for a flight and were informed that *this was the day* they were going to have a catastrophic crash killing the crew, and likely all of their passengers, what would they do?

Suddenly get sick and go home? You bet! Wouldn't you?

Of course, that is an exaggeration, but the point is that airline crews generally do a fantastic job of flying safely because they are *prepared well for their job* and feel confident that their training and good judgment will make possible their handling of a problem, even if they were never trained for that particular problem. Billions of miles flown safely every year testify to the reasonableness and practicality of that arrangement. Being constantly spring-loaded for an emergency would actually be counterproductive.

When you get up every morning to start your day, do you say to yourself, "I am probably going to be killed today in an automobile accident"? If you felt that way, you'd turn off the alarm and stay in bed, wouldn't you?

Another reason why being spring-loaded is impractical is that usually, as adults, we expect that we can handle normal problems, including most emergencies that may come our way on a daily basis. Or if not, we expect that we will be able to get the necessary help to prevent fatal consequences to ourselves or our family. Is that not true?

What then is the way we should live our lives without being frustrated by living on the edge, set to the emergency detent? The following are a couple of scriptures that I think can provide any of us with confidence without our having to be spring-loaded to the "Armageddon today" mentality as the hierarchy has convinced its members they should be. These may help anyone to develop a balanced viewpoint.

First of all, Micah 6:8 says, "And what is Jehovah asking back from you but to *exercise justice* and to *love kindness* and to be *modest* in walking with your God?" (NWT) The NIV says, "the LORD require…To *act justly*…to *love mercy* and…to *walk humbly*" (italics added to both).

Applying the above qualities, in one's life, does not give a person the right to look down on others, thinking he or she is better than anyone else regardless of the choices in life they may choose to make.

Recall the Apostle Peter's words to Cornelius at Acts 10:34 and 35: "At this Peter opened his mouth and said: 'For a certainty I perceive that God is not partial, but in every nation the man that *fears him* and *works righteousness* is *acceptable* to him'" (NWT; italics added). The NIV says, "Does not show favoritism…accepts from every nation and does what is right."

Acting in such a way, applying basic Bible principles as well as treating others the way we want to be treated and acting in accordance with other points from Jesus' Sermon on the Mount (Matt. 5–7) won't assure that any of us will be the "sharpest knife in the cupboard," but these actions do pretty well guarantee that we will be acceptable to God. That's a worthwhile and attainable goal.

The next chapter includes a test that will address choices we may face. I am sure you will find it intriguing, fun, and no doubt enlightening, and you will be glad you took time to consider it.

CHAPTER 13

IF IT LOOKS, WALKS, SWIMS, AND QUACKS LIKE A DUCK–IT'S A...

- To deduce a fact or conclusion (called deductive reasoning) is to arrive at that conclusion by logic or reasoning.
- If we apply the Duck Test, what will we learn?
- A memory aid: just say de-*duck*-tive reasoning.
- If you don't know the answer to a "multiple choice" question, how might you find it anyway?

Although there are variations to the Duck Test, this is basically how it works. According to *Wikipedia*, "Indiana poet, James Whitcomb Riley (1849–1916) may have coined the phrase [the paraphrased title of this chapter] when he wrote, 'When I see a bird that walks like a duck and swims like a duck and quacks like a duck, I call that bird a duck'" (*Wikipedia*, "Duck test"). The article elaborates by saying, "The test implies that a person can identify an unknown subject by observing that subject's habitual characteristics."

Consider this example: What is a "duck-billed platypus?" The fact that it is called "duck-billed" might incline one to assume that it is of a duck species. Not so; it could never pass the Duck Test, because it is not a duck.

Note the features unique to the "duck-billed platypus." Wikipedia defines it as a "semi-aquatic mammal [not a bird] found in eastern Australia; it is the only mammal on earth that lays eggs rather than giving live birth." Some European naturalists, when first seeing it, thought that it must be an elaborate fraud" (*Wikipedia*, "Platypus"). But the platypus got the last laugh—it was real and not a fraud or a hoax. Its description engenders disbelief, a "you've got to be kidding" response, coupled with a grin.

An evolutionist might be inclined to think that "natural selection" stumbled into a melting pot for this one. A creationist might be inclined to think that God must have found a box of spare parts when it came time to create the platypus, or maybe an angel with a weird sense of humor wanted to have a little fun while helping out a bit.

No matter how one views the platypus' arrival, I am convinced that Mr. and Mrs. Platypus each believed the other to be a perfect match. See if the following description brings a smile. Wikipedia's definition continues. The platypus is an "egg-laying, venomous, duck-billed, beaver-tailed, otter-footed mammal." The male platypus has a spur on the hind feet that can deliver venom that causes severe pain to humans and usually death to smaller animals. Oh, and I forget to mention—it is covered with fur, not feathers (*Wikipedia*, "Platypus").

From these descriptions, do you think there is any way you might think this animal to be a duck? I wouldn't either! Sounds like something from a horror movie that you wouldn't want to meet up with in a dark alley.

Here's another example in the matter of using de-*duck*-tive reasoning. Consider that you are moving to a new state. You are required to take a driver's test at the Department of Transportation, and perhaps you rushed your preparation just a bit (tried to wing it). Now you find a multiple choice question with three possible answers, and you haven't a clue what the correct answer is. How might you find it anyway?

Do you feel reasonably sure that some of the choices offered could not possibly be correct? They don't seem to make any sense. If you could eliminate two of the possible choices by this process, you might arrive at the correct answer by the back door. One question could make the difference between passing or not. Think of the embarrassment if you failed by just one question! Let's try using the Duck Test now—as it relates to this exposé—you may pass.

We have covered a considerable amount of information thus far that paints a picture not just of the good but also the bad, deceptive, and worse, concerning the W/W/H. So I am well aware of the possibility that some of it could be causing trouble for you. I feel your pain; I've been there and experienced the same feelings.

If you have been active as one of Jehovah's Witnesses for many years, you have no doubt believed that the members of the W/W/H are the only ones on earth that have the truth and that anyone who says otherwise is trying to deceive you and is your enemy. I've been there and felt that way myself. But think of some of those who followed David Koresh or Warren Jeffs. Do you think the possibility of deception became problematic for them? Some died—victims of those cults that had exerted near total control over their lives.

After reading the description of a duck-billed platypus, if you became convinced that there is simply no way you could believe that such an animal really exists on earth, would your disbelief make your view correct, or would you simply have something new to learn?

The statements that the W/W/H interprets as apostate statements against it are the very things it has actually said and continuously asserted itself, for 140 years—*about all other religious groups.*

So where can we go from here? Who is telling the truth? How about some de-*duck*-tive reasoning and logic? Let's make some comparisons using the Duck Test to determine what makes sense and what is logical and reasonable. What factual conclusions will surface?

Let's get started; I will cover four areas: 1. Sect-like and cult-like traits; 2. Prophecy; 3. Candor (being open and honest), and 4. Deception, hypocrisy, and lying.

1. *Sect-like and cult-like traits*:

Think back to the Introduction of this book, where I quoted C. T. Russell's definition of a religious sect. Do you recall the six earmarks of a sect? (They are also earmarks of a cult.)

- The mind must be given up entirely to the sect
- The sect decides what is truth or error, not you
- You must accept decisions of the sect

- You must ignore individual thought
- You must avoid personal investigation
- Your conscience becomes enslaved to the sect

Add to these points the two dictionary definitions also previously quoted in the Introduction, for a total of eight Duck Test points:

> Sect: 1. A religious group or faction *regarded as* heretical or as deviating from orthodox tradition…a nonconformist Church. 2. A group with *extreme* or *dangerous* philosophical or political ideas. (ital. added) *Webster's Revised Unabridged Dictionary (1913)*

> Cult: A group of people with a religious, philosophical or cultural identity sometimes viewed as a sect, often existing on the margins of society or *exploitative* towards its members. (ital. added) *Wiktionary.org* - (retrieved: 4/02/2013)

So let's apply the Duck Test, of logic and reason, to the W/W/H and its teachings. It will be very important and helpful for you to stand back and try to be objective. This is *not a personal attack on you*. If you are presently active as one of Jehovah's Witnesses, the only way to benefit from these questions is to be honest with yourself. Think of these deductive points in the same way you would regard things you would use to check a leaking gas line.

What will the qualities of both, logic and reason, using this test, bring to your mind as you consider the following points? Does it (the W/W/H) engage in the following practices?

➢ Does it decide what is truth or error, not you?

➢ Does it believe that its rank-and-file members must accept its decisions and doctrines, past as well as present?

➢ Does it allow personal thoughts, especially ones contrary to its own thoughts? Or are such thoughts and ideas not tolerated?

- Does it allow personal investigation, or does the hierarchy forbid it? (This includes checking the Internet, or other sources, to get all the facts and the other side of the story.)

- Do others consider it to be heretical?

- Do others view it as imposing excessive control over members? (e.g., bedroom policies imposed on married couples; grooming requirements; entertainment choices, etc.)

Can you see that these eight earmarks do, in fact, identify the W/W/H as guilty of displaying both sect-like as well as cult-like traits?

Does this prove that the W/W/H's organization is a sect or a cult? Remember—you are the one taking this test. I have already done so. It is not my business to tell you what you must believe. But it is essential for you to satisfy yourself with regard to logic, reason, and proof. In other words, just what does the Duck Test prove to you?

2. *Prophecy:*

Let's try another example in the matter of prophecy. Think back to chapters 6 and 7 of this book, where I discussed the meanings of words connected with prophecy.

Is it not true, based on the meanings of those words as well as on evidence from the W/W/H's publications that it has been guilty of:

- Proclaiming over thirty prophecies for the end of the world and/or events connected with that end; *all of which failed.* (More prophecies than any other group in human history.)

- Asserting, many times, that the W/W/H is the true prophet of God (since the time of C. T. Russell, its founder, in the 1870s).

- Changing the dates for the end of the world, over thirty times. That would never have been necessary if the prophecies had come true. It was because of continuous failures that the changes were made.

- ➢ Making failed prophecies, clearly demonstrates such prophecies to have come from false prophets.

What do these facts prove? According to the Duck Test of logic and reason, has the W/W/H been shown to be a false prophet? Yes or no? Remember, you are the one taking this test. I already have.

3. *Candor (being open and honest):*

How has the W/W/H fared in the matter of candor (being open and honest)? It has correctly commended the candor of Bible writers. For example, in *All Scripture Inspired of God and Beneficial*, their writers noted, "its [Bible] writers spared **no one, not even themselves**, in the interests of making a *faithful record*" (WTB&TS 1990, p. 341).

- ➢ Has not the W/W/H spared itself, by refusing to admit its failures?

- ➢ What excuses were given by it, after each of the failed prophecies?

- ➢ Has this hierarchy consistently dumped the blame for its failures and false prophecies, on others?

- ➢ Were its trusting followers hurt, financially or otherwise, by those failures?

- ➢ What has been the W/W/H practice, when members of its organization have called attention to its failures or deception? Were such ones labeled apostates and then disfellowshipped and shunned?

- ➢ Who did the same things, but called this process "expelling from the synagogue," in the first century?

IF IT LOOKS, WALKS, SWIMS, AND QUACKS LIKE A DUCK—IT'S A...

- ➢ Do you think that the W/W/H has followed the example of Bible writers or of the Pharisees, when it comes to "openness and honesty?"

- ➢ What does the Duck Test prove to you—this time?

4. *Deception, hypocrisy, and lying:*

In the matters of deception, hypocrisy, and lying (addressed in chapter 9), what has been the record of the W/W/H?

- ➢ Who, in the past, has it identified as the governing body? Who appointed those claiming that position? Was that position seized by them in the same manner in which I had seized a toy airplane?

- ➢ Were they appointed by Christ (as they originally claimed)?

- ➢ Does their history show that they seized or stole that position—more than once?

- ➢ Has not their story in this matter changed again, even in 2012 and 2013? Why do you think they made that change?

Many other examples were provided about these issues in chapter nine, but for now, you have completed all of the questions on this Duck Test.

What do the facts prove in these four areas, using the Duck Test of logic and reason, for the W/W/H? What have they proven to you?

Remember that I have already taken this test, and I passed. How did you do? Hopefully you passed also.

Now let's consider the following.

REVIEW QUESTIONS:

1. Has the application of the Duck Test helped you? I sincerely hope that has been the case.

2. If you are not one of Jehovah's Witnesses at the present time, do you feel better qualified to ask some pointed questions before committing yourself to becoming one?

3. If you are presently associated with Jehovah's Witnesses and you have serious reservations about your involvement, what could help you if you discerned the need for a change?

4. What things do you already have going for you that would come under the heading of valuable assets to help you make a wise choice?

Chapter 14 will provide some helpful suggestions for anyone who may discern the need, and has the desire to escape from the W/W/H's organization. He or she may not really know how to go about it due to very real fears and anxieties about making such a drastic change.

Three factors that will always be present for any type of escape will be addressed and illustrated by three real-life examples given in the next chapter. The end result may not always turn out well, so having *a workable plan* is essential!

Chapter 14

ESCAPING THE SPIRITUAL ABUSE OF DECEPTION, MANIPULATION, AND TYRANNY OF AUTHORITY

- What causes one to feel the need to escape?
- What desperate measures have others taken in their efforts to escape?
- What is needed to make good an escape from someone, something, or some place that is unacceptable to one?
- How can one distinguish between what is possible and what is not, for an escape?
- What help is available for one who chooses to escape from the Watchtower/Witness organization?
- Where can such help be found?

When one feels the need to escape, there are at least three factors that become problematic:

1. How serious is the need to escape?

2. How many are going to make the attempt?

3. Who may be trying to prevent one from escaping?

Three examples from the past:

- My multiengine airplane instructor who escaped from Cuba: his family first and then himself in 1963.

- Desperate people trying to escape from Vietnam (in the 1970s) in the wheel wells of airline jets.

- Two families from East Berlin, Germany (September 16, 1979), who made good their escape by means of a hot air balloon with a gondola.

First example: In 1963, Fidel Castro was prime minister of Cuba, and life in Cuba was rapidly deteriorating for most Cuban people. Fear was mounting over what the new dictatorial government was due to bring to that nation.

- In May of that year, while living in Ft. Lauderdale, Florida, I started learning to fly a twin-engine airplane, a Cessna 310. Flights have been documented in my *(Pilot Master Log);* I had my eye on getting an airline job!

By that time, my instructor, who had been a captain for a Cuban airline, had defected to the United States. The insidious changes in Cuba had compelled him and his family to get out, at any cost. Using deception, he got his wife and son out first; there had been no other way to accomplish it. Then he, as a captain, flew his scheduled trip to Mexico City, deplaned, and simply *walked away*—from everything! After recovering his wife and son, he was successful in gaining asylum in the United States.

Along with his family, this very talented and highly skilled instructor was starting a new life. His qualifications as an airline captain were a huge asset as an aircraft instructor. Enter a much appreciated multiengine instructor and a fantastic opportunity for me to benefit from his knowledge and expertise.

All three problematic issues had been present before the family had made its escape:

- A desperate need, from their viewpoint.
- He, his wife, and his son all needed to escape.
- As an airline captain, he was a scarce commodity in Cuba, so the officials would not be willing to simply let him go without a fight. However, he and all of his family members did get

out successfully, but with little more than the clothes on their backs.

Second example: This example, attempted at very great risk for the refugees involved, occurred during the 1970s when I was a first officer (copilot) on the DC-8. I never was assigned to fly any of United's: Military Command Charters (MACs) into or out of Vietnam, but I do recall vivid pictures in the newspaper of desperate refugees who had climbed into the wheel wells of airline jets, hoping to escape from various airports in that country.

However, some of the pictures showed people actually *falling out of the wheel wells.* The doors had opened for the gear to retract, just after takeoff, and out these people went, with only seconds to live before they would hit the ground—a terrifying few seconds of unimaginable proportions.

Usually when one finds it necessary to escape, there will be a material loss. For the vast majority of those attempting to escape in jet wheel wells, the results turned out to be a loss, not just of their material assets but of life itself.

And what were the risks? They included an outside air temperature of forty to fifty degrees below zero and virtually no oxygen in the wheel well at thirty thousand feet or possibly higher. (Even while flying my plane, I personally used oxygen any time I was flying above fourteen thousand feet, which was a standard operating procedure required of the pilot in command.)

The atrocities of the Vietnam War pushed desperate refugees to risk everything, including almost certain death, in their efforts to escape. Only a very small handful of such desperate people have ever survived those risks, trying to escape not just from Vietnam but from other countries with undesirable regimes as well.

Third example: This example involves two men, Peter Strelzyk and Guenter Wetzel, as well as their families, who escaped from East

Germany before the Berlin Wall fell. As is usually the case, they got away with little more than the clothes they were wearing. They made good their escape attempt in a gondola suspended below a hot air balloon that they fabricated themselves. Disney made an intriguing movie (*Night Crossing*) about their daring and successful escape. Congratulations to them and all successful escapees.

But the times when people have felt compelled to escape from an adverse situation or an adverse location are truly innumerable. Sometimes their efforts have met with success and at other times, not. What can make the difference?

The remainder of this chapter focuses mainly on normal people, just like you and me, who for reasons of their own feel or felt compelled to escape deception, manipulation, and tyranny of authority foisted on them by the W/W/H; for many these problems began in their childhood. This hierarchy has been responsible for considerable distress for them and their families; they would tolerate no more. The only way out, is/ was to escape—period!

Since the same three problematic factors present in the previous examples of literal escapes were factors for these people also, how could these problems be dealt with and overcome? What help may be available from unexpected sources for people in similar situations to theirs?

Let's take the previously mentioned problematic issues, one at a time, to see not only the problems but also possible solutions.

First Factor: How serious is the need to escape?

For many, such as my wife and me, the W/W/H teachings were foisted on them as youths. A whole lifetime has raced by, and the end of the world never came as had been promised, and yes, even guaranteed.

Recall Prov. 13:12, which says, "*Expectation postponed* is making the *heart sick*, but the thing desired is a tree of life when it does [finally] come" (NWT; italics and brackets added).

Do you recognize the fact that it was not God or Christ Jesus who promised over thirty specific dates for the end of the world or events connected with it; it was the W/W/H. The hierarchy's prophecies all failed, and *it has never admitted this*, apologized, or in any way taken responsibility for its failures. Do you see why broken promises and failed prophecies could become a major factor in motivating many who were former Jehovah's Witnesses to escape?

Such people as my wife and me are no longer willing to tolerate the "carrot in front of the donkey" mentality that the W/W/H uses to keep followers working for its interests and enrichment. We have all caught on, but the hierarchy has just kept that carrot moving while its promises and prophecies have continued to fail.

I am so disappointed with myself for having taken so long to catch on to this deception and to do something about escaping. Cognitive dissonance, you'll recall, helps explain why it can be so difficult to see and act on the problems.

But even if you have long been associated with the W/W/H and its organization, you may not be aware of the fact that the scriptures never command or require that Christians (the rank-and-file JWs) must go door-to-door for God or for the hierarchy, to look for new recruits. So what is the reason, why, it insists on this? It does so in order to prop up its failing organization. (It has one of the highest membership *turn-over rates,* of any religious organization in history.) Even now, it is beginning to reap what it has sown from its deception, manipulation, tyranny of authority, and hypocrisy.

> ➤ A side note: The usual scripture that the W/W/H uses in demanding that every Witness must go door-to-door can be found at Acts 20:20. Here, the Apostle Paul is speaking of himself, "teaching the elders… from Ephesus, house to house."

> ➤ There is not one single scripture that says any rank-and-file Christian (a regular guy or gal) ever went door-to-door looking for new recruits. The only ones recorded in the Bible as having

gone (house to house in a religious context) were the apostles—to teach and encourage other elders in Ephesus, according to that scripture.

- ➢ So, this hierarchy's demands are a deception and a lie, nothing more than a ploy to get free labor.

- ➢ Do you discern why many former JWs, would feel the need to escape from being manipulated and used by the W/W/H to work freely as recruiters, for the aggrandizement of its organization?

- ➢ What if you had been used by a crooked financial advisor (such as Bernie Madoff) and had lost a few hundred thousand dollars? Would you feel inclined to trust still more phony promises he made, to see if he could play with more of your money and lose that too?

- ➢ Is that principle any less harmful when applied to the W/W/H's phony and fraudulent promises?

Second Factor: How many will attempt the escape?

In any escape attempt, a big question is what the total number will be of those needing and being brave enough to attempt the escape; the larger the number, the greater the risk and need for planning. The same will be true for those wishing to escape the W/W/H and its organization. Remember, there are those who wish to keep a stranglehold on the escapees, if possible.

You may recall, if you saw the movie involving the escape from East Germany, that at first, only one family made the attempt, and they were not successful. They nearly got caught. For the second attempt, both families tried and succeeded. Fear had to be overcome, and it was. That daring escape attempt did become a successful reality—for all of them!

In the case of my wife and me, some of our children are not even considering the possibility that there could be some deception coupled with hypocrisy being practiced by the W/W/H. Some of them are still in the mode of "follow that carrot." What can I say? We have been where they are, but they have never been where we are. Likely, much more time will go by before they will catch on—if they ever do. We hope, especially for their sakes, that they will. We are very thankful that we did, and that we made good our escape.

Third Factor: Who is trying to prevent one's escape?

- ➢ The W/W/H has billions of dollars at stake because free labor and contributions are disappearing; these losses are already happening as many make their escape. Do you think the hierarchy is likely to allow that to continue happening without a fight?

- ➢ This hierarchy has over one hundred and forty years of experience in duping millions of people with over thirty failed prophecies by means of the "carrot and the donkey" trick. It has, so far, gotten away with simply dumping the blame on others, and it "keeps that carrot moving." It has worked so well; why change now—get the message?

- ➢ Additionally, it has its pet disfellowshipping and shunning procedures, which are purposely designed to generate fear and anxiety for anyone wishing to escape from its sect-like stranglehold.

- ➢ It is, even now, trying to find new ways to blackball (find and disfellowship) any previous believers who have simply fallen through the cracks into inactivity.

- ➢ The numbers of former JWs who have caught on to the W/W/H's deception, hypocrisy, and tyranny of authority and who have abandoned its organization is exponentially increasing. The departure of believers that started a few years ago as a trickle is turning into a torrent. Who will be able to withstand it, when it becomes a tsunami?

How to Make a Successful Escape:

Based on what one wishes to do, a plan for how one can hope to accomplish it becomes essential.

If one is presently a Witness or has relatives who are, let's talk about assets that are likely already available that could assist one in escaping when the need arises.

- ➤ Recall that when one starts studying with JWs, that person is encouraged to "burn his or her bridges," so that the only support group that the person will have left is Witnesses. The W/W/H attempts to steal from that one a valuable asset (his or her natural family) and replace it with a highly controlled and controlling new family.

- ➤ But remember that a bridge that has been burned down can be rebuilt. Certainly an inconvenient task; but by no means is it impossible. Millions of one-time believers and followers of the W/W/H's manipulative organization have already proven to be successful in their escape—congratulations to them all.!

Despite having turned away from previous friends or family members, (at the bidding of the hierarchy and by the person one was studying with), the escapee will likely be pleasantly surprised at how forgiving and understanding those same people will be, if and when, that person desires to rebuild those bridges—been there, done that.

The W/W/H has never had the honesty to admit fault and accept responsibility for its manifold errors and deceptions, and say it was sorry, or ask for forgiveness. But if an escapee is not afraid to be honest and truthful about how he or she now feels, and what he or she has done, that person will undoubtedly have success. Reasonable efforts to be honest and sincere in trying to re-establish those lost friendships will likely be met with appreciation and even enthusiasm.

> As a Witness, one has learned how to give Bible talks and how to meet new people by having developed one's communication skills. This person still has those skills, and they can be used in a sincere way and without the Witness agenda. They can be used to overcome the awkward feelings of starting from where one left off or starting all over again. Remember my flight instructor after his escape from Cuba? It will feel like the escapee has started a new life too!

> One will be amazed at how much time becomes available, no longer having to fill up a Witness agenda. There is now time to listen to one's friends and neighbors without trying to trick them into studying the Bible and pressuring them to start drinking that W/W/H (Jim Jones' style) soft drink!

> Using some qualities, (that the hierarchy has pulled away from, in order to meet its agenda), such as truth, honesty, and integrity, will now go a long way toward helping the escaping one to deal with others as they would like to be dealt with. (The Golden Rule)

One other area deserving some attention, especially by past members of the W/W/H organization, is the following question.

Who Will Pay for Those Stolen Years?

There are many examples in the past of countless persons who lost money or worse yet, years of their lives or even life itself because they believed the fraudulent claims of a religious hierarchy, financial adviser, political manipulator, or perhaps a kidnapper. Recall the following infamous people.

- Religious cult leaders: *Jim Jones; David Koresh; and Warren Jeffs*
- Phony financial advisor and Ponzi scheme trickster: *Bernie Madoff*
- Political tyrant, deceiver, and manipulator: *Adolf Hitler*
- Treacherous kidnappers, liars and deceivers: *Philip and Nancy Garrido*, who stole eighteen years from Jaycee Dugard

In all six of these examples, their victims lost a great deal; not just money, but also years of life, and yes, sometimes even life itself.

Beyond stealing people's lives by killing them, there is the matter of stealing people's lives in the form of years stolen. This is done by others controlling these people. In effect, the thieves of these years keep these people imprisoned by means of deception and by using them for their own agendas.

There is no way for the victim or victims in any case to recover life itself, if they have died—that will be in Christ Jesus' hands. In the case of years that have been lost, there is likewise no way the clock can be turned back to recover them. So, rather than worrying about what cannot be done now, focus, instead on what may be a workable course of action, from this point foreward. What assets do you have that may make escape an easier endeavor for you?

> ➤ There are factors you could consider that may not have presented themselves to your mind up to this point in time:

For example, at times, the perpetrators of the wrongs are forced to pay at least something monetarily to their victims. At other times, some seem to get away without paying completely or not paying at all for what they have stolen.

In our discussion involving the W/W/H, note that the Watchtower Bible and Tract Society (the mother corporation of that hierarchy) has billions of dollars in cash and assets; these could be tapped to repay, to at least some degree, those countless numbers of persons who have had whole lifetimes stolen from them, by doing its bidding.

Millions of such persons have been tricked into a less than comfortable or sometimes even substandard style of living, especially when old age sets in. Why? Because the W/W/H had dogmatically assured them that "the end will come, "so soon" you will *never grow old.*" That's the *first lie.* Or, "There is no need for higher education, because "Satan's system will be destroyed so soon" that getting a higher education would be a waste of time." That's the *second lie*.

Are you in either of those categories? Who do you think should shoulder the blame and pay for those lies and deceptions by it, especially when there have been very real and tangible losses?

Many personal Witness friends of mine are presently dismayed with the W/W/H, because in some cases they still have to work to support themselves, even in their seventies and older. I can't even imagine it. I have been securely retired for more than twenty years, since I was fifty years old, because of refusing to buy into that mentality.

I did pursue my flying career, and what a difference that decision has made in our lives. I am sorry for those who did "buy in" and for the "loyal" ones who are still buying into that deception. What a nightmare it has been, or will yet become, for so many!

Is there anything that can be done to stop that harmful trend? Will the time ever come when, perhaps through a class action lawsuit or by some other means, that the W/W/H will be forcibly called to account? Likely only time will tell, but I sincerely hope so. One thing is for sure: no amount of money in the world can adequately repay the hapless believers and others like them for their hardships and their losses.

What About "Sifting"? (Luke 22:31–34)

The W/W/H is quick to tell rank-and-file Witnesses that if anyone leaves the organization, it is because he or she is being "sifted out by Satan." This is a deception when it comes to what is really being talked about in these verses in Luke. The hierarchy is attempting to give that scripture a Watchtower spin. As usual, it will help you to read the whole context of this scripture first.

Notice that the context is definitely not talking about Christians in general being tricked by Satan and sifted from the congregation. No, rather, Jesus was telling the Apostle Peter what he was about to experience, by being cornered because of accusations from those near him during Jesus' mock trial. The account says that Peter was going to deny even knowing Jesus three times before morning.

Did that mean that Jesus was going to throw him out as a disciple, for his denial; or that because of that denial he was going to be sifted out by Satan, so good riddance anyway? Of course not!

Notice that in verse 32, Jesus had made supplication for Peter so that his faith would stay intact and he would be able to help his brothers after the experience he was about to undergo, ended.

The hierarchy's use of the "sifting deal" is just another ruse employed by it, in an effort to try to save face over an embarrassing circumstance, (so many have left its organization already and the numbers are increasing). It could not possibly be the hierarchy's fault that so many are abandoning it... could it?

Additional Considerations:

There is no question that breaking free from a sect or a cult is no easy task. It is rarely, if ever, easy to escape from anyone who is trying to keep you imprisoned. Think of followers of cult leaders such as Warren Jeffs, who felt that the really bad guys were the government officials who were trying to help them break free of the excessive control and sexual perversions of Jeffs, himself.

- ➢ Keep in mind that an escape from anyone or anything is never without cost. There is need for determination and effort. What worthwhile thing have we ever gotten in life that did not cost us something?

- ➢ Many others have "been there and done that," and they can and will happily provide help to whatever extent possible. However, if you need professional help, get it. Think about how badly you want to escape, and you may well find that the benefits to you will far outweigh the costs, whatever they are.

- Additionally, there are websites that can give you help in making good your escape, if that is what you choose to do. Do a web search on "escaping the watchtower," and the results will yield a considerable amount of such help, understanding, and encouragement. You will see that you are not alone and that there are many others who will be glad to help you.

- There have been millions of people in recent years who have successfully escaped the clutches of the W/W/H and its deceptive, authoritarian ways. These include some very knowledgeable present and former insiders such as elders, pioneers, circuit overseers, missionaries, Bethel workers, and even some from the Watchtower's writing and research staff. Their success stories on a variety of websites will likely inspire hope that you too can make good your escape if you discern the need to do so.

- Hopefully, some of the suggestions I have given in this chapter will prove helpful to you if you are trying to escape from the W/W/H. Start by using the assets that you may already have available from your own experiences. Be honest and truthful with those with whom you are trying to restore a relationship; it is essential.

- Remember my airline instructor's counsel after my "wind shear" training and PC? "As long as you are alive, do not ever give up trying to escape disaster." I echo his wise exhortation for any and all victims of spiritual abuse who feel the need to escape from the position they have been trapped in, perhaps for many decades or possibly even, for most of their lives.

I've been there and done that. It is worth all of the effort and energy it will take to escape and you will feel as if you have had a five hundred-pound anvil lifted off your back. That is not an exaggeration. That is how you will feel when you escape from the sect-like and cult-like excessive control by the W/W/H, or from any other type of hierarchy, which exerts such excessive control.

Do you recall my discussion about the ostrich? It has the ability to use its feet for flight (45 mph) or they may be used to fight an enemy with success; even vanquish a full-grown lion with deadly force. Or the ostrich may choose to simply lay its head on the sand and try to become invisible to its enemies, camouflage style.

All three strategies, separately or in concert with one another have been tried by those seeking to escape the W/W/H's spiritual abuse of its members.

There are a number of books that may also provide additional insight and suggestions for an individual; one that has been especially helpful to my wife is the book: *The Subtle Power of Spiritual Abuse, (1991) by David Johnson and Jeff Van Vonderen.*

REVIEW POINTS:

1. Understand clearly how you feel about the need to escape. If you are truly happy within the W/W/H's organization, you certainly have the right to stay attached if that is your wish.

2. Remember the refugees from Vietnam. Try to recognize what is and what is not possible. Be reasonable, and then plan accordingly if you are not happy with where you are and you do wish to escape.

3. Don't be afraid to ask for help. People who have been there and done this can provide valuable insight into the best way to handle various types of problems. Most often, these people will be a support group with no hidden agenda to try to push or pressure you to do anything. Remember, we are free to make our own decisions. This freedom is a God-given right and gift.

4. Don't sell prayer or research short. I am confident that anyone, if he or she has normal intelligence and a desire to do so, could even learn to fly a jet airliner. It is no different in other areas of life, and this includes escaping a sect-like, cult-like organization such as the W/W/H or any other excessive high control group. If you really want to, you can succeed in escaping!

The attitude of trying to save face, refusing to admit fault, and not taking responsibility for one's actions will be highlighted in the last chapter. In that chapter, I will discuss two real airline tragedies that have not been covered previously.

Those accounts will give you added insight into the dangers posed by high control religious organizations that never accept responsibility for their actions; they prefer to be like alcoholics in denial, causing great harm to others.

I am confident that you will find that last chapter, "The Conclusion of the Matter…," both helpful and riveting!

Chapter 15

THE CONCLUSION OF THE MATTER...

- Is "saving face" only an East Asian cultural trait?
- What can be the real cost of trying to save face?
- Have efforts to save face by the W/W/H brought disaster? If so to whom? How, and why?
- How do you think the stated warning, "Do not be misled..." (Gal. 6:7), relates to the matter of trying to save face?
- ❖ Flying: Two tragic airline disasters. Saving face in the first; chain reaction of errors in the second.

Making an effort to save face and refusing to accept responsibility for one's actions is nothing new. It shows up in conflicting stories of the supposed "truth" (i.e., the facts of what went wrong) nearly every time there is a danger of exposure of wrongdoing.

Many times, saving face is depicted as only an East Asian cultural phenomenon, but the practice is alive and well among all races and nations of people. Discussion around the September 11, 2012, attack on the U.S. Consulate in Benghazi, Libya, is a classic example of this. It shows the lengths that higher-ups will go to in an effort to muddy up the water by denying accountability and evading responsibility (i.e. trying to save face) for serious wrongdoing.

The same phenomenon can be described in the cases of untold numbers of religious leaders, financiers, politicians, and others.

This book has been an exposé of the W/W/H, revealing its consistent cover-ups. Covering up wrong-doing is a habit it is unlikely to break. Let's have a brief review of such efforts by it, before I discuss the air disasters.

- Over thirty failed prophecies...the hierarchy dumping blame on anybody except itself (chapter 6)

- Consistently "Hiding Accountability…and Evading Responsibility…" (chapter 12)

- "If it looks like a duck…" (chapter 13)

Reading this book may have seemed distasteful to some, especially if he or she is presently associated with the W/W/H organization; I sincerely hope any such persons have taken time to check the many references in this book, documenting the hierarchy's actions. Every one of them can easily be checked and verified. If any reader is inclined to believe that the statements, contained in this book are not true, and yet he or she has failed to check them out, who really has the problem? A hint - It is not me, the whistle-blower!

Two airline disasters involving: 1) saving face and 2) a tragic chain of events relating to this exposé, follow:

- ❖ Japan Airlines (JAL) Flight # 715, September 27, 1977. This disaster occurred three years before airline "Crew Resource Management" procedures (CRM) came into existence. The JAL DC-8, which was flying a segment from Hong Kong to Sultan Abdul Aziz Shah Airport in Malaysia, never reached its destination; it crashed four miles short of the airport. The causalities included eight out of the ten crew members and twenty-six out of the sixty-nine passengers.

Under the "assumed cause," the very limited Japan Airlines *Accident Report*, which was short on details, said: "the accident was caused by the Captain descending below the minimum descent altitude (MDA) without having the runway in sight…and the Copilot failed to challenge the Captain's breach of company regulations." CRM concepts had not yet been learned and applied by this crew.

After the crash occurred, it was reported to United Airlines pilots at a proficiency check that a UAL captain had been traveling as a passenger on that flight and had survived.

THE CONCLUSION OF THE MATTER...

He reported to United's Training Center that while he was evacuating the plane, he could see that no one had come out of the cockpit. As he forced the cockpit door open, he saw the captain, copilot, and flight engineer still in their seats, with their seat belts and shoulder harnesses still attached. He urgently shouted, "Come on! Get out of here!" But the captain turned and looked at him and answered, "We stay, we die."'

According to the accident report, "The remains from the crash in the soil surrounding the estate [where the plane came to a halt] can be found up to this day."

The cockpit voice recording is reported as [conspicuously] "missing" for confirmation of what occurred on the flight deck. The account that I just related from our PC Instructor is in fact what we were told about that accident.

This account seems to corroborate the notion of the face-saving efforts typical of many from Eastern Asian cultures, though these efforts are not exclusive to them. As it was reported to us, "This is not the way to conclude an accident." United has always counseled cockpit as well as cabin crews, "After an accident has occurred, do everything possible to get your passengers out alive. But when things get too hot, don't delay—get your own ass out of there!"

The cost of lives in this accident was thirty-four out of a total of seventy-nine souls onboard. Perhaps more of them would not have had to die; it appears that at least some of the deaths could be chalked up to the face-saving efforts to mask and avoid shame or guilt.

The second accident was far more tragic and unnecessary:

- ❖ The date, September 7, 1983, saw a Soviet MiG (SU-15 interceptor) take down Korean Airlines flight KAL-007, which had invaded Soviet airspace. It was a night flight scheduled from Anchorage, Alaska, to Seoul, South Korea, carrying 269 passengers. Every soul onboard perished.

Cold War tensions at that time between the United States and Russia were the highest they had been since the Cuban Missile crisis of 1962.

The transcripts of the communications between the Soviet Air Defense Command Center and their SU-15 interceptor were released. Ten years after the incident, a portion of the cockpit voice recorder conversations was released, which covered the period from just seconds before the missile attack occurred until splashdown.

The time from the MiG SU-15 intercept, at 18:11-z (Coordinated Universal Time) until the missile was fired at 18:25-z was *14 minutes*.

According to the transcript from the Soviet Air Defense Command Center on Sakhalin Island, the MiG pilot had attempted to contact KAL-007 twice at 18:13-z and at 18:14-z, but the crew had not responded to him. KAL-007 was not monitoring the "emergency frequency" that the MiG was using. They should have been; it is a standard operating procedure.

The flight recorder for KAL-007 revealed the chain reaction of events that had occurred, ending in tragedy.

The following points come from the "KAL Flight 007 *Flight Accident Report*."

- "Heading" was selected for the autopilot, as the flight began its departure from Anchorage.

- The flight was cleared by Anchorage ATC to a heading of 245° for intercept to its first way point (Bethel). The inertial navigation system (INS) was selected, but it was only "armed to intercept."

- A chain reaction of tragic events had started [1st link]. The heading the flight was given did not allow intercept to "Bethel." The plane was *outside* the maximum *automatic intercept distance* of 7.5 nautical miles.

THE CONCLUSION OF THE MATTER...

- The crew *never got a "lock-on" green light* from the INS, confirming that they were indeed headed to that way point (Bethel). [2nd link]

- Another air traffic controller failed to call KAL-007's attention to *the fact* that the flight was *in reality off course* when the crew reported over the "Bethel waypoint." [3rd link]

- The cockpit crew *never noticed their deviation*, which they would have if they had cross-checked their instruments and computers. [4th link]

- They *did not monitor* (set one of their radios to the *"emergency frequency"*) an action required by standard operating procedures. (So the MiG pilot could not contact the flight, even though he tried to do so, twice). [5th link]

- It was *"customary,* within KAL, for pilots *to 'shortcut' their flight path* in order to win the company's fuel-saving bonus." (That action predisposed the crew to being a little off course). [6th link]

- The Soviet Union at first *assumed KAL-007 to be a U.S. RC-135 spy aircraft.* (That was a military version of the Boeing 707.) That was why the *MiG did not approach KAL-007 close enough to be seen* by the crew. [7th link]

- The Russian military was *planning on conducting illegal rocket tests* of its SS-X24 missile that night, (in violation of the SALT II agreement). There is nothing quite like *a guilty conscience* to keep one spring-loaded to the "emergency" position for fear of being found out! [8th link]

- At 18:20-z, Tokyo ATC cleared KAL-007 to begin a climb to thirty-five thousand feet (a normal clearance, because the aircraft had burned off enough fuel to make the higher cruise altitude possible and save more fuel). The plane started that climb, but it was just after the MiG had fired warning shots in front of the plane. But, because *there were no tracer bullets in that round of fire, the KAL crew never saw them.* [9th link]

By this time, the MiG pilot believed he was looking at, and was *locked on to, a spy plane* disguised as an airliner, so he interpreted the climb as an evasive maneuver to get away and get out over international waters.

- At 18:25-z, the MiG pilot squeezed the trigger—it was the last straw. [10th link] The tragic fate of KAL-007 was sealed.

There is no indication that the crew of KAL-007 had any idea where they were (over two hundred miles off course) or that they had been fired on by a Soviet MiG. They thought that, for whatever reason, they had just experienced a rapid decompression. They lost control of the 747; the flight recorded data ended at 18:27-z and they disappeared from radar at 18:38-z. The chain reaction had ended in a very unnecessary tragedy with the loss of 269 lives.

JAL-715 Recap:

The first accident, involving JAL Flight 715, occurred because the captain started descending from the MDA without having the runway in sight. The *approach should have been aborted* and a go-around initiated; this was mandatory without the runway in view.

The *copilot should have objected* when the captain continued his descent with no runway visible. He did not; recall this was before *CRM training* became the norm for all cockpit crews.

The accident occurred, and apparently the whole cockpit crew stayed put; so they did not get out of the plane alive. Is it not incredible that the voice recording never showed up? Without it no one can ever learn, for sure, what was really said in the cockpit that day; sadly eight out of ten crew members perished.

THE CONCLUSION OF THE MATTER...

It has been impossible for me to find confirmation of what became of that JAL captain; the words of our United Airlines' captain (whose voice may have been on that voice recording) urging the crew to evacuate - and other things he reported to our training center in Denver would also be available and perhaps helpful if it were found.

Why are there no available details about the accident or even about which crew members died; information readily available for every other accident that I have checked? The concept of saving face and trying to evade responsibility appears to be the most likely explanation for this.

It gives credence to the idea that some people will do anything to avoid acknowledging accountability or accepting responsibility for their errors. It was clearly the captain's fault for continuing the approach after he reached MDA and the runway was not in sight. A "go-around—missed approach procedure" was mandatory. It was not initiated. The captain did not follow the standard operating procedures (SOPs), and as a result, lives were lost.

Do you see a similarity to the faulty mentality of the W/W/H and its way of dealing with failure? I have documented one hundred and forty-plus years of its refusal to accept responsibility or even to acknowledge accountability for over thirty failed prophecies, among other things. Instead, this hierarchy has consistently hidden or denied facts (even those contained in their own literature) in an attempt to save face, bringing great harm to millions of trusting believers.

Trying to hide shame, guilt, or responsibility by remaining on the ill-fated aircraft did not excuse the JAL-715 captain. Do you recognize that the W/W/H has the same type of record in that *it has never* been willing to accept blame or responsibility for its many errors?

KAL-007 Recap:

In the second tragedy, involving KAL-007, there was no face-saving issue involving the cockpit crew, because they never knew what hit them; the crash cost all 269 lives. A chain reaction started when the cockpit crew did not confirm that the autopilot was tracking the INS rather than being in the "heading select mode." But that was not what finally sealed their doom.

Any of the information in the links from two thru nine, above, could have broken the chain reaction and prevented the tragedy for KAL-007. How might that relate to the problems the W/W/H has faced?

Have there been opportunities for the hierarchy to detect that its course, the way it has been heading, has been faulty? Has its course of conduct also been part of a chain reaction that could have been interrupted? How many of its members have suffered needlessly because it has refused to change its course in spite of many obvious warnings for it to do so—warnings that could have stopped the wrongdoing and continual damage to itself and its members? Rather than warnings from ATC radar controllers, the W/W/H has received countless warnings from its rank-and-file as well as from former upper echelon members, over a period of two lifetimes. The hierarchy has ignored them all; bringing tragedy to millions.

How many failures do you think it should have taken for it to catch on to the fact that something has been radically wrong in the course it has been taking?

Since 1975, instead of providing dates for the time of the end, and/or events connected with it, they have just used words like "soon" and "imminent," with the same results—namely, failures. Criticism of the failures seems to raise its ire more than anything else that can be said to or about the hierarchy. Why? An example may help to explain this phenomenon.

A number of years ago, while at a gathering, I overheard a friend of mine mention to another person whom I had never met that, "Jim is a captain for United." The person, who had seen but never met me, made the comment, "He sure doesn't *look* like a captain." (Well… *excuse*…me…)

THE CONCLUSION OF THE MATTER...

I didn't say a word, although I could have whipped out my wallet and confronted him with my FAA Airline Transport (ATP) Certificate—but I didn't. (Wasn't that kind of me?) I just smiled, because it didn't matter what I looked like to him, or whether I met *his "ideal"* of what an airline captain should look like. It *had not* been a valid criticism. But, it does demonstrate a point.

What usually angers one most, when criticism is given, is when it is *valid and we don't want to hear it.* In this case involving me, it may have been true that I didn't look like an airline captain. (What did he think airline captains should look like, anyway?) But I was one, and I could prove it. So who cares, anyway?

However, if I had *not* been an airline captain and had only asserted that I was a captain, the criticism could have led to my being exposed as a liar and a fraud. Then how would I have felt? Liars and frauds will always get angry when they are exposed.

Can you discern why criticism of the failures of the W/W/H angers it so much? *It is valid—it exposes them,* so it stings!

Remember that in the cases of Jesus and Stephen, highlighted earlier in this book, it was their *valid criticism* of the Jewish religious hierarchy or Pharisees that so inflamed the Pharisees against them and prompted them to kill both men.

The W/W/H has consistently complained about anybody questioning or exposing its failures. But the question is: What is the fastest way to silence critics who call attention to one's failures? It is really very simple, just *admit the failures, pay the price* exacted because of such failures, and *stop doing the wrongs.* The criticism will stop, like a small car running into a freight train. The hierarchy has never been able to figure that out. This is in spite of the fact that it has given counsel to others, especially rank-and-file Witnesses, that they "must admit their wrongs or they risk undermining their own credibility."

This is especially true in judicial matters; because of not confessing all of one's wrongs or *telling completely on one's self,* during a judicial hearing, it is viewed as "a clear lack of repentance on the part of the accused, and hence, solid grounds to warrant disfellowshipping action" by the judicial committee. They have never heard of, or at least *will never allow* any accused one to plead the **FIFTH!** It works better that way for a *"cloak and dagger"* operation, in a Kingdom Hall back room, don't you see?

Considerable counsel to the W/W/H has gone ignored. The whistleblowers, who could not be silenced, have been labeled as apostates, disfellowshipped, and then shunned by all of Jehovah's Witnesses (including their families)—all of this because the hierarchy will do anything and everything possible, to save face and hide exposure.

Do you recognize that all those links in the chain, literally thousands of warnings that could have changed its off-course heading, have been ignored by the hierarchy? But the warnings have been valid. The hierarchy has simply refused to admit wrongs, or to recognize that mercy "trumps" judgment, or at least that it should. As long as that remains the case, a downward spiral of the organization will continue, along with loss of free labor and financial support.

What Time is it anyway?

The wise man King Solomon wrote about the fact that there is an appointed time for just about everything from birth to death and in between (Ecc.3:1–9). I would like to call your attention to verses 1 and 6: "For everything *there is an appointed time…*a time *to seek* and a time *to give up as lost"* (NWT and the NIV make the same point). Many people who have been associated with the W/W/H over the years got involved because they were seeking something. They believed that the Witness recruiter, who called at their home, seemed to have just the ticket!

It sounded so wonderful, almost too good to be true—incredible—"How could I have missed it?" They wondered to themselves.

- ➤ Jehovah has chosen you to study. You are so special.

- ➤ The end will come before you grow old.

- ➤ You will survive, along with just a handful of other very special people—just Jehovah's Witnesses.

- ➤ Perfect health and everything you ever wanted or could imagine, and it's all free! How does that saying go? "If it sounds too good to be true…"

REVIEW POINTS:

1. The W/W/H has made and published over thirty prophecies and predictions for the end of the world and its associated events.

    ➢ History proves they have all failed!

2. The hierarchy has asserted that it alone is God's favored prophet and it alone has and tells the truth.

Recall prophecy number 30 from chapter 3. "True, there have been those in times past who *'predicted an end to the world'*, even announcing a specific date. Yet **nothing happened**...They were **guilty of false prophesying.** Why? What was missing...? Missing from such people were God's truths and *evidence that he was using and guiding them"* (*Awake!* - October 8, 1968, p. 23)

Additionally please recall that the *Watchtower* (January 15, 1974, p. 58) notes, "What about truthfulness? **Do we really respect the truth,** or are we willing to **twist the truth a little bit** to get out of an inconvenient circumstance... **A liar...is serving the Devil.**" And remember Deut. 18:20, where it says, "However, the prophet who *presumes* to speak in my name a word that I have not commanded him to speak...**that prophet must die**" (NWT and NIV).

3. It is not the whistle-blowers who have condemned the W/W/H. Its own literature and actions have condemned it as the following:

    ➢ A false prophet

    ➢ Serving the Devil

    ➢ Deserving of death

Have you discerned the good, the bad, the deceptive, and worse on the part of the W/W/H?

The only possible way for the W/W/H to *defuse valid criticism* of itself, is to admit fault, pay the price for wrongdoing, and change. Will it, like the little old lady from chapter one, be big enough, brave enough and honest enough, to acknowledge accountability, accept responsibility and make those changes? Its history over the past one hundred and forty years seems to scream—*No way!*

What is really required of all mankind? Note Ecc. 12:13, which says, "The *conclusion of the matter*, everything having been heard, is: *Fear the* [true] God and *keep his commandments*. For this is *the whole [obligation] of man*" (NWT). Why? Verse 14 continues: "For God will bring *every deed into judgment*, including *every hidden thing*, whether it is good or *evil*" (NIV - italics added to both). The W/W/H is no exception! It too will be called to account and could be forced to swallow a very bitter pill because of its own wayward course.

It is a fact that all persons have the right to their own views (religiously or otherwise), as guaranteed by the U. S. Constitution; it is not the right of me, the W/W/H, or anyone else, for that matter, to try to *force* personal views on others, whether adults or children. You have seen, in this book, that doing so, can easily leads to child abuse.

If you consider yourself to be a Christian, you likely recognize already that such ones have an obligation before God as noted in the above quoted scripture (Ecc. 12:13). I do believe that we will all, eventually be forced to take responsibility for the decisions we have made. No wrong-doing will be able to stay hidden; the hierarchy should especially take note of this fact!

Recall Acts 10:35 - God is not partial; but in every nation, the man, or woman, who *fears God and works righteousness*, is acceptable to him. We would do well to inform ourselves of his requirements and follow them. It was the *common honest people* in the first century who heard and responded to the message that Jesus was giving; we can and should honestly and sincerely follow their example, and not that of a religious hierarchy (such as the Pharisees) and certainly not that of the W/W/H, in our day, who have followed the Pharisees' presumptuous wrong-doing and denial of responsibility!

History's record is filled with accounts of those in authority who abused it. Of particular note was Captain Edward Smith of the *RMS Titanic*, who ignored warnings that should have *struck terror and caution* into the heart of any captain. He ignored the warnings that could have been lifesaving because he had an agenda: he was hoping to set a new speed record across the Atlantic Ocean. A great idea and a worthy ambition, but *not on this night, nor on this trip*—the risks should have made it out of the question even to contemplate such a venture. The result for his passengers made that point indelibly clear.

On April 15, 1912, most of Captain Smith's passengers had no way of escaping the *Titanic* alive. He had not been deceptive, but he had made a terrible mistake and downplayed, at least in his own mind, the magnitude of the risk he was taking by ordering that the *Titanic* continue at a dangerously high speed which resulted in a horrific, never to be forgotten disaster!

I have traveled above Mach 1 (the speed of sound), which is almost eight hundred miles per hour. But no one can travel fast enough to escape from himself or from his record; that applies to Captain Smith all right, and it most assuredly holds true for the W/W/H. not even it can out-run itself, especially in our transparent world!

Additionally it has done massive harm to, not just 1,502 people (the number who sank with the Titanic), but it has also been responsible for severe life-long harm, deception and damage foisted on millions of innocent adults, as well as their children!

The W/W/H is at the helm of a *Titanic*-like organization. Massive damage has already been inflicted on its organization because of its blatant arrogance in the way it deals and has dealt with its trusting members. Many observers believe that the hierarchy is going down. The massive hemorrhaging it is experiencing through the departure of hundreds of thousands and even millions of rank-and-file JWs is sounding the death knell for it. How much time does its organization have left to stay afloat? I don't know, but I have already abandoned that sinking ship. What about you? The choice is yours and yours alone to make.

This fatally crippled, *Titanic*-like organization is bound to descend into the depths of oblivion. A most fitting "Conclusion of the Matter…"

An ominous scene:

- The ocean—calm and still
- The silence—eerie and foreboding
- Eyes—anxiously piercing the darkness to see

Time has *finally* run out for the W/W/H! As it slips beneath the icy waters of years of arrogance, consistent deception, blatant hypocrisy, lying, cover-up, lack of mercy, as well as tyranny of authority—a most appropriate, compelling and deserved farewell—

THIS EPITAPH -

The Watchtower/Witness/Hierarchy
Has Finally Reaped What It Has Sown!
- Galatians 6:7

AMEN!

REFERENCES

All Witness publications are © by the Watchtower Bible and Tract Society of PA (WTB&TS, PA), and Published by WTB&TS, NY, Inc. All books before January 1, 1923 are "Public Domain" (P/D)

_____. 1889, 1902, 1908, 1917. *The Time is at Hand.* New York: WTB&TS.

_____. 1897, 1911, 1917. *Studies in the Scriptures.* Vol. 1-3. New York: WTB&TS.

_____. 1917, 1918. *The Finished Mystery.* New York: WTB&TS.

_____. 1924. *The Way to Paradise.* New York: WTB&TS.

_____. 1931. *Vindication.* New York: WTB&TS.

_____. 1973. *Comprehensive Concordance.* New York: WTB&TS.

_____. 1977. *Thayer Greek-English Lexicon of New Testament.* Grand Rapids: Baker Book House Company. (Public domain)

_____. 1984. *The New Strong's Exhaustive Concordance.* Nashville: Thomas Nelson Publishers. (Public Domain)

_____. 1985, 1989. *Reasoning from the Scriptures.* New York: WTB&TS.

_____. 1988. *Insight On The Scriptures.* Vol. 1, 2 New York: WTB&TS.

_____. 1990. *All Scripture Inspired of God and Beneficial.* New York: WTB&TS.

_____. 1977, 1979, 1981, 1991. *Pay Attention to Yourselves and to All the Flock.* New York: WTB&TS.

_____. 1993. *Jehovah's Witnesses-Proclaimers of God's Kingdom.* New York: WTB&TS.

_____. 2005. *Organized to Do Jehovah's Will.* New York: WTB&TS.

_____. 2010. *Shepherding the Flock of God in Your Care.* New York: WTB&TS.

Made in United States
North Haven, CT
20 May 2023